The Indian Software Industry

The Indian Software Industry

Business Strategy and Dynamic Co-ordination

Parthasarathi Banerjee

First published 2004 by
PALGRAVE MACMILLAN
Houndmills, Basingstoke, Hampshire RG21 6XS and
175 Fifth Avenue, New York, N.Y. 10010
Companies and representatives throughout the world

PALGRAVE MACMILLAN is the global academic imprint of the Palgrave
Macmillan division of St Martin's Press, LLC and of Palgrave Macmillan Ltd.
Macmillan® is a registered trademark in the United States, United Kingdom
and other countries. Palgrave is a registered trademark in the European
Union and other countries.

ISBN 1–4039–0503–7

This book is printed on paper suitable for recycling and made from fully
managed and sustained forest sources.

A catalogue record for this book is available from the British Library.

Library of Congress Cataloging-in-Publication Data
Banerjee, Parthasarathi.
    The Indian software industry : business strategy and dynamic co-ordination / by
    Parthasarathi Banerjee.
        p.   cm.
    Includes bibliographical references and index.
    ISBN 1–4039–0503–7 (hdbk.)
        1. Computer software industry—India.   2. Information technology—India.
    I. Title.
    HD9696.63.I42B35 2004
    338.4′7005′0954—dc22   2003065676

10   9   8   7   6   5   4   3   2   1
13   12   11   10   09   08   07   06   05   04

Printed and bound in Great Britain by
Antony Rowe Ltd, Chippenham and Eastbourne

Contents

List of Figures and Tables

Figures

Tables

Acknowledgements

The author and publishers wish to thank the following for permission to reproduce copyright material: Elsevier Science Ltd, publisher of the journal *Technovation*, for fig. 1, p. 597, *Technovation* 23(2003), and table 1, p. 259, *Technovation* 23(2003); and Sage Publications, publisher of the journal *Global Business Review*, for fig. 3, p. 126, of issue 4(1) and fig. 1, p. 246, and table 3, p. 252, of issue 4(2). Thanks are due to the editors Dr George Hayward of *Technovation* and Professor C.S. Venkata Ratnam of *Global Business Review*. In addition the author thanks several colleagues and the Director, Professor Rajesh Kochhar, of NISTADS, where the author is currently working; and also several students at the XLRI, Jamshedpur, whom the author has taught or guided. And he is grateful to the Adviser, NISSAT, New Delhi, Dr A. Lahiri, for a project grant, part of which proved useful in writing this book.

1
Introduction

Enterprises in the throes of discovery have an aura of magic around them. In the world of software this becomes many-splendoured with a certain *joie de vivre* that it generates, quite distinct from what obtains elsewhere: a sense of wonderment, surprise and eventual delight; a coming within reach of power and profits; possibly through a little tweak in technology with a touch of novelty, opening up vistas that have always seemed so near and yet so far. In professional management terms, this waving of the wizard's wand, as it were, is nothing more than an effective recovery of strategy from a technological paradigm. This book is about exploring the journey from rules and norms to solutions, specific solutions prized out of the armoured covers of sector-specific industrial structures and often resources-determined mindsets. Originality is the fountainhead for such strategy. It then progresses into the realms of the economics of innovation to give itself a solid foundation from where it becomes possible to retrieve a new language of strategy and of innovation. In this highly natural yet dynamic world, the profit motive, backed by ingenuity, lends support to many of the arguments that evolve in this flow of events. The Indian software experience is a unique demonstration of how this process – the coalescing of the economics of surprise and novelty and the economics of knowledge – works. This forms the basics of the strategy theory.

The story of Indian software firms, their remarkable growth and resilience against grave odds, is hardly new. From a position of near-zero credibility as a second-rate manufacturer of industrial ware, stymied by an agonizing paucity of resources, to becoming the champions in Silicon Valley, the story is well recorded and data is publicly available, thanks to the efforts of the NASSCOM (National Association of Software and Service Companies: www.nasscom.org). This book steers clear of the beaten statistical path and engages in a discovery of the thought process, the unique strategic moves and follows them into the realms of entrepreneurial surprises. The continually evolving economics of surprise and novelty and the economics of knowledge warrant another look at strategy theory. A study in Indian software would provide generic conclusions around our concept of strategy as novelty.

Most critics have frowned on the dependence of Indian software on services; many have prescribed that software firms should undertake the well-known and tested path of 'development' of products. Yet others have suggested that Indian firms, dependent as they are on servicing global firms, should forge new alliances with large global partners. Doomsday prognosticators have warned of imminent failures. This book defends the services strategy of software firms. Such a strategy seems to have provided to the service supplier a strategic leverage, which has been analysed in terms of demand management. This novel strategy adopted by Indian firms has ensured unique management of knowledge wealth by the owner. Knowledge of software business resides in manpower and, strangely, firms in India managed to excel in a high manpower turnover scenario. This warrants an explanation. This book argues that the flow of manpower indeed provided to the Indian incumbent firm a strategic leverage on knowledge and its usability for surprise profits. Further, such a profit did not emanate from technological advances or innovations. Nor did small software firms need much organizational innovation. Indeed, they depended on normative expectations. Expectations on future coordination between several firms in a partial market provide both dynamism and sustained windfall profit to these. The success of Indian software firms, therefore, implies a strategy for governance and for surprise profits.

Exploring anew

This book is a departure from most received theories and explores the Indian software route as it learnt new modes of doing business. Such success is not generic to software and, indeed, several new business models have been generated which can be profitably replicated in other areas of business. This book does not undertake the task of developing a grand theory of generic strategy, which may be beyond the realms of possibility. Instead, it explores several new learnings and puts together a few such theory-pieces. These may not form a single coherent theory but, collectively, narrate a story about social capital, public policies and public spaces. It also explores how such spaces and policies are implicated in partial markets where firms cannot stand alone but must act upon each other's structure and processes. Knowledge, as in software, permeates every nook and corner of a business of which several dimensions belong to public spaces, some to the structure and some others to the strategic processes of influencing and bringing about surprises. Indian software provides several examples which this book seeks to analyse rather than provide any grand theory. Nor does the book endeavour to build theory based on the facts around software successes. It brings to the reader a collage of Indian software experience that will hopefully provide a pragmatic perspective.

There are several grand theories or grander traditions: the Industrial Organization approach, including several kinds of structure, conduct performance assertions and game theoretic models, evolutionary theories and corresponding case studies, resource-based approaches or several intermediate variants of competency-based ideas that provide us with a rich yet incomplete landscape. This landscape is possibly oblivious of certain traditions provided by economic theory; the rich repertoire bequeathed by Marshall and Shackle is a case in point, as they are immensely rewarding. Each important tradition or theory or approach has made global assertions and has proved to be prescriptive or normative. Some authors have looked back at Marshall and a handful at Shackle. Fewer still reconsidered certain rich traditions of thinking on strategy. This book does not attempt to issue prescriptive or normative guidelines purely because the global canvas is too large and often beyond the capacity of intelligent comprehension. A strategist acts on a local scale following what Simon has observed generally. Pragmatism emerges as an important guide and achieving the surprise element is, above all, the key to definitive strategy. While this strategy evolves from governance, it also informs governance at every stage. Handicapped by a paucity of resources, the strategist must dovetail the two to increase immensely the scope of governance not only over what the incumbent possesses but also over a much larger group of firms not under its direct control. Thus, typically, the Indian software firm, small and with limited resources, has successfully to leverage itself to move to a position of power from where it further enhances its circle of influence. This need not necessarily be explained by another grand theory with globally prescriptive assertions or powers of predictions. Surprise must stand beyond predictability. It must govern to earn windfall profit. Strategy, thus, cannot be prescribed; it would comprise piecemeal engineering. This is what this book explains.

The Indian software experience defied predictions. Almost all the large and small software players are first-generation entrepreneurs. Most did not receive structures or finance for their strategic moves from firms established as big players in other mature sectors of industry. Contrary to feelings in some quarters, this was, in fact, a boon, especially because it spared the nascent industry the redoubtable intervention and support from the government. What it was endowed with, instead, was a milieu of ubiquitous presence of institutions of knowledge, flow of manpower and novel business models. These were what primarily provided the nurturing ambience, allowing small start-up software firm to grow into enterprises. Had large corporate or large financial intermediaries bequeathed structure, finance, policies and strategies, the entire milieu would have been infected with all the reactive and inertial deadweight that old institutions and ossified organizations possess. Divested of this, the software firms became nimble footed and more than countered the loss of weight that the association of big names might have lent and the attendant mileage in terms of credibility that may have followed. Nevertheless, the software firms did run into a credibility gap with overseas clients refusing to take them seriously in the initial days. Small, software start-up ventures with little reputation, smaller wherewithal and an almost zero domestic market are never the best candidates for a global vote of confidence. Yet, these firms brought in strategic surprises in the globalized business based upon several partial markets to acquire the reputation. They constantly negotiated vicissitudes to sustain growth in what would certainly be an act of combined heroism though it is difficult to identify anecdotal heroes, as it were. There are several financially successful and unsuccessful strategists who contributed to this book with nuggets of information around different pieces of their strategic moves. These have provided the patchwork pieces for the comprehensive software strategy quilt; pieces that may be likened to nests within nests that this book presents. Thus, even without presenting a neat theory or prescription, this book provides essential insights for new theories and new perspectives for readers seeking to chart out their own road maps given any contingent situation.

The software business is about knowledge. The understanding provided here is based on the cognitive dimensions of strategy. Strategy is in the mind. Knowledge, both representational and beyond representation, sustained by several kinds of information implicates the cognitive sphere of strategy making. Yet strategy is, above all, determined by economics. Striving for higher rates of profit ensconced in the normative milieu of the interdependent and pragmatic would permit venturing into several paths, circumscribed by limitations of the minimal kinds only. The strategist's mind, finding itself in strange interludes, even vicissitudes, has to embrace them with pragmatism and with the nimbleness that contains the surprise element. The economics of knowledge has several aspects. In the public sphere comes its strategic and organizational structure specific aspects. While identifying this public sphere, one could reduce the paradigm on tacit knowledge and asset specificities to inconsequence. Public policy making for knowledge as a factor of production, unbridled by and least constrained by reactive property rights, therefore, appears as a corollary to the arguments here.

Given this background, the software success seems to have had little to do with autonomous advances in technology. The domain of technology has been restricted severely by trading in property rights, in technology assets and commitment to the paradigm of tacit knowledge. Chroniclers of innovations often leaned on either the technology restricted assumptions as they currently are, or on the structure of industry described through several structural or otherwise equilibrium-seeking assumptions. Both these presumptions are suspect because software has overcome both these barriers. Software successes are not as much technological as they are strategic. Similarly, success in software depended upon a novel kind of demand management where changes in industry structures and changes in firm organizations proved important. Strategy in software – which is also a process – looked for disequilibria.

The salient arguments of this book follow. The next two chapters present major theoretical arguments and the subsequent four chapters extend those arguments supplemented by Indian software examples. To reiterate, this book refrains from providing or analysing publicly available data on Indian software. Readers may directly move on to the detailed arguments and skip the rest of this chapter.

Strategy, governance and need for a theory

Strategy seeks to maximize personal gain. This gain or pay-off has multiple components and several languages. It is not possible for an agent to achieve unrivalled pay-off ensured by an absence of governance. Yet that is what the strategic intent is. It is only in the absence of any possibility of such unrivalled pay-off that an agent agrees to be governed, or abide by rules or whatever of competition. Tacitly, competition conforms to governance. Strategy in contrast looks beyond competition, for the moment of surprise or novelty when the apple-cart of governance, based as it is on rules and co-ordination, can be turned upside down.

Conflating governance with strategy is commonplace when strategy leads to governance over other structures. In the final analysis, it is individual intention that is the agent moving the structures ahead, keeping a system dynamic. It is motivated by the need to maximize personal gains and is the core of strategy. To achieve this, strategy seeks to govern the process of strategy formulations by others in the business. It follows then that strategy is all about hastening governance through the employment of a structure. Thus, strategy not only seeks to shape the structure of one's own business organization but also strives to shape structures of other business organizations in the strategist's strategic milieu. Governance is the pay-off of a strategy. It is argued here that a piecemeal engineering of theories, rather than a grand theory capable of explaining and predicting activity outcomes of several economic and organizational aspects together, is the most pragmatic approach.

Structures, processes and partial markets

Structure results from strategy and can be defined in terms of a 'structural sort' generated around some interfaces and some nodes, which are called confluences. The constituents of such a construction include the chief of the organization, its important stakeholders, senior executives along with the organizational wealth, including finance and knowledge, its knowledge employees and its allies. A structure changes according to the demands of strategy and small software firms often change structures rapidly to take strategic covers. This is named 'umbrella cover'. A particular structure is thus just one amongst several possible modes of business structure. A structure is woven around interfaces between structural entities and around nodes, called 'confluences' here. The types of interfaces (structural entities) and confluences remain constant over changes in organization. Such interfaces and confluences go on to describe a minimal structure.

A strategic make-up has, apart from the structural sort, five types of organizational processes which maintain the dynamism of an organization. The logic of strategy confines it to a partial market, named strategy milieu and defined through an incumbent–adversary strategic antagonism. An (incumbent) strategist seeks to score a win over an adversary and in this strategic duel, there appear two more types of strategic attitude holding organizations. There are four types of organizations, each with five processes. The resultant twenty processes belonging to the strategy milieu become the desired subjects of governance, which the strategist wishes to gain control over. Influences over processes enable the incumbent to shape the structures in a milieu when necessary.

The process participants act on certain beliefs. Thus, in order to influence processes, a strategist needs to know the conditions leading to the belief. This knowledge is referred to as strategic knowledge and it provides the conditions for strategic moves, which are different from strategic acts. The latter is behavioural and can be observed. The former can only be inferred.

Knowledge variations

Knowledge participates in strategy in three modes: as strategic knowledge, factor of production, and knowledge wealth. Strategic knowledge is about manoeuvering conditions leading to beliefs of the processes under scrutiny. It cannot be descriptive or procured from the market. Knowledge, as a factor of production, is descriptive, has least strategic worth and can be bought and sold, procured from the market or from the public domain. Knowledge wealth, as a component of the structural sort constitutes structure and is mostly not descriptive. This knowledge has strategic worth. Each knowledge employee is an epistemic generator, enhancing the knowledge wealth without being able to share or pre-reconcile the generated knowledge. There can only be a partial co-ordination among these employees in terms of what they possess as lexicons – collections of names and situations. This fact of co-ordination takes place under the direct influence of governance as an outcome of strategy. An organization, therefore, accumulates, to the extent permitted by its strategic initiatives, a revisable lexicon that reflects its idiosyncratic strategy. This knowledge cannot be tacit.

Strategy shapes the structural sort through both strategic moves to influence the processes and its strategic acts on the constituents of the structural sort. The chief of an organization, for example, shapes the knowledge wealth – a feat in its own right – not so much through efforts of co-ordination or through promulgation of rules for knowledge formation as through allowing conditions of default, which set in several norms. Given the multiplicity of knowledge situations, dealing with uncertainties and the ignorance of the inter-employee epistemic status, employees generate knowledge and share such knowledge driven by expectations. The norms provide boundary conditions and stability to such expectations.

Prescription or pragmatism

A strategic action is a strong commitment because it cannot be reverted and neither can its consequences. A fact altered by an act is another fact. A model or a theory of strategy cannot take into account an exhaustive informational account of facts leading to a strategic action. Further, an act may be provoked by the momentary passion, which again cannot be described through an exhaustive informational account. Together, these two constraints render it impossible to verify the justification of a strategic act because such a fact or such an action cannot be recreated. It follows then that no action can be claimed to be the 'best' or the 'optimal' one.

To find a guide to action, one may follow an epistemic practice of relating to the efficacy of the theory-pieces gathered from several received theories. This efficacy provides a guide to action. This is not about a higher degree of truth or better power of prediction. The strategy theory maps out efficacious actions towards reaching the goal or the final good of a strategy undertaken. This is a pragmatic account of strategy aiming for governance. All conceivable agents are empowered by the proposal of undertaking actions for achieving governance over others of strategic concern.

Partial market and structure

A strategic goal defines a locality but is itself influenced by the disposition of the strategist. This disposition reflects the strategist's belief, which is a state of mind. Beliefs might not be causally active in the formulation of the goal; however, beliefs condition the reckoning of a goal.

The strategist's specific market is determined by the strategic goal and is conditioned by his beliefs, as reflected in the strategic moves. Each market is thus both subjectively and objectively (or socially) formulated. Each such particular market is formed around a strategic actor, named the 'winning strategist'. A firm as a winning strategist deploys a sort of structure, a set of processes, a set of strategic moves and a set of strategic actions in a strategic milieu.

There is, however, a tacit recognition of the difficulty, if not the impossibility, of drawing a strict boundary for an organization. While a structural boundary exists, process and organizational boundaries are vague. A structural sort based on strategic moves and strategic actions is different from an organization. Understandably, there are situations when a structure hibernates or when a structure closely approximates organizational processes. There are other situations when a structure appears sharply against other structures and against the organization's own processes. The variability of the structural form, it is argued here, owes itself to the strategy of an organization.

Structural sort

A structure is a certain mode of assemblage, described here as structural sort, woven primarily around interfaces and confluences. An adumbration of received literature suggests that the structural sort is woven through seven types of interfaces:

(1) the chief,
(2) senior power holders,
(3) the material domain over which the chief's authority extends – in short, material domain,
(4) the umbrella cover,
(5) wealth and finance,
(6) knowledge employees and
(7) allies.

This structural sort sustains an organization through organizational processes. While the structure provides the armour at times of confrontation, processes alone can mobilize organizational resources, which a structure can deploy in an act of strategy. Five types or categories of processes are recognized here:

(1) sustenance of leadership by the senior managers,
(2) the agenda that elevates the firm to an organization,
(3) structural features of the organization,
(4) financial resources under control of the firm,
(5) the prospect of liability/threat (or punishment).

Processes and the structural sort together make up an organization's conditions for and its capability of strategic move.

Strategic milieu

Strategy is a deliberate attempt by a structural sort to govern and influence the dynamics of processes within the organization and in other organizations in the strategic milieu. A strategy concern must, however, remain limited by its reach, defined here as strategic milieu. This is a partial market and structured around: the winning strategist, its opponent, the follower of the middle path, and the careless firm. A strategic milieu is defined by the domination of the winning strategist and opponent pair. The followers of the middle path and the careless are such firms that choose to continue on strategic courses that lie in-between and are careless about the dominant strategic move. There are other types of firms in this milieu as well: those that have entered into strategic alliances with the winning strategist or, conversely, entered into strategic commitments with the opponent.

Interpreting Marshall's partial market on two modes, first, as a fraction of the market and secondly, as the processes of exchanges and contracts, shows that they are incomplete and are kept incomplete. Moreover, not all transactions are known or are knowable and, indeed, foreknowledge of transactions would exclude novelty. This '*not knowability*' implies disequilibria. Strategy enjoys disequilibria and seeks to create disequilibria. The winning strategist selects such moves and acts of strategies that are disequilibria seeking.

Strategic acts and moves

Strategic moves are disguised intentional acts, undertaken specifically for influencing the conditions of belief of other processes. Behaviourally, a strategic move is indistinguishable from a strategic act. Not all acts are strategic behaviours though even if most of them are intended to achieve a purpose of influencing conditions to belief. A distinction between strategic acts and strategic moves is thus in order. A strategic move is based on descriptive psychological states and it can be for: (1) an alliance, (2) a confrontation, (3) fluidity, (4) nonchalance, (5) prevarication and (6) dependence. In contrast, a strategic act can be: (1) of appeasement, (2) rewarding, (3) discriminatory, or (4) as punishment. A strategic move is not observable and hence strategic behaviour can be discerned by observation on strategic actions alone. A strategy make-up is complete with, first, a structural sort; secondly, processes; thirdly, strategic moves; and finally, strategic acts.

Knowledge wealth in structure

Knowledge as organizational wealth is not a pure asset. It evolves alongside structure, is sticky and cannot be procured from a resources market. It is not tacit though. A firm requires the services of a distinct knowledge to organize the dispersed knowledge, which contains the 'content'. The organizing knowledge is epistemic in terms of content and different from the dispersed knowledge. This is called strategic knowledge. It influences the conditions for knowledge wealth in all the processes in a strategic milieu. Dispersed knowledge again has several incarnations. A structural sort contains dispersed knowledge wealth (and not the strategic knowledge) as its constitutive element. The structure considers this knowledge as wealth.

The generation of substantive knowledge is never the outcome of behavioural response; it is the result of attitudes (aversion, desire, hope, despair, intention and such others) of the holder of dispersed knowledge. Consequently, a holder never exhausts the possibility of generation of substantive outcomes. An objectively given strategic situation with the same parameters might provoke alternate knowledge outcomes from the same holder but at different instances. Each generation satisfies a contingent attitude. These attitudes together create conditions of belief or knowledge.

The knowledge employees comprise the wealth component of the structural sort and serve as a dispersed set of epistemic generators. They leave little room for knowledge by description – such knowledge is descriptive and lends itself to description – because individuals do not store as much from descriptive sentences as they retain from epistemic engines and lexicons. Knowledge employees conceive little of their knowledge in the form of descriptions. However, the structure needs to have descriptive knowledge about lexical content.

Three types of knowledge

Knowledge in relation to business can be subdivided in three categories: knowledge as a factor of production; knowledge in structural sort as wealth; and strategic knowledge. Of these, the first belongs to the public domain; the second belongs to structure and the third to strategic moves and intents. The first is exclusively knowledge by description; the second is only partially knowledge by description – it is idiosyncratic, though not tacit – and the third is not descriptive but is based on attitudes and intentions while not being tacit. Tacit knowledge, even if it exists, is outside the schema of the book. A structure is thus exclusively for 'doing', with the knowledge about the deed to be done.

Strategy as surprise and pre-reconciliation

Strategy is about surprise profit. It is not about competition and it goes far beyond the pre-reconciliation assumed a priori by competition. Earning windfall profits, creating a novel turf where competition will take place, generating new language of expectation and shifting the boundary of the unknowables, in Shacklean terms, are the goals of strategy. Pre-reconciled knowledge cannot, by definition, bring in strategic advantage. A firm uses a language of co-ordination and the goal of strategy is to help overcome this constraint of co-ordination. Co-ordinated knowledge or pre-reconciled strategy cannot produce novelty or surprise.

Discarding paradigms

The paradigm of generative linguistics or of biological evolution has influenced much contemporary thinking. This book begins its inquiry with an examination of the relevance of biological evolutionary principles and generative linguistic principles to this domain of knowledge-strategy linkage. This linkage is seen to be unsupportable. A firm does not have an innate structure or a generative routine. In the absence of such innate or generic foundation, there cannot be any firm-internal residence of the idiosyncratic aspects or distinctive competencies of a firm. Strategic gains are for influencing, guiding or otherwise deforming the strategic intents of other parties. Knowledge can be of strategic advantage only if that knowledge can enable a dominant party to leverage such strategic gains. Such knowledge is defined here as strategic knowledge. Knowledge that all parties can access from the market or that can be generated by any party is knowledge by description. It has competitive significance only.

Strategic knowledge is thus non-representational or knowledge not by description. In other words, strategic knowledge is not a bundle of information. It is not tacit either. It is not about knowledge of routines or about adhering to routines and rules or even about the competitive behaviours of others, which are in public domain. Strategic knowledge is about conditions of knowledge and about conditions of belief that other parties have. Conditions of knowledge and conditions of belief reflect intentions. Strategic knowledge plays with intention.

Strategy process

Competition is decidedly behavioural. A strategy is considerably different and must refer to winning. Strategy must begin from a state of rivalry and simultaneously strive to go to a state beyond rivalry made by the 'winning' firm. Thus, strategy is not a game of poker: the firm, which is 'desirous to win', does not make a competitive move as in poker. It creates situations to which others will have to respond. Strategy cannot treat a firm as a homunculus. It involves the actual business processes, recognizes its own organizational structure and own organizational systems, and considers the influence its strategy can make on the agenda, processes, structures and systems of its competitors. An executive, therefore, while choosing strategy considers an array of fields.

Strategy as competition

A strategy make-up cannot be captured by the competitive behaviours or the signals that a firm sends to its competitors. This make-up cannot be reduced to competency, dynamic competency or core competency. Competency recognizes internal dimensions and limits that to generative innateness. A make-up, constituted by the internal and external dimensions of a firm, is never innate. External dimensions might refer more to games of co-ordination but are never limited to that, as this book argues. Internal dimensions too might refer to co-ordination, albeit with less intensity. With the boundaries between external and internal dimensions frequently changing, there appear to be no organizational boundaries at all at times.

It follows then that strategic concern of the winning-strategist firm is about influencing all the relevant categorical processes of these four principal types of firms in the strategic landscape. Each of the four types of players has five processes relevant to strategy to constitute a strategic state of affairs. The total of these twenty processes constitutes the strategic landscape. A player can move strategy in any of the six modes. These modes describe the appropriateness of the mode adopted to the percipient move-maker. Decisions regarding strategic actions are based on the particular mode of a strategic move, as are strategic actions. No behavioural or observational narration can capture this descriptive psychology of strategic thinking.

Strategy and knowledge

This argument would indicate that knowledge about knowledge generation issues pertains to issues of strategic knowledge. However, knowledge generated remains as information. The 'what' of knowledge, the 'how' of knowledge are issues that are strategic because they decide the influences on the strategy landscape. This knowledge, however, is different from the knowledge generated as content-only. A content-only knowledge appears as a bundle of information to each except the person who generated it.

Strategy is essentially concerned with knowledge that can influence processes and has little to do with content that is completely describable. Such content can influence behaviour and decisions but can be outsourced and be utilized solely for gains in competitive performance, corresponding to a given technology and a given industry structure. A firm can trade in knowledge content. A firm has an advantage only if it can locate, secure and deny others the access, or otherwise influence creation of contents. Influencing creation of contents in the public domain would not provide a firm with a privileged position vis-à-vis other firms. A firm would be privileged if knowledge creation and utilization in all the twenty processes in the strategic landscape can be warranted to conform to the strategic moves of this firm.

Strategy for profit

Strategy overcomes co-ordination, which supplies some preliminary 'data' required only when a firm wishes to make an investment or decide on the quantity that can be produced or whether an entry barrier can be overcome with current productive technology. If the firm wishes to earn a Schumpeterian entrepreneurial profit, or a 'profit' *à la* Cantillon (following Shackle's (1972) exposition on profit – which says profit appears as 'surprise' and as something beyond both expectation and convention) however, the firm must get beyond the co-ordinated or pre-reconciled conventional 'profit'. A business strategy is about surpassing reconciliation boundaries or the boundaries of competition. Strategy is thus about getting beyond the reconciled and co-ordinated arrangements. A strategy is also about disguised actions, about denial, about opening up a new game or a turf. Strategic co-ordination is thus an adjustment of disclosures; a *tâtonnement* of degrees of completeness in knowledge by description; and is often disequilibria-seeking.

Strategy as influencing beliefs

Strategic moves attempt to alter the conditions of belief. The new belief conditions on offer must, in turn, appear credible. Credibility of a belief condition offers scope for belief revisions or at least for a new 'translation'. It need not replace an old belief. The process owner (individuals and collectives) makes inferences on the credibility of a new condition of belief by observing strategic actions of the winning strategist. A strategic move cannot be observed but must be inferred. Strategic actions, in contrast, are observable facts.

Every player in the strategic landscape observes strategic acts of the others and no one responds only behaviourally. Each seeks to fathom the other's intent and then, based on one's own content of intention, displays a particular strategic act. The content of intention is not at all the content of knowledge of a belief holder. Strategic moves causally implicate these contents of intentions while achieving the other feat of warranting a certain rule following. Rule following, however, is not based on innate characteristics and is fallible. The act of following rules that are almost always unwritten is the outcome of the content of intentions.

Rules are followed because intentions perceive strategic advantage in following a rule. Further, rules can be followed because there is a real threat. A strategy fails to perform if there is no threat. This threat alone provides scope for imaginative intentions, which seek to source from each following of a rule a certain novel strategic advantage. A winning strategist, as earlier argued, seeks to guide these intentions in processes belonging to the strategic landscape. Once rule following can be controlled in this manner, a strategist fulfill his objectives.

Knowledge and co-ordination

The contents of knowledge exhibit true co-ordination and can be procured from the market or through firm-internal mechanisms by relating to lexicons. Content helps adjust the efficiency of a firm to the benchmark efficiency, which is a common knowledge. Adjustments or the *tâtonnement* bring together firms to the same or similar status of knowledge content ownership. Knowledge content is a factor of production and similar to equalization of factor efficiencies, equalization in knowledge content driven efficiencies appears as the goal of competition. A market driven by equalization of efficiency of knowledge content is dynamic because an equilibrium reached will be surpassed immediately by the disequilibria generated by a new combination of knowledge contents. No firm can have a strategic advantage from such combinations of knowledge contents, though.

This ignorance or its converse, the mutual knowledge, is about the content of the beliefs or about the content of the conjectures. These are not about the conditions of beliefs. Conditions of belief reflect intention along with imaginative and emotional states of mind. The belief content is reconciled only partially, that is to the extent of conjectural reconciliation, which is not about reconciliation of strategic acts. Strategic acts would get reconciled only if players are rational by prescription. Contrarily, a person acts on 'momentary' emotion. Mere conjectural reconciliation does not ensure either reconciliation of conditions of belief (strategic move in this book) or of strategic acts.

Strategic intent

All this comes alongside an intention of giving up rationality. Every strategic act of winning sets up a new structure of game and for every strategic act of winning to be accomplished both the common knowledge and mutual knowledge about this rationality get self-violated. Victory comes through violence on rationality. Again, a profit must appear as a surprise and fall outside a range of envisaged possibilities, according to the Cantillon perspective on profit. Surprise in strategy is unlike this. A strategic act by the winning strategist appears as surprise to all the processes in the strategic landscape but cannot be a surprise to the protagonist. In profit, surprise is subjective. In strategy, surprise belongs to the inter-subjective or objective domain. Strategic knowledge is intended to be causal and this prevents strategic knowledge from being pre-reconciled or co-ordinated. Knowledge content, in contrast, is co-ordinated. Intended causality allows the undertaker of strategy a structure uniquely its own. A firm is strategic because of this intended causality and not because it exhibits a distinctiveness on certain routines or knowledge contents or distinctive competence.

Knowledge wealth and software competence

Knowledge as wealth relates to the structure and is only partly descriptive. The observations on the Indian software firms here are surely limited because data-based description of Indian software firms, constrained by this intrinsic limitation on descriptive explanation, renders any narration on the knowledge wealth of these firms inappropriate and insufficient. The association between knowledge wealth and structural sort is a-causal. Thus the narration on knowledge wealth can never attempt to have a predictive power. Competency here has been defined as an epistemic capability, which is not 'knowledge about' nor a capability 'for'.

Over several small surveys of software firms and meetings and interviews with them – with responses often necessarily query-determined – managers and entrepreneurs suggested that an indicator of competence be defined not on the basis of an alignment or a strategic fit. Respondent executives or entrepreneurs suggested several possible modes of combining resources and knowledge wealth in order to secure high organizational or structural competence. They also rated the relative importance of types of epistemic generative capability of the knowledge employees or of their groups working together in a process. Executives and entrepreneurs were asked about the strategic goals of R & D in software; they were provided with a few epistemic categories and were asked to give weights to each according to their strategic relevance. It appeared that firms accorded priority to certain structural features that characterized knowledge wealth.

Knowledge wealth in those structural features contributing to innovations in products or projects and services, and the academic background of an employee, especially if considered in terms of higher degrees and grounding in research, received the least weight. Importantly, the higher degrees representing experience in research did take care of certain aspects of the factor of production. Knowledge wealth is a structural feature, being different from knowledge as a factor available in the public domain. Executives and entrepreneurs held opinions on structural sorts relating to knowledge wealth differently. Differences in relative importance or relative arrangements of the constituents of a structural sort, therefore, indicate differences in strategic intentions.

Linkages of software firms

Sticky knowledge, derived from the market, is usually internally readable within a structure. Also, firms with more earnings from products seemingly tend to employ more marketing people while those with few marketing personnel tend to earn most of their revenue from repeat customers, with whom they entered in general into long-term contracts. A long-term marketing arrangement indicates an alliance type of a relationship. In fact, all customer relations types indicate formation of alliances, which are sometimes explicit as in an 'offshore development centre' or maybe 'long-term/one-time' in nature, or else are somewhat less explicit as in profit and loss sharing, value-based contracts. Most such marketing agreements discussed here fall under the strategic move types: 'fluidity', 'prevarication', or 'dependence'. The constituents of the structural sort are influenced by these strategic moves. Knowledge wealth pertaining to different types of agreements is, however, different.

The absence of marketing alliance partners or of allies, with whom strategic technology development can be undertaken, is indicative of certain specific types of knowledge wealth. It seems that Indian firms, often protected by dependency type long-term contractual obligations, fail to muster the sticky knowledge that they acquire from marketing into knowledge wealth.

The survey data also indicated that firms considered existing clients as the most dependable ally, as it were, to proceed with new product launches or for following up with any strategy to enhance or innovate upon product/service superiority. Building up reputation and brand has not been the frequented mode, possibly because firms are often small. This data further indicated that technological achievements, R & D, and value propositions are well accepted modes of strategy. In short, the most preferred strategic mode appears to be dependence on the large customer as a quasi-ally and to forge with it long-term contracts, while simultaneously emphasizing the technological superiority of one's product or services, if necessary through R & D.

The lack of division of labour across domestic firms led to a situation of little complementarity amongst domestic firms. The path dependence on outsourced business processes forced this lack of division of labour. This path of a typical Indian software firm led it to specialize in techniques, which could offer little complementarity amongst domestic firms. Only a few Indian firms have global alliances, which in turn would seek complementing capabilities, which Indian firms with their techniques dependency find difficult to offer. Their other salient features include a minimal dependence on collaboration or alliance for project marketing and a high percentage of revenue from repeat customers. Perhaps the most significant feature is around the sources of information on market opportunities. Market agents and direct talks with interested companies are the most dominant group of sources. Several firms offer products only with own brand names; few undertake to develop products bearing the collaborators' brands.

Resident competence

Market competence is derived from structural competence. Knowledge of the market and employment of this informational knowledge to other constituents of the structural sort generate structural robustness. The nature of the market matters and outsourced businesses must remain dependent on the path dependencies of the customer firms. Competence must then refer not only to firm-internal structural coherence but also to aspects of co-ordination with structures of outsourcing customers and with existing or expected groups of customers. Umbrella cover as a strategy takes care of this aspect of correspondence. Structural correspondence must appear in correspondences across several constituents of the firm such as its knowledge employees and allies. Market competence then reflects structural robustness internally and from the various aspects of correspondences. The co-ordination between internal constituents of a structural sort and co-ordination with structures or strategies of clients jointly determine the competence of a software firm. The example (see Chapter 4) of market competence from a small set of data was captured through a total of nine modules, each a simple ratio. Market competence is the sum of all these modules, each reflecting a ratio on the constituents of a structural sort or on co-ordination across structures. Data indicate that firms were nearly equally evenly distributed over structural compulsions. Firms sometimes opted for minimal co-ordination while others opted for maximal co-ordination with equally greater numbers of firms choosing paths intermediate between these two extremes.

Competence in knowledge wealth captured through indicators or market competence refers to competence in the structural sort to yield to the new demands. This competence to reshape is the ability to take umbrella cover. An organization reshapes the structural sort whenever necessary and resources allocation appears as a result of the yielding of the structural constituents.

This aspect is well captured through investments that the firms made. The value of such investments is deeply embedded in the inter-structure relations of co-ordination. The invested capital appears to be moving away from the domain of undisputed authority and control structure of the firm's structure. Similarly, declared information on R & D and on other investments in intangibles is a function of the strategies and of the market. Very low values of R & D suggest several possible states of affairs, including the institutional rigidity in the Indian market and its subservience to very large customers in the USA. There is little competition between the domestic firms. Competition – or whatever is there of it – between domestic firms, is forced to mediate through the external market. Strategic moves of the fluidity and prevarication types warrant an Indian software firm holding enough assets in liquidity. Ratios are not indicative of investment in durable assets or commitments to asset specificities. Instead, they are indicative of the choice of a particular liquidity. Liquidity is an insurance against lack of knowledge on another's structural sort. Liquidity is also an enabler of fluidity and growth in the direction of scope. Structural fluidity and the holding of assets in a fluid mode suggest that Indian firms are opportunity seeking.

Software strategy on fluidity and profit

This fluidity cannot be reckoned in terms of the Schumpeterian innovator's profit, especially in terms of Schumpeterian technological innovation. Schumpeterian profit is not entirely anticipated. It is an expectation meeting with success. This is the first understanding of a profit, which forms the basis of an action and requires co-ordination with existing knowledge. Schumpeterian profit is not entirely speculative. Shackle and Keynes refer to Cantillon's ideas on profit, the first of which is based on speculative valuation of the current states of affairs, and working on this hypothesis often leads to a counter-expected outcome in the form of windfall trading revenue surplus. This counter-expected surplus is the windfall profit of Keynes or the resolutional profit of Shackle. Speculative profit emerges from a state of ignorance. Resolutional profit emerges from a novel recognition of reality. Structural liquidity is the expression of ignorance. Knowledge is scarce and expensive.

Lack of knowledge on what choices could be made and on which durable asset or committed action the liquid asset can be spent results in both deferments of decisions and holding on to liquidity.

Strapped for resources and stymied by size, Indian software firms have to deal with poor liquidity sapping their strength. What precise strategic moves or what structural appearance of the incumbent could appear as an inducement to others – to invest more in liquidity, strengthened with social investment vis-à-vis investment in durability – is the subject matter of strategy.

Fluidity in software firms

The dilemma of a software firm lies in choosing between fluidity and size. If its strategy is to grow large and to market its products, it must make strong structural commitments and substantial investments in durable assets, including its manpower. Such investments and commitments would, however, force this firm to lose its fluid strategic moves, its asset liquidity and umbrella cover. Indian firms have lower commitments to the current competition, hold proportionately higher liquidity and are less committed to current structural sorts. Firm competency is derived from structural sorts, primarily from the ability to assume an appropriate umbrella cover. It is argued here that competency to switch across products and services also refers to speculative profits and limitations that might arise owing to constraints imposed by demands of co-ordination. Speculation is engendered by ignorance and is possible with fluidity in strategic moves. An Indian software firm could then undertake liquidity in a structural composition.

Routines and strategy

The received literature concedes that an organization's routines include higher-order routines that govern learning itself. They enable a firm to maintain behavioural continuity. Learning from the past and accumulation of such learning help behavioural continuity. The received theorist argues that competency is defined through this unimaginative accumulation. Acts of skill occasionally exhibit spurts of insights, which are not the outcome of reorganization of learning. Continuity denies opportunity and space to acts of insights, speculative inventions and innovations. A conscious attempt at cumulative syntheses brings about acts of insights, which do not result from learning or the competencies, or accumulations of such knowledge. It follows that competence can have little reference to behavioural continuity. Innovation then is necessarily out of disequilibria and is guided by the desire to bring about strategic surprise.

A structure is different from the organizational processes and evolves through strategic acts and not through strategic moves. Innovation, as defined here, implicates competency of a structure to transform or adapt itself to another structure. Structural switching is thus not simple structural change made through accumulation of knowledge but results from strategic acts that are different from strategic moves. This switching competence, it is argued here, warrants both firm internal and external aspects. Competence then refers to a market. It is further argued that competence refers to a partial market. A market is often identifiable in terms of peers or closest rivals. The resources market, even if in local equilibrium, can then be determined by rivalling strategies. Resources that a firm draws from the partial market are dependent on the firm's strategy. Simple competency to draw upon resources too would thus be dependent on firm structure and strategy.

Strategy and resources

Second-order resource is dependent on second-order competence that refers to the structural aspect of knowledge, defined here as knowledge wealth. Switching must also take place at this second level and must, in order to be reflexive, keep provision for an even higher third level. This reflexivity can come from third-order resources that have attributes only. It must be equivalent to decisions. Competency of a firm structure is this third-order competency or the dynamic competency and this alone can ensure innovations while keeping behavioural continuity. In simple competency, rule content and rule form are indistinguishable. Second-order competency retains only abstract contents and provides path-dependent learning. A core competency is, however, a pure rule, even devoid of abstract resources. It enables a firm to be a creative innovator and look for potential and imagined or speculated strategic milieus. These milieus cannot be extrapolated and hence derived from accumulated learning. Problem-solving too is tied up with the existing milieu third-order competency – as pure decision rules and as reflexive reasons – and looks beyond this immediacy of context. It creates its own strategic milieu. It can generate several novel umbrella covers or possibilities of the incumbent's structure. An umbrella cover as a switching mode is a ploy for both defence from strategic attacks and a form that assumes novel attacks. Structural transition that demands the lowest structural transition or switching cost can be achieved by this highest competency.

Strategic demand management

This is an internalist's account that did not care for the strategies of other firms in the partial market. The Indian software firm's dilemma over whether to develop a product or to deliver sophisticated project solutions is not derived from considerations on internal competencies though. It is derived from the problem of demand management, which is a novel idea.

Structural transition of a software firm takes place in response to the possibility or potential of demand management. Software-based organizational change is strange and this strangeness follows from the fact that while in ordinary changes, the change agent and the changed organization are distinct, temporally sequential and causally related; in information-based organizational changes, temporal sequence, causal order and distinct separation become elusive. Client firms cannot distinguish between changes in information from changes in business, and the client must procure software from such a supplier firm as is in dynamic structural co-ordination with the client. Therefore, software-based changes refer to structural co-ordination between two firms that are jointly producing to meet a demand. This implies that the software firm is no longer simply a supplier and the client firm is no longer a customer. The demand management refers to a new mode of co-ordination. Vertical integration proves to be uneconomic in such a joint demand management. Joint authority is impossible. The switching competence of a software supplier must thus refer to its ability to effect structural changes in its client's structural sort.

Strangely, this demand is generated by the dynamics of structural changes and can be managed only interactively and through mutual co-ordination between client and supplier. The product strategy of a software firm fails to derive demand from changes in structural sorts brought through mutual interactions and through mutually sustained structural switching. A software service, in contrast, is suited to that objective through speculative destabilization of its customer's structure. The supplier aligns with selective constituents of the structural sorts of the customer through structural switching. The switching competence of the supplier is then reflective of competence to co-ordinate demand management. The software services strategy is more capable of bringing about switching in both the client and the supplier. The absence of a strong strategy on product cannot then be described as weak. The software supplier's competence to switch between proto-products and services appears to be sound. A proto-product is a non-dominant product with non-global market and a short life cycle. A proto-product is specific to a particular strategic milieu.

Products or services as strategy

Product development by a software firm is often a supplementary act, which sustains its principal occupation of providing software services. A simple ratio of average man-days spent on development of a product to that spent on an average service project appears to be a good indicator of the structural capability to switch across projects through intermediate differentiated products. Structural competence to switch from product to services and vice versa, however, may be considered to be somewhat different. The structural competence of a firm to switch across services can be reckoned in terms of a 'service-product-service' strategy. Switching without intermediation of a reigning product platform can be likened to 'service...[product]...service' strategy. Intermediation by product is definitely underemphasized in this latter case where structural switching is necessarily simpler. The switching coefficient must reflect the structural ease with which a firm can switch its structural sorts. The capability to make a decision on the attributes of a structure, without being constrained by the contents of the structural sorts, is both a core competency and a competency of the third order.

Data and market characteristics

Demand management through structural transformation cannot refer to several issues of co-ordination that arise in a partial market due to a strategy for surprise profit. Structural transformation makes use of knowledge as wealth. Strategy for profit makes use of strategic knowledge. Manpower flow and use of information secured from this manpower are the keys to this strategy.

The quality of manpower is private information and experience alone cannot reflect this quality. Contract or negotiation remains incomplete if information on quality remains private with an opportunist employee. Quality information can, in a limited manner, act as a weak signal failing to reach the entire market. The strategic milieu, which is shared by structurally isomorphic firms, can be reached by this information and such a market remains 'uncleared'. Quantity signals define and clear a market that is macro. The incumbent firm or individual resource holder, however, acts in the micro domain where quality information proves superior to quantity signals. The partial market of strategic milieu thus trades in quality signals – such a market without market clearing status may be called 'meso'.

Knowledge, unlike a typical factor of production, is not an accumulated stock. Production and consumption of knowledge must go hand in hand, making knowledge a special type of joint production. Local quantity of manpower generation, its flow and quality are influenced or determined by firm strategies and acts undertaken by individuals. Production and consumption of manpower or knowledge thus refer to joint production. Tradability of knowledge as an asset is influenced further by the fact that knowledge always has a generalized and a particular aspect. Quality pertains to the particular and strategy is concerned about the particular.

Asset balance and strategic profit

Production of knowledge is not technologically determined and price of knowledge is not just as per demand. Nor does holding knowledge as idle stock carry much prospect. Knowledge can be reproduced, rehearsed or generated anew. Liquidity ensures a higher pay-off from a holding and liquid knowledge can refer to abstract generalization of knowledge. Obtaining unique prices thus fails. Knowledge prices exhibit several degrees of locality and knowledge is not homogeneous. A large number of local markets in knowledge, dictated by firm strategies, thus influence decisions pertaining to prices, investments and holding knowledge as asset balance. A typical software firm holds liquid fund and liquid-knowledge manpower in the form of 'waiting' and from which the firm cannot earn even an interest income. Liquid ideas or prototypes or completed solutions to a futuristic business opportunity are held in expectation of speculation. The balance between the three types of assets, namely liquid money, knowledge in waiting and knowledge in regular business, will thus not be determined by the prevailing interest rate in the market and the money supply.

The stored knowledge-asset formation balance in a software firm cannot be a tradable asset. Tradability implies that all firms have information on the worth of any such balance and that lowers the speculative profit value or the strategic value of such knowledge asset. The ingenuous mode of holding such knowledge is quality manpower, which cannot, however, hold the knowledge as specific or tied up or tacit inaccessible content. A software firm looks for a social net of professionals that acts as a buffer, to which it can shunt its temporarily excess manpower and from where it can hire them again. This social net must keep on reproducing knowledge.

Knowledge held back from immediate consumption represents the first type of distributive aspect that recognizes the future. The distributive aspect of social net spreads over two more horizons. Diffusion or imitation follows innovations around the future frontiers of knowledge. This results in distribution. The second mode of distribution is through a flux of manpower into the social net that gains in new knowledge and reproduces or generates new knowledge in several organizations.

Software manpower as asset

For a firm, manpower and knowledge are not simply technologically determined cost-based production or assets for the purposes of exchange. Even as internal assets they remain distributed over structural sorts of that firm. In contrast to the asset specificity perspective based on tacitness, a routine software writing or on the job experience leads to a tradable outcome. The degree of tradability of knowledge is a function of the market for knowledge and is not at all related to the supposedly existing tacit–explicit domain. Tradability is an outcome of two factors, namely, strategy and market for knowledge. Knowledge out of routine practice is most tradable and is easily accepted as a tradable asset. Knowledge sourced in structural practices is less recognizable as an asset. Finally, knowledge sourced in operations of manoeuverings on processes of other organizations is the least tradable and has the lowest value as an asset. Asset value depends on strategy and on the existing market for knowledge where these two factors operate in reverse directions.

To trade in knowledge assets or to procure differentiated knowledge assets from the market, a firm must simultaneously force its structural sorts to accommodate divisions of labour inside the organization in accordance with the market. The period of production refers to the time taken by the market to be commensurate with the quality-seeking strategic division of labour initially undertaken inside a firm. A firm begins with quantity information from the market to select a domain to work upon. Through strategic divisions in knowledge internally, this firm generates quality signals at a later period. Investment in the generation of domain knowledge does not preclude a firm from generating knowledge that represents further specializations on that domain and these qualities guide the other firms in the market to replicate similar qualities. Quality information then, following a period of production, leads to quantity signals. Tradable asset knowledge is context dependent and the abstraction of context leads to qualities that are not easily tradable and that are held for strategic purposes. Generalized structural or strategic knowledge cannot be communicated and, therefore, cannot be traded as an asset.

Divisions of knowledge and software

The strategy of a software firm hastens divisions in internal knowledge ahead of the market and the firm acts as the source of dynamism in the market. Enhanced internal divisions raise transaction costs of the firm. A firm does not restrain divisions in knowledge and increase differentiation. The enhanced degree of specialization or what might be called a strategic edge explains the increase in transaction cost. Quantity demands based on strong market-wide signals require accumulation of such quality-based finer divisions to take place over the short period of production in an economy. A quantity signal follows a period of production, which is long. Strategic decisions of a firm depend primarily on the weak quality signals. Quantity information decides the resources availability in the market while quality information decides the strategy of a firm.

Investment in yet-to-be tradable assets appears as 'asset formation balance' with little current market value but with strategic import and with deep distributive implication. This balance is equivalent to the R & D balance and generates yet-to-be-tradable assets with least site-specificity. The current bargaining by a software firm depends on what competency it can exhibit to its clients. This competence relates to the quantity identified broad divisions of knowledge such as domain competence. Competence alone cannot provide the firm with a speculator's or Cantillon profit. To get to that, a firm saves up resources as an asset in balance and in the form of finer divisions of knowledge that are currently not tradable. This balance influences strategies of product, of consultancy and of services.

Normative co-ordination

The indefinite boundary of a software firm and the interdependent capabilities and processes of firms in a milieu have thrown new challenges to the relevance of strategy for co-ordination. The interdependence of firms, which is coterminous with interoperability of the products of these firms, cannot be considered as pre-reconciled. The interoperability and co-ordination in software are emergent and not results of *ex post* reconciliation. Concurrent co-ordination leads to an equilibrium and interoperability forces movement towards equilibrium. We argue that there must be a variant of information other than the two mentioned as business and technical, that can shift a firm from equilibrating interoperability to a process of disequilibria. Co-ordination of expectation on expectation, it is argued here, achieves this without keeping the boundary of a firm sacrosanct or definite. This third variant of information precipitates co-ordination of expectations. Parties to an exchange of information act based on expectations through mediation of norm. Normative co-ordination is a process and refers to capabilities residing beyond firm boundaries. If firms have to concurrently expect or hold expectations on expectations on a set of innovations, resource or structure-based strategy should give way to a normative expectations co-ordinating norm.

Human resource is the carrier of this third variant of information. Interoperability can be pre-reconciled, timeless and non-sequential. It can also be an input–output system of an interdependent succession of events that apportions in time intermediate products. Technology can be incorporated in this latter system that does not depend on pre-reconciliation and on equilibrium conditions. It is argued that a strategic move influences and orients the moves by other firms and is dependent on the expectation on expectations, or normative co-ordination of several intermediate software products through an act of deferment of the consumption. Deferment elongates the period of production and elongates the divisions of labour. Deferment constitutes capital and increases the rate of profit. Strategic knowledge increases capital and the rate of profit.

Deferment as software strategy

Deferment is not pre-reconciled and it allows opportunism and cheating and technological changes. Deferment is capital and is not due to a 'market failure'. Richardson thinks delay is undesirable and institutions including vertical integration alleviate problems of delay. Systemic innovation takes place as per pre-reconciled plan although it prolongs delays. Autonomous innovations would experience shorter delay. Following Shackle, it is argued here that systemic innovations must appear through an uncertain mechanism of 'orientation' of expectations. The delays and their lengths are attributable to this orientation. The longer the delay or the 'average period of production', the higher is the capital usages or cost. An average period is as per the plans made by all participants to the production net in an epoch. The short period is as per the plans made by participants for a systemic technology while a period even shorter is as per plans made by those few who participate in an autonomous technological innovation. The lengths of periods are determined by economic states of affairs including increase in divisions of labour rather than by technological innovation. Technology alone can determine efficiency and the velocity with which an intermediate product might move. Strategic moves bypass technological determination by inventing and innovating further on economic organization of production. This takes a firm beyond Schumpeterian technological profit or rent to the Cantillon surprise profit or the strategic profit.

Deferment takes place through a norm, which is neither a rule nor a routine. A norm sets in injunctions. Ordinary co-ordination depends on durability that reduces uncertainty through commitment and reciprocation. *Ex post* plans and existing technological paths are durable too. The novelty in technology or innovation and reduced durability of investment allow economic agents to engender differentiation of labour and increase in lengths and circuits of a production net. Divisions of labour across firms or across several groups are contingent to a situation of expectations and are fluid. Co-ordination of long deferments demands an institutional solution, which normative co-ordination provides but vertical integration, as an organizational solution, does not. The evidence from Indian software points out the undesirability of vertical integration as a solution that is preferred consequent to a pre-reconciled plan and durable investment.

Irreversible commitment means a closure to increase in the division of labour and the deferment. Cantillon profit vanishes under these situations. Irregular writing of software represents reversible investment in manpower as held or held-back assets that offer prospects through deferment. The volume and frequency with which such assets are held back depend on the opportunity cost of withholding, expected gain in the irregular business and the frequency with which one might strike bargains. The portfolio of a software firm consisting of manpower in regular as well as irregular business, the money held and the manpower that can be hired from the social circuit, depend on which part of the logistics of expectation a firm is in.

Manpower turnover and normative co-ordination

Normative co-ordination tells us that the competency of a firm is decided not internally but evolves interdependently over time on expectations on expectations. A future surprise comes through a moderated process with each small surprise as a strategic step in broaching ignorance. Ignorance as a counterfactual to the current knowledge of the *ex post* states of affairs must be based on current knowledge on what others are not expecting. In normative co-ordination, price and quantity data are irrelevant because those refer to the past.

Information exchange in typical co-ordination does not refer to internal processes and structures. Software firms look for carriers of information that can interpret, generate and creatively employ information on internal processes. This firm requires intermediate goods because deferment necessarily requires elongated intermediation. Manpower flowing between firms can satisfy both these requirements. Information-in-expectation has as goal disequilibria and it refers to ignorance. Expectation is a function of ignorance. Common knowledge cannot provide the foundation to expectation. Definite knowledge shapes internal structural sorts while ignorance cannot shape structural sorts though it can influence internal processes, which are the sources of expectation.

Job switching defers consumption. Decisions on deferment by a firm do not depend on the quantity signal but on the turnover rate, which is indicative of the period of production averaged in that partial market. This partial market rate is unrelated to quantity. It reflects asymmetric information-generative capabilities of the personnel and is an indicator of the expectation on the rate of profit in that market. Thus, internal processes of a firm are directly dependent on the partial market parameters. The differences across firms are a function of delay. The uniqueness of a firm depends on delay function, which is a representation of learning. Deferment by a firm is represented in the learning of that firm. This partial market deferment acts as a norm that a firm ought to follow. Potential gains of firms do differ owing to differences in learning or the knowledge-generative dimension of the time period of deferment. Potential gain is thus a function of time that has been named as the delay function here. Firms normatively co-ordinating must consider each other's delay functions.

Manpower flow and strategic profit

If firms with a static average period of production continue increasing divisions of knowledge in the short period, new, incoming divisions replace some divisions. The nature of intermediate goods must also keep varying in that case. Normative co-ordination must then exchange not only varying information but also varying intermediate goods that contain capital in the process of deferment. Knowledge resident on an individual alone can ensure this property of capital. This not-yet-complete knowledge of an individual can be completed through inter-firm normative co-ordination. Firm uniqueness depends on the ability to guide generation of information and deflection of the expectations of other firms. Information-in-expectation is the foundation of innovation, which is beyond Schumpeterian technological innovation and which supports increase in Cantillon profit. Here the private space, common to a partial market that brings together the internal processes of firms in a milieu through repeated exchanges of intermediate goods, is named 'Shackle space'. A Cantillon innovation, different from the Schumpeterian, requires the continuous creation of Shackle space, created through repeated flows of intermediate goods.

2
Strategy, Structure, Knowledge

Co-ordinating conflicts

Strategy and governance are related. Governance has wondered since the time of Adam Smith how market dynamics is co-ordinated or how individual choices get pre-reconciled. From a firm's perspective, strategy issues have considered how best to govern and mobilize competencies, resources and processes for one's own advantage and to the exclusion of other firms. The regulator or legislator perspective, however, considers the firm's strategy in terms of its effect on social welfare and adherence to or coherence with the other principal or minimal sets of social goals. There has thus been continual recognition that the strategic acts of firms maintain the market dynamics while the market responds by governing co-ordination amongst conflicting and incoherent demands. A closer look at this phenomenon led to the admission that the issue of governance was primary and perhaps more basic. The strategy of a firm governs such processes, as around authority, loyalty (Simon, 1991; Williamson, 1996) and agenda, which lead to distinctive traits of a firm and to the mobilization of resources by the firm. Similarly, social regulations or the prescriptive and normative boundaries set by principles of rationality and the rules of a game govern the strategic behaviours of the agents in a market. Governance, it appears, inheres through strategic considerations.

Strategy, however, must strive for a domain unrestricted by governance. Governance insists on pre-reconciliation, which ensures governability and co-ordination because that ensures continuation of governance over dynamic movements. Strategy, in contrast, aims to ensure maximization of personal gain. This gain or pay-off has multiple components and several descriptions. A more philosophically acceptable term for pay-off could be personal dessert or good. Seldom does an agent agree to apportion a pay-off without any constraint of governance. The absence of governance possibly ensures unrivalled pay-off. A strategic intent works for such unrivalled pay-off. Only in the potential absence or in the absence of expectation of such unrivalled pay-off does an agent agree to be governed. More specifically, the agent then agrees to abide by the rules of competition. It is tacitly agreed here that competition conforms to governance, while strategy is always on the lookout for the moment of surprise or of novelty, to overturn the rules and the co-ordination endowed governance apple-cart.

A strategic move or an act can only be effected through a structure. There is thus one agency that owns a structure and has the strategic intention and at least another counter-structure over and above which the pay-off would be secured. The general belief is that firms are such structures. Contemporary theories suggest that the processes of a firm are the latent structures. When the governance function of the firm is amiss, these processes must get pre-reconciled or co-ordinated by an entity more extensional than the firm. Certain theorists suggest that institutions or, sometimes, the 'particular markets', serve this function of governance in a more loose sense. Pure market governance, as through signalling of prices, is vague and hazy although there are theories taking that position. It seems more pragmatic and less theoretically ambitious to consider strategic structures as an individual, a firm, the processes and the particular markets or other similar institutions.

This book examines these structures as residences of governance as well as of strategic moves and strategic acts. They are engaged in a strange interplay: between strategy and governance passing through the vicissitudes of these structures, which is the theme of the present inquiry. It stems from dissatisfaction with currently dominant theories on the interplay that prompts this departure from select strands of these dominant theories. Implicitly, it is being argued that this inquiry does not make departures from 'a theory' but departs from certain strands of 'a theory'. This chapter presents a collage of strands from theories that often proclaim their absolute separation. The dissatisfaction primarily arises from the conflation of governance with strategy. These are not dramatic polarities opposed to each other. The desired outcome of strategy, it is argued, is governance over other structures. This dramatic engagement takes place over several kinds of structures. The dissatisfaction also stems from the defining of strategy. Ultimately, it is individual intention that acts as the agent moving the structures ahead, keeping a system dynamic. It seeks to maximize personal dessert, gains, good or pay-off. This intention – using different languages and adopting different measures – as it is pointed towards personal gains, demonstrates such observable features as exclusion of others from partaking of the gains. It is argued that this intention is the core of strategy. Excluding others from the gains or influencing others to become imitators or followers are definable in terms of maximization of personal pay-off. Finally and ironically, strategy seeks to govern another's strategy formulations. This is a governance function of strategy. This chapter looks into this strategy, the structures through which such a strategy acts and the governance issues, including that of co-ordination, which seek to regulate the unsettling intent of strategy. This current exposition on the Indian software experience will largely be explained through portraits of the dramatic acts.

The essence of the new logic

Strategy seeks to hasten governance and is realized through a structure. Indeed, strategy is the principal reason for the formation, evolution and sustenance of a structure. Having shaped the structure of its own business organization, strategy strives to shape structures of other business organizations in the incumbent's strategic milieu. In the governance over structures and over formation as well as implementation of strategies by these structures lies the abiding good of the incumbent's strategy. Governance is thus the pay-off of a strategy. This is a significant departure from the received theories, which have either neglected or minimized the importance of governance or argued that governance and strategy are parallel and coterminous. Several such theories from transaction cost economics (TCE), evolutionary economics, including competency theories, industrial organization (IO) or even resources perspective can be compared in this scheme of reasoning.

This departure may be construed as steps towards building an alternative theory but is essentially a far more modest attempt, arguably because a grand theory – capable of explaining and predicting activity outcomes of several economic and organizational aspects – is uncalled for. The argument here resembles piecemeal engineering. This pragmatic approach does not claim to be based on any grand theory or even a set of models with good predictive powers. It examines pieces from the existing repertoire of theories and accepts as an explanation whichever seems most plausible, correct and appropriate. The preoccupation with the power to predict is unwarranted because research shows that such powers are not innate to theories. Instead, they result from the influences on a subject and retroversion of the subject and object of a theory. It is also not clear how strategy theory can be tested. A strategy largely deals with beliefs, is based on intents and consults knowledge. A strategy first deals with the cognitive and the mental; secondly, with powers as noticed by the incumbent; and with knowledge, information and rationality as the third priority. In lieu of a theory, one can proceed with a task of weaving several designs. Each such design borrows from received theories but collectively the designs differ from any of such theories.

Structure, as conceived here, results from strategy and differs from structures as in scaffolding. Such structures have been termed 'structural sort'. The four constituents of a structural sort include the chief of the incumbent organization, its important stakeholders and senior executives, its wealth, including finance and knowledge, its knowledge employees and its allies. This sort includes the material domain over which governance prevails and it includes an ensemble of organizational forms named 'umbrella cover', which this incumbent organization may revert to.

The strategic make-up has, apart from the structural sort, five types of organizational process that maintain the dynamism in the organization. An incumbent strategist seeks to win an adversary. In a strategic move between the two, there appear two more types of strategic attitude holding organizations. The logic of strategy demands that it should not be global but remains limited to a partial market constituted by these four actors. This partial market is called a 'strategic milieu'. Each organization in this milieu has five processes, making the twenty processes in the milieu the desired subjects of governance. They are what the incumbent strategist wishes to gain control over.

Structural sort is thus one key player amongst several making up the strategic initiative. Knowledge participates in strategy severally and three types of knowledge are described here: strategic knowledge, knowledge as a factor of production and knowledge wealth. Strategic knowledge, it is being argued, is about conditions for beliefs in the processes under the lens. Knowledge, as a factor of production, is descriptive and can be bought and sold or otherwise procured from the market or from public domain. This knowledge cannot be strategic. Knowledge wealth, however, constitutes a structure and is also mostly not descriptive. This knowledge is strategic because strategy modulates it and is, in turn, modulated by it.

Quest for a theory?

Is one seeking for 'a' theory? The answer is presumably in the negative. It is not possible to present a bundle of facts whose axiomatic generalization leads to a theory. In any case, contemporary investigators have discarded such an approach. One could offer, instead, a collection of models, which according to the semanticist is a theory (Suppe, 1974). This collection of models would not pass the coherence scrutiny even if it did appear meaningful. Thus, this account would be closer to a pragmatist's account. Models presented in this book do not aspire to be explanations of certain states of affairs. An explanatory account often looks into the 'why' of facts, and models here do not provide such answers. The current quest is thus not for typical deductive – nomological or inductive – statistical models of explanations as offered by Popper (1959) and Hempel (1965). These models do not fit into a larger whole – a worldview – or Weltanschauung's position, whose details are unspecified but whose presence is felt through the mode in which the models are organized. These models get organized in the total belief systems or cognitive worlds and such organization is not 'known' but can be felt. The philosophy here stems from a sense of unease with the seeming discordance between what the parts of the models might lead to. One redeeming fact is that a model can be entirely pragmatic (Papineau, 1987; Putnam, 1995), being able to explain only a fragment (Van Fraassen, 1980). Another model might explain the other fragment even though the two are not logically coherent or causally connected. A model or even its fragment might be able to offer what has been described as an inference to the best explanation (Harman, 1973). A small background of the beliefs or models might even unconsciously support such inference to the best explanation. However, this background does not present a coherent whole nor does the model collection appear as one.

The unease referred to earlier stems first from the background to belief contents not being known and enhanced by the fact that possibly even the belief contents forming the basis for the book are not coherent. There is an undeniable influence of the paradigm (Kuhn, 1962). However, only parts of the model here might have 'noticed' the paradigm and selectively lifted significant terminology from generative linguistics or from evolutionary biology on the basis of specific attention to them. In fact, most often lifting such terms did not make these borrowing theories more formal. Neither has reference to facts by these borrowing theories made them more substantive and relativized. Borrowed terms, it must be remembered, have served the purposes of rhetoric and in inter-theoretic dialogues as between industrial organization approach (IO) and evolutionary approach to strategy. These terms have been employed in an entirely non-formal but a substantive sense. Such borrowed terms, therefore, have only noticed a paradigm and have not even attempted an inference to the best explanation or they might not have sought coherent justification. Paradigms did not work then. Rhetoric took the lead and brandished terms, such as 'distinctive competence', in an otherwise significant discourse. Obviously, the models here too have borrowed such terms, which have been relativized terms and entered into rhetoric.

Understandably, the current account will be quizzed on the truth it contains. Contemporary theorists have taken a position that the predicate 'true' does not 'describe' the proposition but 'endorses' it. This endorsement could be sought in the pragmatic fact of meaningfulness and in the truth provoking actions to desired results. This account might simply be focusing on its ability to provide a basis for action. This surely involves a shift from the propositional account. The truth of a model need not then be sought in its correspondence or in its verifiability. However, other accounts from psychology for example, which provide a descriptive psychology that provides a 'correspondence' account of truth, are being employed. This does not, however, imply that a correspondence account of truth is necessarily being endorsed. Nor is it being implied that the recourse to several models as opportune and pragmatic devices signifies a reverting to a deflationary account of truth. A deflationary account of truth validates a proposition as true when there is a fact, which validates this kind of a truth. One then needs possibly infinite accounts and equal numbers of facts. Here models are being used to account for partial generalization. Models can endorse the truth of certain actions that need to be undertaken for strategic gains. The models used here are restricted to this modest claim.

More limitations to strategy theory

Facts in strategic affairs are not impervious to actions undertaken by a strategist. A strategic action in this sense is a strong commitment. An act cannot be reverted and the consequences to an act are irreversible. An altered fact is a new fact. A model or a theory is not defined on strategic acts. A model cannot take into account a complete and exhaustive informational account of facts leading to a strategic action. Further, an act is provoked by the momentary passion. Passion cannot be described through an exhaustive informational account. Together, these two constraints render it impossible to verify the justification of a strategic act. Most importantly, such a fact or such an action cannot be recreated. An act is situated in a context. The temporal relations between an act and its context create a fact. Such a fact cannot be recreated. An act that delivered an end result at one moment might not recreate a similar result later. No action can be claimed to be the 'best' or the 'optimal'. As history proves, lost heroes are easily forgotten, while strategy-gaining actions get role model positions. Narratives on strategy too create role models, as do theories generated out of contingent facts of 'success'. Verificationism has, however, not died. A large number of evaluative, prescriptive and deontic 'decision-cues', often provided to practising managers on a regular basis, are, in fact, based on this paradigmatic verificationism. Predictability is only another offshoot of this paradigm.

In this sense then, predictability, the much-acclaimed quality of a theory, stands on quicksand. Predictability depends on the actual impact of the predictive theory on the preforming of a belief, opinions and possible actions of a strategist. The predictable outcome is the result of the impact. The object of a theory then becomes that subject who is a participant in the making and in the testing of that theory. The object of theory has 'appropriated' as a subject the results of the theory in a reflexive manner (Schutz, 1971). A theory of strategy cannot be chosen out of a set of contending theories based on its predictive power or similar operational characteristics.

Further, a strategist undertakes an act based on believed readings of a complex situation (Hayek, 1973–8, vol.2; Simon, 1979a, 1979b) and, therefore, incompletely readable. Strategic states of affairs are not repeatable because there are commitments and hence the situations are un-'Galilean'. Finally, an action of the strategist has 'unintended consequences' (Hayek, 1973–8, vol.1). A strategist is satisficing and only intendedly rational (Simon, 1983a, 1983b) and it is argued here that the strategist is thus 'limitedly' rational. Even while presented with enough informational account of a situation, a strategist looks for 'typical' and believed 'prospects' (Bell, Raiffa and Tversky, 1988; Kahneman and Tversky, 1979; Kahneman, Slovic and Tversky, 1988). In order to read a situation informationally, all undesired information is overlooked and 'attention' paid to or 'notice' taken of what the strategist as an intentional agent had failed to achieve. In the process, the strategist develops a body of metaphors and metaphoric cues that helps to notice information that the 'intention' has been seeking. Game theorists, in particular (Aumann, 1976; Dixit and Nalebuff, 1991; Schelling, 1960) have attempted a heroic retrieval of such a strategist by inducting in their theoretical framework a normative and prescriptive rationality, whose norms and deontic imperatives forbid a likely departure. A departure, Gibbard (1995) argued, has consequences which the agent as a self-seeking person cannot entertain. However, the concern here with game theoretic rationality as a norm is that apart from human limitations in processing of information, or in paying attention, or in foreseeing unintended consequences, a strategist's action most reflects (in the Hobbesian sense) the dominant passion at the moment of action. Even rational and well-informed human agents commit themselves to actions provoked by momentary passion. A thinking Cartesian mind, it would appear, stands apart most often from the passionate provoker.

This seems to imply that it would be difficult to locate a 'typical' subject and 'ordinary' economic agent, whose strategic behaviours can be theorized. The first difficulty is with the behaviour-based study and the second difficulty is with recovering 'ordinary' agents from both the socially constructed milieu and the labyrinth of personal idiosyncrasies. Taking the latter aspect first, using what Gibbons (1987) has described as the hermeneutics of recovery and of suspicion, one observes a near impossibility in recovering or otherwise being sceptical about the 'ordinary agent', who is immersed in several layers of socially constructed reality. It is even more difficult to recover the 'type' from the idiosyncratic belief holder. To overcome this latter difficulty, Davidson (1984) invoked the 'principle of charity'. This argues that even in order to achieve recovery from personal idiosyncrasies, on the one hand, one needs to be charitable enough to accommodate the beliefs, desires, aversions and such emotions of others. On the other hand, theories should accommodate the propositional attitudes of the individuals. It is contended here that surprise and novel moves are non-accommodated more. Most parts of decisions are not pre-reconciled. Operationally, a decision that is reasoned and rational and even unique appears to be an accommodated or pre-reconciled decision arrived through a *tâtonnement* – because the operationalization takes place in an institution, which is pre-reconciling. The unique decision is thus made into an accommodated or charitable decision. Charity appears to be even larger when instead of decision, the actions are turned into co-ordinated or accommodated actions by the prevailing institutions. Institutions do effect the job of translating the unique actions or decisions.

The second point raised here about behavioural symmetry, described by Geertz as the 'thin' description, is an equal suspect. Recorded behaviours are as observed in the context of an institution such as the believed truth that records are observer or institution (or milieu of observation) independent. Behaviourist claims that an observation by anyone or at any time records behaviour identically. Each 'observation', it is contended here, is but an 'attention' or 'noticing'. Intention notices and the Cartesian mind can be reported to. Putatively then, the same behaviour is noticed as different behaviours. A strategist certainly observes behaviours of other strategic players in the milieu but such observation does not endorse behavioural modelling by an unnoticing 'observer'. Moreover, a theory based on recorded behaviours must, according to Geertz, be a 'thick' description by incorporating values and propositional attitudes into a description or in an explanation of behaviours. Game theoretic accounts based on conjectures of the players are indeed a step in this direction of a thick description. However, outcomes are predicted under the assumption that players are rational and game structures are either a common knowledge or mutual knowledge (Brandenburger, 1992; Brandenburger and Dekel, 1989). If these assumptions do not hold, this theory cannot offer a thick description.

Minimal retrieval

This account has so far presented the limitations to theorizing on strategy. Limitations mark out a territory, for example, by informing one what might not be expected of a theory or what the theory might not contain. Limits do not prescribe the contents of a theory. Thus, a sort of 'negative freedom' has been achieved and one has the positive freedom to include several models or explanations in this vague journey to theory. One might not wish to complete a theory or even an explanation. The contents of the theory then remain unspecified and the theory will always have an incomplete listing. Each listed model or explanation in this theory-sort is then specific to the instantiated situation. The listed explanation cannot lay a claim on a larger set of situations. Moreover, explanations or models belonging to this theory-sort might possess characteristic assertions or belief systems that are not congruent or coherent. This is a sort of piecemeal engineering approach. One is not making a Quinean claim (1986) relating to normative epistemology. Quine referred to the 'technology of truth-seeking' and a normative, which becomes descriptive when the terminal parameters are provided. A contemporary game theoretic approach is closer to this Quinean normative epistemology than what is being argued here. This normative consideration is driven by efficiency or efficacy.

This account too is epistemic in nature. It is concerned about the efficacy of the theory-pieces. However, in this understanding, efficacy relates to action. Efficacy for Quine implies power to attain a higher degree of truth; efficacy for Williamson (1999), for example, implies power of prediction. In this proposal, efficacy implies a power of guiding action to the desired result or the good. A strategy theory maps out actions that are efficacious in achieving the goal or the final good of a strategy undertaken. This account is close to a pragmatist's account. A strategy study, according to this approach, should be delineated from studies on other aspects of management on the basis of the good that a strategy study proposes to bring about. The epistemic concern here is not related to normative epistemic considerations or to any reliably produced true belief, which according to Goldman (1986) is knowledge. An epistemology might be able to guide an arrival to knowledge (which could be normative, according to Quine or conceptual, according to Goldman). It could be argued though, that knowledge is that which guides a right action (Castaneda, 1975, 1989). Therefore, understanding knowledge is not singularly conceptual or singularly normative or prescriptive nor even singularly descriptive. Kornblith (1985) and Harman (1986) are close to this position because they argue the difficulties involved in separating the normative from the descriptive. Stitch (1990) also points out the influence of values in the belief-acquisition process and this proposal too argues that conditions to belief are immensely important to the acts undertaken. This proposal is pragmatic on two counts: first, it shows the importance of belief conditions to actions undertaken; secondly, it differentiates knowledge claims based on the final good aimed at through actions.

The argument here is that a strategy theory is different from other theories on management because the former offers a unique good. The division of knowledge, according to this understanding, is based on separations between different goods. Every knowledge undertaking according to this perspective must be defined by the good or the dessert to which one is entitled by this knowledge. In other words, knowledge entitles its seeker to a definite and particular good. A particular theory must principally address how to achieve a particular good. The next question is what is the good of a strategy theory. What specific good can be achieved through strategic actions? Several authors (for example, Ansoff, 1965; Porter, 1980; Schelling, 1960) have pointed out the importance of 'influence'. Perhaps no important piece of writing on strategy has failed to bring out this aspect of influence in such different terms as deterrence or barrier. Most often authors have painted pictures where influence appears to be one among several other goods. Game theorists ordinarily have used pay-off with wide connotations, including economic rent and influence by power. Evolutionary (Winter, 1964) and competence theorists, including the resource theorists, have used notions of influence that are necessary to manage processes and resources internal to the organization for strategic ends. Transactions cost theorists have definitely used governance as a key word. Organization theorists (Mintzberg, 1979; Weick, 1979, 1995) have used various notions of power and influences. Finally, theorists of strategy process (Foss, 1996, 1999; Foss and Mahnke, 2000; Foss and Robertson, 1999) and bounded rationality (Cyert and March, 1963; March and Simon, 1958; Simon, 1979b, 1983a, 1991), the latter in particular, have strongly emphasized the importance of power and influence.

Difficulties remained with such coinages though. Except such authors as Simon, Schelling, and others, most proposed a panorama of good achievable from strategic acts. It appears that these theorists are often interested exclusively in seeking out good as being of immediate economic worth. An influence brings about economic worth. However, it is argued that an economic worth can have or indeed does have multiple connotations. Sustenance of economic worth or raising barriers to other potential entrants or allocating knowledge resources for a possible future gain are all economic worth, achievable through exercise of certain authority. Such an authority over the processes under consideration remains an abiding good.

Strategy for governance

The proposal here is categorical. The good or the final goal of strategy is to achieve governance over a state of affairs. Strategy is for governance. Subsidiary to this principal good are several kinds of pay-offs, most of them being immediately measurable in terms of economic gains. This governance is equivalent to Simon's 'authority'. It is cherished by a single agent, an organizational process, a team and an organization or even by a group of organizations. Thus, all conceivable agents are empowered by this proposal to undertake actions for achieving governance over others of strategic concern. The governance over a milieu of strategy ensures several subsidiary good of strategy. It can thus be claimed that governance is the good of strategy. Other aspects of managerial studies are, *inter alia*, concerned about achieving good that is different from governance. This, as the principal objective of a theory of strategy, differentiates strategy theory from the rest of the theories.

This chapter began with observing a tension between governance and strategy. This tension is often prevalent at the fundamental level of theory construction. Received theories have painted a picture where governance inheres through strategy while strategy seems to look for good for purposes other than that of governance (this is true even of Williamson, 1996). This proposal overcomes this major lacuna and governance is observed as the central claim of a theory of strategy.

Strategy milieu

A theory must aim at delineating locales in which it can be applied. The scope of this theory has been delimited by pointing out several limiters such as non-verification and non-coherence. It is also pointed out that the proposal is necessarily incompletely specified. The question now is: how far can a strategy aim to govern? Is the domain of governance aimed at a theoretical global? Can a strategy aim to govern every possible entity in a domain globally captured through certain generalizable parameters, for example a global market? Should such a theory limit itself to a domain when its parameters are known or can be specified by the implementer of strategy?

It is proposed here that a strategy theory is always limited to a 'particular market' (Marshall, 1919, 1920, 1925; Pigou, 1925) or 'a specific milieu'.

A strategy theory must include, it is argued, as its core, a particular market. The Industrial Organization approach (for example, Porter, 1980) or the Structure, Conduct and Performance Paradigm have evolved around the concept of an industry segment. The game theory part of IO recognizes competitors, substitutors, complementors and such others and thus constructs a milieu. Evolutionary theory is relatively more unspecific in this regard. Competency theory (Teece, 1986; Teece and Pisano, 1994, for example) recognizes a milieu. Such constructs of milieu are, however, often vague or quasi-global. Resource theory of strategy is perhaps most global because its resources markets are in global equilibrium.

This proposal further restricts the scope of milieu and brings it down to a Marshallian particular market. Marshall primarily considered a territorially local market. The argument here is for a particular market, not necessarily restricted by territory but by several other features (note a local circuit in a Braudelian market was sometimes not territorially local). Moreover, this construction of locality permits its consideration both within and outside an organization. Locality could be in terms of description, technological domain locality, strategic alliances locality or regional or resources market locality. Locality is a construct of the mind of the strategist who, limited by bounded rationality or by dwarfed ambition, grapples with a certain limited state of affairs, as it were. A state of affairs is a possible world. It is a believed world. The strategist reckons with this small or large state of affairs. Such a state of affairs has certain characteristic features, which will be dwelt upon.

Does the strategic goal or good define this possible world of locality? Or, is this because of situational features, which are independent of the strategist's intentions? The point is that – following an explanation of situation provided by the situation theorists, stating that a situation has both objective features and subjective or attitudinal or value-based features (see Barwise and Perry, 1983) – a strategic goal (in a Quinean sense, whose parameters draw out the road map of locality) defines a locality but is also under the influence of the disposition of the strategist. The disposition of a strategist reflects his beliefs. Beliefs might not be causally active in the formulation of the goal. However, beliefs condition the reckoning of a goal (Ryle, 1949). A belief as a state of mind can be causally implicated in the strategic actions of an agent. Beliefs are attitudes reflective of desires, aversions, intentions and such emotions of an agent towards the states of the world (Stalnaker, 1987). Belief states themselves are thus possible worlds: the several ways the world of strategy or the milieu of strategy could be. Beliefs thus notice 'a milieu' or 'a particular market' and it is the strategic intention triggering off a belief that causes a strategic action on this milieu. Here, one is recognizing a difference between a reason and a cause. A strategic goal is noticed by virtue of reason that is triggered or conditioned by beliefs. A strategic act in contrast is caused by an intention, an element of what gets reflected in beliefs.

The particular market of a strategist is then formulated by the strategic goal as well as conditioned by the beliefs of the strategist. The beliefs of a strategist will later be formulated in terms of a concept called strategic moves. Each particular market is thus both subjectively and objectively (or socially) formulated. A milieu or a strategic array is sustained by 'confluences'. Confluences are a part of the structure of a strategist. Each such particular market is formed around a strategic actor, named the 'winning strategist'. A firm as a winning strategist deploys a sort of structure, a set of processes, a set of strategic moves and a set of strategic actions on the strategic milieu. The following paragraphs examine this in detail.

Strategic make-up: strategy and structural sort

Chandler's work (1962; also Clark, 1961; Hounshell, 1984; Lazonick, 1991, 1992; Williamson, 1979, 1981) on strategy and structure has had a paradigmatic influence (Teece, 1980) on the later thinking on this subject. Chandler, and others following him, notably from economic theory of organization (Hart, 1988; Hart and Holmstrom, 1987; Holmstrom, 1990; Holmstrom and Tirole, 1989), looked at structure as the site that allows accumulation of gains in efficiency. For Chandler, structure is necessary to gain from capital and a structure results from the efficiency differences between employment of capital through organized and unorganized modes. Perhaps Barnard (1962) was among the first to notice singularity, in the form of a chief executive, in an otherwise even and quasi-homogeneous organization. March and Simon (1958) and Simon (1961) brought to the fore an array of hierarchy as detailed administrative necessity and additional appendages to the chief executive. Chandler's work mapped out large corporations and their divisional, departmental and otherwise replicated large administrative hierarchic structure. A very large literature has since then analysed the rationale and the functioning of such large structures. This mode of description on structure may be called the scaffolding description. A study of this sort on structural scaffolding and information passages met with criticisms from several perspectives, such as labour processes, regulation theorists (Boyer and Durand, 1997; Boyer and Mistral, 1982) and later from those who argued that information technologies were bringing down hierarchies (Antonelli, 1988, 1999). Several accounts of organization based on processes (Arrow, 1974; Simon, 1991; Weick, 1979, 1995), however, provided a position intermediate and sufficiently well grounded in theory. These accounts did not dispose of structural scaffolding altogether though. Instead, they emphasized the importance of processes as though these were the real structure to be retained and supported by the structural scaffoldings. In fact, Chandler too recognized that his account of scaffolding was based on the rationale of retention and channelization of authority throughout functional scaffolding by means of channels of information. Structures are permeated through and, some authors argue, inhere through, processes.

This account of structure departs from scaffolding theories of hierarchic, divisional and such other structures by making room for the dynamic processes that exist in a structure. This account will also keep processes separate from a structure and as the dynamic life-giving force of an organization. Tacitly, this account recognizes the difficulties, if not the impossibility, of demarcating a strict boundary to an organization. It is argued that the structural boundary exists but process boundaries, and similarly, organizational boundaries, are vague. Strictly speaking, one could argue that a strict boundary exists as a special case. In continuation, it is emphasized that this account on structure is an account of a structural sort. A structural sort is based on strategic moves and strategic actions. An organizational structure in this scheme of things is not static and inert. A structure of this sort assumes its structural forms according to the strategies undertaken in response to the strategic forces in the milieu. Understandably, there are situations when a structure hibernates or when a structure closely approximates organizational processes. There are other situations when a structure appears sharply against other structures and against the organization's own processes. Variability of the form of a structure, it is argued here, comes from the strategy of an organization.

The scaffolding of a structure has several limitations. Such a structure, it is argued, is rigid and often not robust. The proposed structure here is designed to be plastic (P) (changing shape appearances upon strategic demands) and is purposefully robust. A scaffolding structure is built around arms and is not structured around the structural nodes. As a result, a structural transformation has most often been envisaged as changing of a few arms (arms are similar to organizational units, SBUs – strategic business units, or profit centres, divisions or departments). Nodes at the arms-interfaces have been neglected in this consideration of structure. This proposal reverses the order. Here, a structure is woven around interfaces between structural entities and around nodes, named 'confluences'. The types of interfaces (structural entities) and confluences remain invariant over demands of strategy or over time. These types of interfaces and confluences then can describe a minimal structure. Of course, arms get appended to structural interfaces and sometimes, though informally, to confluences. Structural arms are important as well. Strategic demands effect restructuring by deleting, removing or creating arms around these interfaces. Such an interface-based and confluence-centred structure, it is argued, is not rigid to transformation, making this structure robust.

A structure from this perspective is not monolithic. A structure is a certain mode of assemblage, named a structural sort. This structural sort is primarily woven around interfaces and confluences (or one might call these nodes) but is not limited to only node-centric features. An adumbration of received literature suggests that the structural sort is woven through seven types of interfaces: the chief; senior power-holders; the material domain over which chief's authority extends, in short, the material domain; umbrella-cover; wealth and finance; knowledge employees; allies. These interfaces apart, there are nodes or confluences where organizational processes meet. Confluences are sites of visits, though mostly informal.

Describing structural sort

A structural sort cannot remain vibrant without even one of the afore-mentioned seven types. All are essential in this minimal description. Briefly, the chief is the final authority but is not necessarily the absolute authority. The important processes and decisions and important arms of the structure must visit the chief. Weakening of the 'chief' necessarily indicates a weak structure, possibly unable to pursue a strategy. The senior power holder is a stakeholder and is often also a senior executive. Several formal and informal links in an organization visit these power holders regularly. Most organizational narratives overlook the real struggle for power amongst these senior executives or otherwise senior power holders. A chief is weak when overshadowed by such power holders.

The material domain reflects the domain over which business authority (such as business decisions) of the chief prevails. A material domain can also be defined as the domain over which a business adds value. Ordinarily, this is called the organization. However, a chief's business decisions around production and distribution and such other functions often prevail over its dedicated suppliers, franchisees or even over alliance partners. Strictly speaking, these are not under the same organization. This terrain is defined as a part of the extended organization. A classic example is Toyota. In other words, the boundary of an organization is flexible and this boundary can both expand and shrink, even if no divestment or mergers and acquisitions have taken place.

An umbrella cover is like a hideout. A structure under attack (or perceived attack) often responds by resorting to several techniques of concealing or protecting itself. When the controlling group in a business is a minority shareholder, it often resorts to perceived takeover threats by increasing equity holding drastically or else through the creeping acquisition route. The territorial expansion or an intensification in the same territory of a business, entry or exit decisions, are some other examples of such umbrella cover. Sometimes an organization under threat undertakes restructuring, providing another instance of an umbrella cover. An organization might open itself to any new technological advance. For example there are cases of firms deleting business processes or divisions while opting for advanced information technology, such as enterprise resources planning (ERP) implementation. The objective is to be in tune with benchmark requirements of the ERP at all times. A benchmark of this type is expressed in the Baumol, Panzar and Willig's (1986) organization in a perfectly contestable market.

These are only some examples of the umbrella cover. A typology of such covers is possible.

A firm resorts to umbrella cover only under conditions of threat (Porter, 1980). Conditions of opportunity do not demand taking such a cover. Umbrella cover necessarily implies that the firm shrinks to its one or multiple core. This implies that core competency is defined as that support, which a firm under threat or perceived threat resorts to. This manner of defining a core avoids the circularity involved in Prahalad and Hamel's (1990) or Teece, Pisano and Shuen's (1997) construction. A firm's 'fundamental business' has been defined as the core by Teece *et al*. Williamson (1999: 1093) observes 'it comes perilously close to saying that a core competence is a competence that is core'. Prahalad and Hamel, however, recognize the Japanese threat and in response exhort American firms to discover cores. A core is not something given innately but is a structural response to strategic needs. Thus, the core into which an organization takes umbrella cover varies and shifts according to the type of threat. An umbrella-covered organization has a shrunken core and as argued here, a typology of such covers is possible. A few can be outlined here. Several authors have recognized a cover under high technology or advanced knowledge. A reverse mode of cover is afforded by a highly plastic organization. Another approach is to cover an organization by raising defensive legal protections.

Wealth and finance are part of the structural sort and attention is especially drawn here to knowledge wealth. A cash-rich organization is often a prey to an acquirer but a knowledge-rich organization, even if acquired, cannot be assimilated and put to a profitable line of business by any and every acquirer. Contrarily, an organization with finance and wealth can acquire other firms or put its wealth for structural expansion and strategic advantage. It follows from this that knowledge employees are important constituents of the structural sort. An organization with a higher ratio of knowledge employees to total employees is structurally rich. The point is that knowledge empowers such an enriched organization with greater innovative potential and higher adaptive capacity. Such a firm would be better placed to respond structurally to a contingent strategic demand. Allies and alliances have been studied by a large number of investigators in recent years. Organizational allies can be found in unrelated businesses, amongst strategic alliance partners, or amongst suppliers and customers, and amongst the complementors. Received literature has often indicated reciprocal alliance-specific asset development by firms. Allies and alliances have been reckoned as those who have made commitments. A commitment refers to structural transformation that is of mutual gain to both or multiple parties. Allies, therefore, are part of the structural sort.

A discussion on structural sort will remain incomplete without taking note of the place of confluences in the structural sort. A confluence is a site of visitations. In contrast to the common understanding of node (in a network) as a static structural holder and a point thus common to several arms of a structure, a confluence is a site, located anywhere in an organization and which receives visitations, formal and informal, of processes and resources. Through a confluence, an organization is revitalized recurrently. Further, a confluence is also a site of power. Several senior executives and others who wield organizational power occupy this position. The structural sort discussed here has few confluences within it. However, several other confluences remain outside that structural sort.

Beyond the structural sort: organizational makings

A structural sort organizes organizational processes that sustain an organization. It positions the processes. A structure serves as a base for the purpose of confrontation though processes alone can mobilize organizational resources, which a structure can then deploy in an act of strategy. The proposal here recognizes five types or categories of processes: the sustenance of leadership by the senior managers; the agenda for transforming the firm to an organization; the structural features of the organization; financial resources under control of the firm; the prospect of liability and threat (or punishment). Processes and structural sort together make up an organization's conditions for and capability of strategic move.

Processes revitalize an organization and, indeed, constitute the foundation to the structural sort. The last process, threat, is the most effective because it influences the beliefs of strategists and strategy groups (such as a process). Threat acts as a reason and, following the earlier discussion on the difference between reason and cause, one may also notice that threat does not act as a cause, or as a direct cause. Threat is an exemplar. Internal to the organization, a threat remains valid because, ultimately, the master–servant laws control most job situations. The threat of excommunication, loss of social prestige and relevance to the organization or the possible loss of a chance to lead a technologically challenging project are examples of such fears.

Extra-organizationally, a threat gets communicated most often by the law of tort and its liabilities (Rizzo, 1980). There has been a distinct shift, since Kelsen and recently in Hart (1961,1983), in the interpretation of the law of contracts towards limiting contractual obligation. Without going into the heart of the legal debate, it may be emphasized that no organization can be conceived without support from master–servant laws and without the power of adjudication – though vested partly with the legal institution (Jain, 2003; von Savigny, 1988). Such an organization is fiction.

Simon (1991) recognized the 'ubiquity of organizations' in a modern economy and emphasized that an organization be legitimized by its ability to motivate employees and by its efficiency. Motivation and efficiency, Simon argues, rest on four processes: authority, rewards, identification and co-ordination. The five processes indicated in the proposal here are close to

Simon's argument and the departures from Simon's position are much less significant compared to the differences with several brands of evolutionary (Nelson and Winter, 1982, 2002) and intra-organizational ecologists (Hannan and Freeman, 1989). The latter has two major strands: first, those who emphasize environmental determinism versus strategy (Bourgeois, 1984); secondly, those who emphasize the importance of selection and retention in organizational change (Hannan and Freeman, 1984). Somewhat intermediate between these two positions are those who argue that strategy and ecology are not antagonistic. Instead, these are framed together in the processes of variation, selection and retention (Burgelman, 1991; Weick, 1979). Variation, selection and retention refer to various strategic initiatives inside an organization. This implies the need for an agency for the selection of those initiatives by a structure and the retention of selected strategic initiatives in several forms of learning and competency modes of structure. Unlike Simon or as in the present argument, ecologists and evolutionists de-emphasize the processes of authority, threats and such others and tacitly assume an innate structural mode on which selected and retained cues perform an upwardly spiralling evolutionary journey. An organization, according to ecologists, necessarily has a clear boundary and its variations making processes too are distinct. Structure to the ecologist or evolutionist responds to strategic demands. While agreeing with this, one does not share their position that structural changes take place over tacitly given innateness.

There is a distinction in the present schema between the structural sort and the processes. Processes are not innate. Processes allow one to recognize the shifting boundaries of an organization and, even more importantly, that internal processes are influenced by strategic moves made by other organizations and their processes. The structure of an organization then assumes its role to keep under control the structural sort as a robust entity through the mechanism of processes under its command. As a result, there is no need for an innately given structure. Moreover, strategy in this perspective is a deliberate attempt by a structural sort to influence the dynamics of processes belonging to its own organization and to other organizations in its strategic milieu. Strategy, it is argued, is to gain governance. The immediate issue of governance relates to internal processes while these issues are under the influence of external structural sorts. Hence governance must reckon with those other aspirations of governance issuing from organizations and respective processes in the strategic milieu.

There is thus another important element in this proposed strategy make-up. This element is constituted by other organizations of strategic relevance, which are not or cannot be global. The understanding here is that a strategy concern must remain limited by its reach. This reach is defined as a strategic milieu that is a partial market. Such a milieu is structured around the winning strategist, its opponent, the follower of middle path, and the careless firm. A strategic milieu is defined by a dyadic relation – the domination of the winning strategist and opponent pair. It follows then that the follower of the middle path and the careless are firms that choose to continue on strategic courses in-between or are careless about the dominant strategic move. There are other types of firms too in this milieu: those that have entered into strategic alliances with the winning strategist or, conversely, who have entered into strategic commitments with the opponent, for example. A milieu in this proposal is thus exclusively dependent on the strategic moves and strategic acts. This milieu is not given beforehand or is not a given as in SCPP or as in IO. The industry segment that a winning strategist belongs to does not define a milieu. Nor does the territory define it. A strategic milieu is defined by the strategies of the winning strategist. Strategy defines who is the opponent and who are the followers of the middle path.

This mode of milieu representation is categorical. A category ordinarily has only one firm of consequence and each such firm has five processes. A winning strategist thus has twenty processes, contributed by five processes of each of the four types of firms. The strategic acts and moves of the chief and, to varying degrees, of the senior power holders, including even persons at the confluences at times, take into consideration all or a significant number of these twenty processes for strategic manoeuvring. Moreover, persons under the spell of or belonging to a particular process often behave as a team as well. Such a team, by virtue of sharing plenty of common beliefs and a common mode of action, often behaves as one person. A chief failing to act strategically on these processes virtually gives up those processes to the manoeuvrings of other strategic players. The present construction of a strategic make-up thus borrows freely from several putatively different theoretical positions. It agrees with the agency theorist on the importance of agency in strategy but does not limit agencies to a select principal and, therefore, to one firm only. The agent here can be manipulated, is an opportunist and suffers from *akrasia* or weakness of will. Such an agent thus has little loyalty to the firm whose principal has 'entered into a contract' with him. Loyalty is a process that must be kept revitalized by the strategy process of the firm.

Partial market and strategic milieu

A strategic milieu is a partial market. Marshall's (1920, 1925) term 'partial' may be interpreted in two modes: first, because it is a fraction of the market and, secondly, because market if defined on completion of a process of exchanges and contracts, remains incomplete here. In other words, a chain of exchanges and contracts is surrendered and kept incomplete. The latter is not a case of market failure. For Coase (1990) and Williamson (1985), a firm is based on only those exchanges that fail to function efficiently or involve less transaction cost when inside a firm than out in the market. Transaction cost minimizing exchanges are thus independent of firm strategy or intents of the economic agents. In the present case, however, the strategic milieu intentionally terminates a series of exchanges at such interfaces as are convenient to the strategic intent. What happens here is akin to what happens with an organization when some parts of a long chain of exchanges and contracts are accomplished inside the firm boundary while some other longer parts get accomplished outside the firm. The apparently abrupt cut-off applied to the long chain by a strategic milieu is the feat of the act and moves of the winning strategist, who attempts to secure a milieu for his actions. Undeniably, the bounds of rationality and limitations of information at one's disposal influence the setting of a milieu. It may be argued though that the milieu is located by the logic of strategic action and is affected in its selection of opponents and such others by the power of strategic action.

A game can be won against one. This winning leads to further wins and each step of a game has only one principal adversary. This is the logic. A strategy must necessarily define this adversary. This actor–adversary act implicates two more categorical modes of reactions to this drama (Burke, 1969). Thus, categorically, an act of strategy implicates four agencies. There are five processes constituting each firm in these categories and hence the logic implicates all the twenty processes. A market that gets completed by these processes is thus partial not because of a market failure or because the transactions cost warranted a demarcation between transactions to be carried inside this milieu and externally but because the logic of strategy demands so. This implies that a strategy cannot be global. The locality of a strategic act and of a strategic move can be territorial, technological, product-wise or industry-segment wise, for example. The strategy chooses the particular milieu it would make the moves in.

TCE warrants that all those transactions that get carried over internally are governable, economic and lead to efficiency. According to TCE, the internal–external divide must be unambiguous. Transactions must all be known beforehand. Here, one begins from the premise that all transactions are not known or 'knowable'. This is because foreknowledge would exclude novelty. Not knowability implies disequilibria. Strategy enjoys disequilibria and seeks to create disequilibria. The winning strategist selects those moves and acts of strategies that are disequilibria seeking. Further, the governable transactions of TCE are given up in this claim. The TCE sets up firm boundaries on this consideration on governance. In contrast, it is argued here that governance being the strategic objective, transactions that would get considered as governable often do not belong to the winning strategist (by virtue of claims of property rights, for example) who, by strategic manoeuvres, however, wishes to govern most such transactions. Therefore, legitimacy of firm boundaries is done away with. This present argument on strategy squarely rejects the property rights perspective on a firm (Hart, 1988). A winning strategist, by warranting that processes belonging (from the perspective of agency theory or property rights theory) to other firms conform to its strategic manoeuvres, enhances the span and scope of governance. In terms of simple economic rent, this increase is beneficial to the winning strategist. Increased access to disequilibria information and enhanced authority to deform processes to the advantage of the winning strategist are some of the gains from this perspective of governance over a strategic milieu.

The construction of this milieu appears feasible because processes are belief led. Belief, unlike knowledge, is loaded with values, attitudes and intents. Belief contents are, moreover, not known to complete description. Knowledge of belief content, as a description, is partial and this knowledge can be elicited only when provoked. The belief state is implicated causally in strategic behaviours. These behaviours are observations on strategic acts. Belief states are indicative of the state of a process. The processes in a firm are similar to state space representations of belief states of the process holders. In order to influence the strategic act (the strategic behaviour) of others, a winning strategist attempts to influence (or govern) such beliefs. To influence a belief, the winning strategist must search for conditions of belief, which it might be able to influence. The outcome of belief contents (which is causally implicated in strategic behaviour) is dependent on the provocations to the conditions of belief. Strategic moves are intentional acts in disguise, undertaken specifically to influence the conditions of belief of other processes. Behaviourally, as in the reckoning of IO, a strategic move is indistinguishable from a strategic act. It is argued here that not all acts are strategic behaviours. Most are perhaps intended to achieve a purpose of influencing the conditions to belief. A separation between strategic acts and strategic moves is, therefore, proposed.

These strategic moves are not behavioural and, to an observer, strategic moves remain unrecognized and undifferentiated from strategic acts. A reading of the extant literature suggests that strategic moves can have six different modes or qualities. They can be for: alliance, confrontation, fluidity, nonchalance, prevarication and dependence. These modes are derived from descriptive psychological states of a strategist (Conlisk, 1996; Dawes and Thaler, 1988; Fischhoff, 1975; Kahneman and Tversky, 1979; Rabin, 1998; Tversky and Kahneman, 1982). In contrast, a strategic act can be observed to be an act of: appeasement, reward, discrimination, or punishment. Since the strategic move is not observable, the strategic behaviour can be discerned by observing strategic actions alone. The strategy make-up is complete with this description on strategic moves and strategic acts. The proposed repertoire of strategy here then includes first, a structural sort; second, processes; third, strategic moves and, fourth and finally, strategic acts.

Strategy and structural sort

A structural sort is not independent of strategy but is determined by the demands of strategy. The articulation of this strategy, through strategic moves and strategic acts, however, influences first and immediately the strategy process. It appears then, that strategy process and the structural sort are implicated together. How would a process affect the structural sort? Received theories are often vague on this. They have mostly borrowed the scaffolding perspective on structure, which later treated the emergence of a large corporate structure as a body necessary to implement both strategy and economic efficiency. Structure in this view is an instrument. It is not known how strategy transforms a structure or vice versa. The alternative perspective on structure from the evolutionary or ecologist underemphasized structure and suggested strategy processes inside an organization, where interdependence between structure and strategy cannot be properly known. However, this view clearly recognizes the dynamic relations between the strategy process and organizational form. Both these perspectives ignore the influence of strategy and structure of other strategizing firms on the structure of the incumbent firm. They only concede that any little influence that might be there could only be indirect and mediated. Structure or even organizational processes, according to them, are close to being impervious and are rather rigid.

In contrast, the structural sort along with the set of confluences are most porous (especially when strategy of the incumbent allows that by default), robust and not rigid. They may assume several forms of scaffolding under umbrella cover upon strategic threats from others. The departure here from the received theories, therefore, categorically lies in asserting that the organizational structure responds plastically to the threats and opportunities from the strategic milieu. The position of Baumol, Panzar and Willig (1986) alone perhaps concedes such an outcome as a benchmark extreme but with the rider that, under the circumstances, a firm cannot have any strategy. The incumbent firm is relegated to the status of a passive recipient of all technological changes in the market and its organization must change accordingly. It is argued here that such a structural death is uncalled for. Structure is vitally important for a firm to exist and there seems to be no other form – like that of an ecologist's processes – which through denial of structure can enlist a firm that can govern even its own internal processes. A structural sort evolves over the life cycle of a firm. It is categorically given but its contents take shape corresponding to the strategic acts and moves of both the incumbent and the strategic milieu. The death of a firm is an important event and strategies take care to prevent such demise. This demise is a structural demise. Processes internal to the firm remain under the firm's governance only as long as the firm structure prevails. As Simon (1991) argues, these processes are taken up by other contending strategist firms (and not by a ubiquitous 'market', as the TCE argues) in the absence of a firm structure.

The structural sort recognizes several elements, which are not recognized as important to a structure by both the strands of the received theories. Knowledge is recognized along with finance as an element of structural sort as are the knowledge employees. The stakeholders or the power holders and the allies of a firm are, similarly, novel elements to a structure, not recognized by both the received theories as pertinent to a structure. Umbrella-cover, in particular, is a new concept that recognizes that the structure of an incumbent firm changes its shape and the firm threatened strategically (as under threats of takeover) takes cover under a certain appropriate structural form. The structural sort sustains a structure, it has been argued, by virtue of its being dynamic. This is also why a structural sort is robust. Primarily, the chief, the central player in the structural sort, causes dynamism. The chief's strategic responses to internal and external exigencies and to the firm's own strategic move, sustains the material domain (over which governance of the incumbent prevails). If necessary, it takes on restructuring as an umbrella-cover. Strategy and structure, it is argued, are inextricably interdependent and a structure is precisely the outcome of strategy. A strategic default causes the structure to fail and an absence of strategy takes the structure to the vanishing point of organizational death.

Knowledge, structural sort and strategy: types of knowledge

Knowledge as wealth is an element constituting the structural sort and needs to be differentiated into three types. This is a major departure from the received theories. Earlier and the traditional views (Arrow, 2000), largely dominated by the neoclassical, held knowledge as another factor of production. This view could not accommodate the internal or structural organization of a firm in its theoretical apparatus. Penrose (1968) brought to the fore how knowledge could act beyond a simple factor of production when organized. The line of thought from Penrose has assumed several distinct forms over the last couple of decades. Perhaps, in all developments, structure has been held to be directing the cause, and knowledge has been assumed as directed. If this were the core of contemporary received theories, the current departure is that knowledge constitutes a structure, or that knowledge, not as a cause, but as an associated reason, is supervenient on structural outcomes. In saying so, one is not denying that knowledge in turn remains influenced by the structure. Knowledge, it is being argued, is not a pure asset. A resource theorist assumes an asset market from where a firm procures its asset. Knowledge co-evolves with structure and this is the essence of what is being presented here. Tacit knowledge (for TCE, evolutionary or competence theorist, see for example, Machlup, 1963; Veblen, 1919) has been presented as a similar category: as an asset it cannot be procured from a resources market, and it is sticky and necessarily evolves with a firm. It is submitted here that tacit knowledge does not exist either or at least, for these purposes, one need not invoke such a category of knowledge, and organizational knowledge is presented as non-transferable and non-tacit.

A structural sort is the outcome of strategies. Knowledge following this logic then is also an outcome of strategies. Knowledge, structural sort and strategy are thus linked by reasonable influences on each other. A robust structure is largely dependent on knowledge at its disposal. Knowledge at the firm's disposal is, however, dispersed (Hayek, 1949, 1978; Minkler, 1993). A firm would then require the services of another knowledge that can organize the dispersed knowledge. Dispersed knowledge has only content. This organizing knowledge, it can be shown, is epistemic and content-wise different from the dispersed knowledge and is called 'strategic knowledge'. This strategic knowledge is different from knowledge as wealth (that is, as part of the structural sort) and as dispersed. It influences the conditions to knowledge wealth in all the processes in a strategic milieu, processes both internal and external to a firm. Dispersed knowledge again has several modes of appearances.

A structural sort contains dispersed knowledge wealth (and not the strategic knowledge) as its constitutive element. The structure counts this knowledge as a wealth. It follows then that a structure needs to have knowledge about locations and possible contents of this wealth as in a data warehouse. Such a warehouse perspective, however, has certain limitations. It is tacitly assumed that the warehouse has a map of location and contents. A location mapping is possible provided contents are pre-specified with the contents known first. A content search would then inform all locations about where, in the organization, such knowledge is dispersed. Some authors have introduced this warehousing model. This model is being rejected here on two grounds. First, this contradicts the strategic knowledge – which busies itself with conditions to knowledge in order to influence knowledge outcome – which cannot engage with content-only knowledge. Secondly, all knowledge contents would have to be known beforehand. The latter is particularly unacceptable.

The holders of dispersed knowledge are generators of knowledge in the form of sentences or in the form of descriptions. Each holder is generative and, while generating knowledge, must access a formal set of parametric set-up. These parameters are both similar and significantly different from the parameters in generative linguistics (Chomsky, 1986, 1993). The latter refers to a common parametric set-up, which generates syntactically linguistic utterances. The references to parameters here are not to that 'deep' level but to parameters set up by conditions of knowledge or conditions of belief. Each holder responds to certain conditions (of belief or knowledge) by generating a certain knowledge content that is meaningful to the holder. These conditions result from manoeuvrings through strategic knowledge by the strategist. A holder first offers to himself a substantive knowledge response. Manoeuvrings create a vacuum that needs to be filled in by new substantive knowledge outcome. This emergent substantive outcome is not a behavioural response to the parameters provoked by strategic knowledge of another; neither is this substantive knowledge outcome communicated to another person in its fullness.

A holder does not have knowledge of contents, hence the warehouse model fails. Further, a holder might not have even knowledge of the generative rules. Only certain types of formal knowledge (an algebraic expression, for example) can be known beforehand in the form of a set of rules or as an algorithm and such like. Some other rules cannot be apprehended (as often in engineering rules of approximations) such as rules described by content-specification, even if probed by the holder himself. A rule, however, can be apprehended as absences of certain known default conditions. This means that without warranting an imperative, a rule might allow freedom to undertake such actions as are not precluded. Even so, a holder generates substantive knowledge outcomes. There is another division here. A holder might respond by first generating a complete listing of substantive knowledge sentences and only then assuming action based on a possible and partial disclosure of the complete listing of substantive knowledge outcome. In case a holder acts first, unthinkingly as it were, the attention to problem-solving and the generation of substantive knowledge sentences happen together and not as a sequence. Thus a holder might not have a prior knowledge of substantive knowledge outcome. The holder might otherwise generate satisfactory substantive sentences but not disclose it. Disclosure is a behavioural as well as strategic response. The generation of substantive knowledge is never a behavioural response but the result of attitudes (that is aversion, desire, hope, despair and intention of the holder). Consequently, a holder never exhausts the possibility of generation of substantive sentences. An objectively given strategic situation with the same parameters might provoke alternate knowledge outcomes from the same holder but at different instances. Each generation satisfies a contingent attitude. These attitudes together set up conditions of belief or knowledge. They also express strategic intent. It follows then that a substantive generation of sentences is a contingent strategic outcome.

Each such substantive outcome is, however, knowledge by description. Such an outcome is content only; at its generation it is influenced by an attitude (such as aversion or intention), at its outcome it appears as a complete set of sentences. Influence by attitude at the moment of generation limits a substantive outcome from claiming for itself the status of complete or exhaustive knowledge account. Hence, even an identical parametric set-up, or identical manoeuvres of strategic knowledge, might provoke different substantive knowledge outcomes. Each outcome would depend on the generator's contingent strategic attitude. It follows then that organizing such outcomes would require co-ordination. Knowledge by description in the context of strategy remains elusive in so far as there are several possible substantive knowledge outcomes, though each is knowledge by description. To restate this, the context of generation of knowledge, represented in the form of certain parametric values, is ontological. It appears then that a strategic context cannot generate a complete account in the form of knowledge by description of an ontological context. Instead, a series of accounts, each complete in itself, but grounded in strategic attitudes, is generated.

A structural sort, therefore, has as its wealth component a dispersed set of epistemic generators. The structural sort does not possess a listing of the complete descriptive knowledge accounts in the form of assets. A firm possesses a repertoire of knowledge by description. However, taken together, this entire set of sentences represents only one possible world, which remains as an incomplete set. A generation of knowledge to come in the next moment (similar to generation of sentences in continuous speech) will not consider the entire history of the generation surrounding an ontological context. Instead, the generation will consider only the episodic reading of some sentences generated previously. The law of small numbers will prevail (Tversky and Kahneman, 1971). This episode comprises the strategic intent and context and implies that there exists only episodic or epochal and privileged memory for a holder. There does not exist a readable complete listing of all previous substantive descriptive sentences. This leads to the conclusion that a structural sort is not constituted around knowledge wealth in the form of descriptive assets as such. Instead, the structural sort possesses a set of dispersed epistemic generators. Descriptive contents are not known completely. Further, the holder's memory does not recognize all previous generations. A firm might, however, keep on record all such listed sentences. Such an approach to creating organizational knowledge data warehouses is shortsighted because a firm is likely to retain millions of pages! An ontological database does not solve the problem as such; it redesigns the search but not the contents as such. From this perspective then, organizational memory is not independent of the strategic context.

Knowledge co-ordination

Hayek's (1949) reference to dispersed knowledge should then refer more properly to dispersed epistemic generators and to descriptive knowledge rather than dispersed knowledge. One constituent of a structural sort is this dispersed epistemic generator that is the knowledge employee. Each such employee enhances the epistemic repertoire over a period and simultaneously increases a lexicon full of names and situations. Following the earlier discussion, epistemic generation or a rule, for example, associates some lexical entries (if necessary by adding to the entries) while looking for exceptions to rules and the meaning of the generated knowledge in the form of descriptive sentences. If a satisfactory sentence cannot be generated, this employee resorts to imperatives such as requesting, ordering or rhetoric. No co-ordination of generative activities was required as long as the demand was self-manageable. However, a single employee alone cannot generate most knowledge outcomes. A structural sort thrives only when situations calling for co-ordinated description of knowledge sentences come in abundance. Co-ordination is thus not a necessary condition for knowledge generation for all times or for all situations. The chief and other power holders, including the allies in the structural sort, try their best to sustain situations demanding such co-ordination. By catalyzing an abundance of situations demanding co-ordinated generation of knowledge descriptions, this group of chief and others continues to reproduce conditions, which sustain the material domain. The material domain, as one constituent of the structural sort, is sustained by exercise of authority. An autonomous generation of knowledge does not require co-ordination and hence need not recognize the material domain. A co-ordinated generation necessarily requires rules, epistemics or lexicons of others. Thus, by calling upon situations provided by the material domain the co-ordinated generation reproduces authority.

Authority is reproduced anew whenever there is a demand on co-ordination. A chief hastens such events of co-ordination by two modes. First, by division of labour and, secondly, by warranting expectations-based outcomes. The former is a recognized mode since the time of Adam Smith. Introducing additions to contemporary discussions on division of labour (Langlois and Robertson, 1995; Leijonhufvud, 1986), it is argued here that such divisions are based on two notions: period and regularity. Any standard discussion on division of labour visualizes a serialization of production. This series is both temporal and spatial. It indicates progression and must be based on regularity in production. Departures from this are noticed in a Petri-net where production can be conceptualized as both synchronous and asynchronous. A net production is conceptualized here as a continuation of communication (recall, a communication is always between a pair) situations. Petri-net (Oberquelle, 1987, 1988) thus enables one to go beyond the necessity of regularity. Milgrom and Roberts (1990) defined a production set-up in terms of complementarities, which is not very far off from Petri's pair-wise communication. In another departure, a cyclical time has been introduced (Alterman, 1988; Valax and Sarocchi, 1989). It warrants expectation, cognition and repetition of productive arrangements. However, cyclical time is limited to an individual whose cognition and expectation of 'what' ought to appear next in sequence and when a group of generations is completing a sentential description (or a meaningful product) constitutes a cycle. Beyond this cycle, however, there should be a period of generation, which belonging to the interpersonal domain must warrant the 'what' next in sequence and the group concurrence on a commonly accepted status on completion of the sentence or product.

This belongs to the domain of conversation. Petri, in fact, constructed his theory on similar ideas on communication without recognizing a period. A period of generation or production refers to a concurrence on completion. Further, a period need not refer to regularity; it could simply be based on a novel and contingent demand. Regularity refers to observed generative behaviours of others. An individual knowledge employee cannot exactly 'know' the epistemic status or the lexical content of his colleagues. 'Unknowledge' and ignorance about other epistemic generators prevent co-ordination between several epistemic generator employees on the subject of epistemics. Co-ordination, however, may resume because he follows withdrawal of egoistic incentives (Caporael *et al.*, 1989). Egoistic incentives, ordinarily prevalent in an organization prevent cooperation and ensure that co-ordination by authority prevails. An employee can, however, infer the possible status and contents of others on the basis of regular observations. This inference remains limited to the generative behaviour in the neighbourhood because the person has limited cognitive power and rationality and a weak will to dominate a global population. This neighbourhood, similar to a partial market, is fundamental in nature. In other words, a small neighbourhood in the organizational set-up accomplishes the regularity in generation or production. A series of such regularity-limited generations or productions get arranged by the controlling authority in the business to set up a business process.

The material domain in the structural sort is thus recreated through these periodic and cyclical aspects. A period, however, refers more to equilibrium conditions when the firm has knowledge of what and how much to generate or produce. Cyclical aspects can refer to conditions of disequilibria as well. A failed regularity or a warranted generation or production going beyond observed pattern may provoke an employee to look for possibilities. A co-ordinated knowledge generation depends on the expectation of a knowledge employee of what other meta-sentences and lexical entries colleagues could provide even though the employee knows that colleagues are opportunists and may 'intentionally' display partial or distorted epistemic behaviours and lexical contents. It is also known that a similar novel situation of generation or production is unlikely to appear soon or is unlikely to recur regularly. Trust then is necessarily undermined (Gambetta, 1988) and transaction cost is necessarily increased. Only the function of governance can ensure reduction in a possible rise in transaction costs (Williamson, 1985). Clearly, the employee cannot complete the generation or production alone. Further, if the governance compels the generation neighbourhood (a group, for example) to complete a knowledge generation, in all likelihood, the group will revert to generating a regularity or period-driven sentence or product. Such a neighbourhood might not come up with discovery (Banerjee and Richter, 2001; Nooteboom, 1999b).

Any novel sentential description (a product as it were) is a discovery (Hayek, 1973–8). The situation described here is complex because no single individual can complete the description; neither can the person revert to the regularity-driven co-ordinated generation of sentence. Left to them, a neighbour- hood, capable of this discovery, would fail to deliver the discovery. Governance alone assures each member of the neighbourhood that opportunism of other members would be kept minimized by its authority (Williamson, 1996, 1999). There is, however, an irreducible core. A threat to opportunism is accompanied by reduced participation by a generative employee, who would now contribute a half-truth or a malformed meta-sentence.

The TCE response, particularly as argued by Nooteboom (1999a), explains a situation where regularity or, for that matter, equilibrium prevails. The transaction costs can be minimized in those circumstances. However, in a situation demanding generation of novel sentences, each generating individual has expectation about possible contributions by others. The costs of transactions refer to several possible worlds and can be only indefinitely approximated. In short, profiles of transaction costs corresponding to each scenario of expected outcomes are not known. The firm governance does not have knowledge on transaction costs as well. Very often, the complexity of the negotiations and the time they may take to complete, precipitate certain norms of expectations. The norms of expectations and of participation in generation are then not designed but appear out of experiences with default situations; a default caused by ignorance on transactions cost. It is argued here that these limiting default cases define norms. Norm is derived from the logic of default, not TCE-minimizing programmes. The firm governance restricts TCE to situations where regularity prevails, and in situations where novelty is demanded, defaults to TCE, namely norms, prevail. The firm governance stays through the negotiations to ensure that norms do not get violated. Governance now has little else to enforce. Only as an exception, a firm governance may stay through an entire negotiation, allowing it to violate even norms and allowing transaction costs to rise immensely, provided the likely pay-off from the novel sentence appears to be greater than the costs of transactions.

Scope of descriptive knowledge

In the structural sort then there is little room left for knowledge by description (knowledge that is descriptive and that can be described). The structure has been charted out and it is understood that individuals do not store as many descriptive sentences as they retain epistemic engines and lexicons. In the space occupied by neighbourhoods, regularity affords scope to descriptive knowledge sentences. However, the periodic (or cyclical) mode depends more on epistemic acts and on expectations. In the case of generation of novel sentences, no descriptive sentence is required. A norm too refers to only default conditions. Overall, a firm has little room left for descriptive knowledge outcomes. It has been argued earlier that organizational memory is also conditioned by strategies (on governance). Memory too demands only a little knowledge by description.

A structural sort, it may be recalled, is based on two constituents relating directly to knowledge, among others: knowledge as wealth and knowledge employees. One has seen how little knowledge the knowledge employees conceive in the form of descriptive sentences. The discussions here also show

how little knowledge wealth of a structure needs to be retained as descriptive sentences. There is, however, a minimal scope for the structure: it needs to have descriptive knowledge about lexical contents. An employee necessarily divulges part of such entries each time the person commences knowledge generation. Moreover, a regular production or generation refers to known lexical items. Similarly, once a neighbourhood engages in production of even novel descriptive sentences it must simultaneously display and divulge a part of the lexical entries. A firm thus has access to some lexical entities, which though not descriptive sentences, are retained in the form of organizational knowledge.

The organizational knowledge is peculiar to an organization. This knowledge is essentially on lexical nominal and on situations. An organization builds up such a repertoire over a period (hence it is episodic) and over a path of business development history. Moreover, the specific individuals who have been working for the firm solely contribute such knowledge. In all this, there are three aspects of episodic knowledge: path dependence, dependence on specific mode and content of work of individuals. To an outsider, this knowledge resembles tacit knowledge though it is not so. Unlike tacit knowledge, this knowledge does not belong to an individual. Its contents are described (though only inside the firm); it is stable and not phenomenal. Several authors from evolutionary and competency theories and from TCE, who locate tacit knowledge as the key explanatory factor or who conjecture a possible organizational tacit knowledge, appear to have flawed reasoning. They seem to overlook that an organization retains description of such knowledge while they treat it more as a trade secret. This tacit-looking knowledge is vastly different from tacit knowledge.

Knowledge and strategy

Knowledge in a structural sort is different from strategic knowledge, which a strategist employs to influence and, if possible, to control conditions to belief and to knowledge held by all the processes strategically engaged in the strategic milieu of the incumbent strategist. A strategic knowledge is different from the knowledge in a structural sort on all the counts, epistemic, pragmatic and such others and also on what each contains. Knowledge in a structural sort or knowledge wealth, is closer to knowledge by description, although it has been seen how limited that qualification is. This knowledge is a constituent of the structural sort. It has to remain engaged in defending, protecting, advancing and in making the structure robust. These goals are achieved through both the knowledge contents and the knowledge employees.

To recount the areas of departure from the received theories: knowledge wealth is not the knowledge engaged as a factor of production. The latter is largely available in public domain and can be bought and sold in the market. Knowledge, as a factor of production, can be combined, assorted, selected and generated by providers, often public research institutions or universities. A rather large number of authors on knowledge – influential among them is Nonaka (Hodgson, 1993; Nonaka, 1994; Nonaka and Takeuchi, 1995; Nonaka, Toyama and Nagata, 2000) – however, have conflated issues. They have equated these two types, including even strategic knowledge under one single omnibus and ubiquitous category. David and others (Cowan, David and Foray, 2000; Dasgupta and David, 1986, 1994; David, 1997, 2001; David, Foray and Steinmueller, 1999) in contrast, and largely following the lead provided by Machlup (1980), have argued that the knowledge economy rests on public generation and public provisioning of knowledge. The firm develops only a component of this knowledge in an idiosyncratic mode. David and others argue that this idiosyncratic knowledge, however, is not at all tacit knowledge. On this score, there is complete agreement with David's and Dasgupta's, including Nelson's (1992) argument.

The above argument in adumbration presents knowledge in relation to business with three subdivisions: knowledge as a factor of production; knowledge in a structural sort; and strategic knowledge. The first belonging to the public domain can be bought and sold through market exchanges, the second is structural and the third remains concealed to the market, being determined by strategic moves and intents. Knowledge as a factor of production is exclusively knowledge by description; knowledge of a structural sort is only partially knowledge by description and is idiosyncratic, though not tacit; and the strategic knowledge is not descriptive but is based on attitudes and intentions, and is also not tacit. Tacit knowledge, even if it exists, belongs to the private phenomenal world. It is argued that tacit knowledge belongs to the moment of knowledge generation and it is a private knowledge.

Knowledge in a structural sort serves a function, which cannot be fulfilled either by knowledge as a factor or by strategic knowledge. Resource perspective on strategy argues somewhat similarly. Evolutionary and competence theorists too concur largely on this issue. However, these groups do not differentiate between strategic knowledge and knowledge for a structural sort. A resource theorist, in fact, does not distinguish between knowledge as a factor and knowledge in structure but argues that firm-internal practices on resource combinations do effect changes in the quality of resources. A factor thus gets converted into a structural component. The argument followed here is that knowledge maintains differences over content, epistemics, control and purpose.

A structural sort, to recall the earlier argument, is retained for strategy. This means that for a strategy to be effected a structure is necessary. This follows also from Simon (1961, 1979b) and Chandler (1962, 1992). What has been added is that strategy generates the structure and the end of the strategy indicates the death of a structure. It follows then that strategy, *inter alia*, actuates the knowledge of a structural sort. A structural sort, it is contended here, is not a static entity. A structure is dynamically recreated through its engagements with the environment: the strategic milieu. A structure is thus exclusively for 'doing'. Knowledge for this structure, named 'knowledge wealth', is then knowledge on 'doing'. Such knowledge wealth is thus a pragmatic outcome. Finer subdivisions of this wealth have been discussed here.

3
The Strategic Knowledge Arena

Strategy is not simply about competition but goes far beyond the pre-reconciliation assumed a priori by competition. Earning windfall profits, creating a novel turf for the interplay of competitive forces, generating a new language of expectation and shifting the boundary of the 'unknowledge' (Shackle, 1988) then provide the ideas on goals of strategy. A strategy, however, need not always be for novelties. A firm could simply be manoeuvring its position vis-à-vis others in order to remain alive. Its growth orientation, while necessary for long-term survival, might not be an appropriate strategic goal if it wishes merely to survive. Knowledge is involved in the creation of a novel turf for future competition, the generation of new languages of expectancy, in shifting boundaries of current knowledge in spectacular ways and has been recognized as an important instrument of strategy. Knowledge engaged for strategic purposes could be called strategic knowledge. Knowledge essential for production or retaining competitiveness, and thus not deployed for strategic purpose, cannot be called strategic knowledge.

The active deployment of knowledge for gaining strategic advantage can, however, be compared with a relatively moderate posture seeking to make good any loss perceived to have been caused by a mismatch between expectations and abilities. Loasby (1986: 52) observes: 'The growth of knowledge is a response to the failure of our existing theories to predict and control a mismatch between expectations and perceived relevant events'. In both cases, knowledge appears to serve the twin purposes of self-reference and reference to knowledge of the other holders. The latter refers to a context of co-ordination which, following Schelling (1960), offers zero-sum competition as only one extreme. Interdependence between knowledge and co-ordination negates much of the possible strategic potential in knowledge. The pre-reconciled movement in knowledge cannot, by definition, bring in strategic advantage. A firm, however, is situated in a co-ordinated sphere where it has been using a language of co-ordinated knowledge. Strategic advantage needs necessarily to overcome this constraint of co-ordination. This chapter looks at the manoeuvrings of a firm that lifts its knowledge activities from the interdependence on co-ordination and allows engagement with knowledge for strategic gains.

The knowledge-strategy linkage

The relationship between strategy or business policy and knowledge that a firm has appears to have been vaguely described by the dominant contemporary theories. Both knowledge and strategy appear as the co-ordinated or pre-reconciled outcome according to certain foundational assumptions most commonly held by these dominant theories. Co-ordinated knowledge or pre-reconciled strategy cannot bring forth any novelty or surprise. Inter-firm differences cannot, in that case, reside in firm-internal characteristics and strategy necessarily gets reduced to a game and knowledge gets reduced to a factor of production. In order to explain differential achievements of firms, some theorists incorporate those strategies that enable a firm to adapt to and assimilate from institutional levels and aspects of knowledge. Here too, nothing generically belonging to a firm can be characterized as the causal engine. Undeniably firms are different. Such differences hold over both performance and strategic acts. Prima facie, there appears to be a generic aspect of knowledge that is kept beyond the realm of co-ordination. Pre-reconciliation and co-ordination appear to be important although they cannot explain the most significant aspect of strategic surprise and strategic knowledge. It is suspected that the intention of an agent differentiates the strategic surprise and strategic knowledge from the co-ordinated and pre-reconciled competitive strategy and productive knowledge.

The paradigm of generative linguistics or of biological evolution has influenced much contemporary thinking. These paradigms have influenced theorization in terms of rules and routines and of competencies and capabilities. The strategy of a firm, according to these theorists, hovers around employing knowledge towards hastening or retaining distinctive competencies that, often, in gene-like structures of routines, learn from variations in environment and adapt competitively through selection of knowledge. In the transaction cost approach, knowledge is retained in tacit structures providing characteristics that are difficult to imitate. In the industrial organization approach, knowledge about competitive behaviours and competitive conjectures of competitors provides the strategic relief.

This chapter examines these proclaimed links between knowledge and strategy. The inquiry begins with an examination of the relevance of biological evolutionary principles and generative linguistic principles to this domain of knowledge-strategy linkage. This linkage is seen to be unsupportable. A firm does not have an innate structure or a generative routine and there cannot be any firm-internal residence of the idiosyncratic aspects or distinctive competencies of a firm in the absence of such innate or generic foundation. If such differences reside in the firm-external institutions, the distinctiveness of firms fails to emerge, given the fact of co-ordination between themselves. One has to accept the Lamarckian system if one agrees with the suggestions of these theories on learning and acquisition of knowledge that can be transmitted over generations of firms. Otherwise, knowledge can be behaviourally utilized for competitive advantages. The argument here is that strategy is not about competitive advantage; strategic gains are for influencing, guiding or otherwise deforming the strategic intents of other parties. Knowledge can be of strategic advantage only if it can enable a dominant party to leverage such strategic gains and only this knowledge is defined as strategic knowledge. Knowledge that any other party can access from the market or generate itself is knowledge by description and only has the competitive significance.

A strategic knowledge is thus non-representational and not knowledge by description. In other words, strategic knowledge is not a bundle of information, nor is it tacit. It is not about knowledge of routines or rule following or about the competitive behaviours of others, which is common to all. Strategic knowledge is about conditions of knowledge and belief that other parties have. Both these conditions reflect intentions and strategic knowledge plays with intention. Commanding a strategic knowledge implies being able to warrant from other parties a certain belief or a certain knowledge, which can subsequently influence strategic acts by other parties. Strategic knowledge is thus not by description. A strategist who seeks to win is driven by an intention that, in turn, seeks to employ strategic knowledge to influence strategic moves by other parties in a strategic realm.

A detailed strategy make-up – in continuation of the strategy model described in the previous chapter, which can employ strategic knowledge – gets presented here. In this make-up, a strategic milieu (in lieu of particular market) of firms can be defined vis-à-vis the dominant role of the winning strategist. Further, each firm is but a set of five processes. Strategic manoeuvring is about leveraging strategic knowledge to influence these processes. The determination of the boundary of a firm is irrelevant in this model. Strategic leveraging, however, does not employ knowledge by description. Beliefs and belief conditions are important for apprehending the attitudes of the other processes, which actually generate the strategic behaviour. Any analysis, based on strategic acts, bereft of any intention, yields an understanding of competitive and behavioural strategy. This analysis looks at strategy that is beyond the domain of competitive behaviour. Such a strategy is driven by intention and recognizes intentional conditions to belief and to knowledge. This strategy can alone bring in surprise because it employs strategic knowledge, which is not co-ordinated; nor is the strategy pre-reconciled. The winning strategist in this model employs strategic knowledge in influencing such belief conditions of others in the strategic milieu.

Strategies and strategic knowledge in Indian software are not being discussed directly in this chapter. This chapter deals with certain theoretical arguments that will be the recurrent themes of this book. Its limitation lie in the ethno-methodological studies on events in Indian software remaining outside its scope. They are necessary in order to appreciate fully the role of intention and belief conditions in the making of strategic surprise and of strategic knowledge. This approach will vindicate the non-adoption of currently dominant theories on strategy, competency and knowledge. As argued in the previous chapter, a Weltanschauung grand theory stands rejected and one would like to look at Indian software from several, possibly even non-coherent, theoretical vantages. This chapter presents one such vantage, which does not claim to be a grand theory; between this and the previous chapter, only some aspects of Indian software are explained. For an explanatory account of the rest of Indian software, one refers to an assemblage of existing theoretical vantages.

Received views in adumbration

Contemporary thinking on the relevance of knowledge for a firm appears to have been greatly influenced by research paradigms employed by other sciences (Ingrao and Israel, 1990). Complexities have entered this field of study, influenced as it is by paradigms from biology, cognitive psychology and evolution in general along with several technical terms and corresponding theories, such as competence and capability and evolutionary economics. The point here is that each science – or each of its paradigms and perhaps all theories belonging to such paradigms (a close equivalent, 'framework', might as well be used) – is more often than not, specific or discrete. The history of development of contemporary, fact-based science suggests that it addresses the specificities of facts first. A theory need not belong to the *Weltanschauung*. Setting aside a coherentist's idea, one can argue about the irrelevance of the contribution of a specific theory to the making of complete knowledge. Contemporary studies on cognition – in particular application of cognitive studies in social sciences – recognize that domain specificity (Hirschfeld and Gelman, 1994) shows that human reasoning follows specialized cognitive abilities to handle specific types of information. Earlier views on the subject looked for fairly generalized human capabilities that could handle several types of demands. Accepting such a perspective, it is maintained that biological faculties or those of linguistic utterances cannot be enlisted to explain cognitive peculiarities, which the human mind might employ to resolve an economic dilemma. Fodor (1983) has described this return to specificity as neo-Cartesian.

Learning from other disciplines

Additionally and regrettably, there is a resurgence of Lamarckian or Lyssenko-brand evolutionism. Nooteboom (2001), for example, calls for a return to Piaget. 'Phenocopies' or the stages theory of Piaget appear to have made a comeback. The Lamarckian strand admits that an individual's learning from its environment gets copied in its gene and transmitted down. Analogically, there are several evolutionary brands of writings on strategic knowledge, which admit to a firm's learning getting stored in such deeper structures as 'routines' and then being transmitted forward, inter-temporally or to the milieu. Those who are afraid of such a Lamarckian return (Nooteboom, 1999a, 1999b, for example), however, turn back to Piagetian thinking. A very brief overview of the Piaget–Chomsky debate (Piatelli-Palmarini, 1980) may not, therefore, be out of place here. Piaget maintained (Kitchener, 1986) that life and cognition could be understood in terms of auto-organization and self-stabilization (Piatelli-Palmarini, 1994), two deep universal principles based on logico-mathematical schemas. The Piagetian organization is necessary and the invariable stepwise sequence in the transition from a lower stage to a qualitatively higher stage. These maturational stages thus represent progress in a strictly unalterable sequence. The random process of a typically Darwinian evolution fails to explain this strict progressive sequence. Piagetian learning is achieved through logical generalization, equilibration, systematization and such like. Piaget (as reported by Piatelli-Palmarini, 1994) expected his theory to be different from both Darwin and Lamarck though his notion of 'phenocopies' is deeply Lamarckian. Phenocopies are imprints of feedback from the environment on the genetic make-up of a species. This is unabashedly Lamarckian. Experimental and theoretical developments since Piaget have generally rejected these meta positions of Piaget.

Chomsky differed in not accepting any of these Piagetian positions that involved deep Lamarckianism and attempted to describe language as a generalization abstraction from the sensorimotor schemata. Chomsky (1986) thus rejected behaviourism (as of Skinner) and empiricism in general while explaining linguistic generation and linguistic competence. The faculty of language is specific (not belonging to other generalizations) and innate. Specific language is generated through computational rules and neither linguistic activity nor linguistic competence is learnt by trial and error. Nor are they a derivative of the sensorimotor schemata. Linguistic rules are derived neither from hypothesis formation and confirmation nor by induction. The problem-solving approach too fails to explain language generation. Supporting Chomsky, Fodor argued for modularity and categorically rejected the stages theory of Piaget. Linguistic knowledge does not advance through Piagetian stages and its competence is not weaker or stronger along a hierarchy. Equally, there is no horizontal dimension of a stage, which means there is no generalized knowledge that, once apprehended in the abstract, can be applied across diverse fields.

Chomsky (1993) offered a minimal programme of this generative grammar, replacing rules by principles and parameters. Learning a language means knowing its lexicon, thereby setting the parametric values. The lexicon is essential to the parametric computational system's generation of utterances in that language. The language of a child is as strong as that of an adult. Utterance or comprehension competence is not increased through induction, trial and error and problem-solving or simply by learning. Problem solving cannot be the driving force in evolution (Lewontin, 1985) because a species creates a problem in accordance with its specific conditions. There can never be any inheritable feedback from an individual experience to its genes or milieu. Equally, novelty and complexity are not enriching, as presumed by the Piagetian. On the contrary, a complexity could arise owing to impoverishment and specialization. Adaptations need not emerge out of necessity. There are many instances of superfluous 'adaptations'. Theses on auto-equilibration, increasing adaptations, autonomizations and such others are often fallacious or redundant. Finally, a 'selection out of a vast innate repertoire is the only mechanism of growth, acquisition and complexification, which we can scientifically understand' (Piatelli-Palmarini, 1994: 340).

Confusions around strategy theory

An evolutionary possibility can only arise after the death of an individual in the species. A firm as an individual – as the 'monobrain' in Machlup's (1963) language – cannot know death or, to use Shackle's (1972) language, temporality (which represents death) in an economic organization has been transformed into a spatial problem. The temporal progress or process of a firm then gets described in a horizontal or a choice space. Temporal discontinuity or the death of a firm is transformed into spatial disjunctions. This economic reasoning transforms strategic causality or temporality into a geometry of choice space. Holmstrom and Tirole (1989) thus argue that the theory of firm must define its spatial or choice boundaries, not temporal limits. Only Schumpeter (1928) possibly gets close to recognizing that the death of an individual firm has something to do with the system of its economy and not just the choice-space geometry. The Evolutionary Theory recognizes time as a parameter and selection from environmental variations as accident, thereby reducing time to a parameter in the evolutionary economic writing. Only if a firm – as an individual of the species of Firm – is fraught with the possibility of a death can there be a possibility of evolution of the species Firm. Only a Lamarckian can claim that an individual firm can store learning from feedback in its deep structures. In the absence of a theory of death of a firm, not even such rash Lamarckian inferences can be drawn. In so far as a firm arising out of failures in market (Coase, 1990) or appearing as a nexus of treaties (Cheung, 1983) or as incomplete contracts over property rights are concerned (Hart, 1988), it cannot be born nor can it die. These approaches attribute the beginning of a firm to an exogenous causality, for example in the birth of a contract. Even the death of that firm is, therefore, exogenous. Thus, when exogenous causes make it less economic, the contract fails and the firm vanishes. In contrast, the application of evolutionism necessarily requires that birth and death of a firm be caused endogenously.

The theorists of knowledge strategy have skirted this issue. A Piagetian theorist (Nooteboom, 2001) argues in favour of the maturational stages of knowledge. Several theorists from the resource perspective of strategic management also recognize the hierarchy of stages in the resource organizations of a firm. The horizontal stages of a hierarchy in which a firm can apply the same abstract principle or decision rule to diverse problems or areas have also been recognized. Linguists and biologists have ruled out a hierarchy in the degrees of enriched knowledge. A similar hierarchy cannot be accepted prima facie in the case of firms. What could such a hierarchy imply in the case of firms? Is one supposed to believe that a larger number of patents or research publications hierarchically enhances the knowledge level of that firm? The objection is that, first, this is not an economic explanation and, secondly, securing larger patents often does not ensure strategic advantage to a firm (Tilton, 1971). A truly maturational stage implies, as it did for Piaget, learning from sensorimotor experiences and then generalizing it logico-mathematically to further upgraded application, thus setting a hierarchic spiral. Closest to such experiences are the firm's trials with the market. Several copy theorists have thereby employed learning from trials and errors as inputs to logico-mathematical decision-making. This, these theorists argue, set in a hierarchy of enriched knowledge. However, trial and error alone can inform behaviour. Behavioural decisions relate to organizational memory and not to any putatively deeper knowledge hierarchy.

The use of technical terms from evolutionary theory (Dosi, 1982; Nelson and Winter, 1982; Weick, 1979) violates the basic premise of specificity. Chomsky has used the term lexicon in a strict sense and for the purposes of syntactic generation. A theory of economics, for example, however, belongs to the domain of semantics and pragmatics. A lexicon common to the species Firm is of no use. A theory of strategic knowledge must refer to specificities of facts in the domain of an individual firm. Terms such as selection, variation, retention and competence or capability have found highly varied semantic connotations in the vast literature on this subject. A term, for example, 'selection', without any supporting definition should be considered as rather useless for the purpose of building a theory. The methodology adopted for theory-building by evolutionary economics also appears to be inappropriate. Technology here is understood as a process and the pragmatism here lies in the market powers displacing an existing technology by another technology. The new technology never invalidates the previous technology but replaces it on putative grounds of superiority. In science, according to Kuhn, Lakatos, Laudan and others, an invalid theory is replaced but in technology, a replacing technology is only more efficient and cannot disprove or invalidate the logic of previous technology (Pearce and Pearce, 1989). Given this, the use of 'paradigm' in the Kuhnian sense for describing progress in technological trajectories (Dosi, 1982, 1988) seems unsupportable.

Conflating categories and trespassing theoretical boundaries have weakened both the theory proposed and the possibility of inter-theoretic debates. There are several such conflated usages. One may refer to the use of the terms 'competence/capability' and 'rule/routine'. Generative grammar's use of 'competence' is strictly definable and refers to certain innate characteristics, a set of minimal parameters (not rules), computational principles and a set of lexical items. Can a firm or even the economic concerns of an agent in that firm have any innate characteristics? Or, does the evolutionary theory of economics and strategy offer a set of parameters, which set generative computation in motion when provided with facts of lexicon, such as the nominal of economic facts? One is afraid that the theory has not done so. In fact, it cannot offer even a rudimentary lexicon. Perhaps there is no lexicon. Even more importantly, there cannot be a set of minimum parameters or, surely, an innate characteristic. Under the circumstances, these borrowed terms have lost technical definitions. Various meanings have been associated with these terms by different authors following current usages of discourse semantics.

Competence cannot refer to a set of 'rules/routines' in the generative grammar. Such a rule following might refer to the domain of semantics. Or, a repeated behaviour might appear as rule following to an observer. The former refers to semantic concerns where violations to following rules might jeopardize communication. The latter is indeed not a rule following. Behaviour refers to memory and what gets memorized does not get stored in the gene or in any other deep structure. This behaviour is necessarily short-term and keeps getting revised. The use of the term 'routine' by Nelson and Winter (1982) refers to behaviour. They have, however, suggested a deep structure ('functioning') routine: one in which skills, technology and organization remain 'intertwined' (Nelson and Winter, 1982: 104). Such routines are acquired through habits and practice. The Piaget–Chomsky debate has shown how information generated from trial and error or from problem-solving fails to get categorized logico-mathematically and how such sensorimotor information fails to be computationally generic. Routine, in Nelson and Winter, appears to be generic or at least, as constraining. Routine in its constraining function will have to define limits on what is allowable and what is not. A behavioural routine cannot be limiting either.

Competence, knowledge and code

Teece and Pisano (1994: 553), following Nelson and Winter, argue that the 'competitive advantage of firms stems from dynamic capabilities rooted in high performance routines operating inside the firm, embedded in the firm's processes, and conditioned by its history...these capabilities generally cannot be bought; they must be built'. This appears to suggest semantically that a simultaneous reference to a lexicon makes an entity exhibit its competence. The deep structures suggested by these theorists, however, are knowledge. This implies that the routines themselves are either the knowledge or embedded in knowledge. A routine has to be a generic structure. Once again, referring to the case of language, it is observed that on the surface levels of language compositions (such as relating nouns to verbs), the grammar used is not described as pertaining to the deep structure. In fact, such a surface grammar changes with time and with languages. The deeper generative grammar generates syntaxes and is not empirically observable from the surface structures. Knowledge is defined semantically and several syntactic structures might serve the purpose of communication, for example. A routine has to be generic and cannot have content. Knowledge without a semantic content cannot be defined. It follows then that the suggested locus of routine cannot be in knowledge content but the locus has to be grammar-like.

Surface grammar, however, varies with time and locales and with languages. A grammar is not knowledge either. A deep structure generative grammar has to be ruled out because Teece and Pisano (1994) argue that the routine evolves with an organization. The locale of the routine is entirely within the firm's organization and thus routine cannot refer to deep structure. According to these theorists, such a routine has been learnt and honed through trial and error. This routine might then resemble surface compositional rules of making sentences. Organizational theorists have employed an extension of this idea while explaining organizational processes as sentential generation. Several problems follow such a conclusion. First, a routine is then not knowledge. A routine can be the mode through which knowledge is articulated. Secondly, routine-generated sentence-like processes or other strategic acts can be meaningful only to internal members of the firm. Thirdly, firms will fail to communicate or co-ordinate their knowledge because an articulated knowledge expressed in an organization's own idiosyncratic language would appear to others as incomprehensible. In fact, this belongs to the private language argument. Fourthly, there cannot be any measure of competency or efficiency because a private language uses its own repertoire of rules and lexicon. There cannot be any yardstick. In fact, Williamson (1999) has observed that the definition employed by these theorists in explaining core competency involves circularity (Porter, 1994).

In order for routine or dynamic capability to provide competitive advantage, the routine has to be idiosyncratic, not imitable and private and should originate inside the firm. These are some of the qualifiers of core competency (Prahalad and Hamel, 1990; Teece, Pisano and Shuen, 1997). Scholars from the field have used several terms that have been defined differently. Dosi and Teece (1998: 284) defined a term 'distinctive competence' that reflects 'distinctive organizational capabilities to co-ordinate and to learn'.

A distinctive competence is a differentiated set of skills, complementary assets and organization routines, which together allow a firm to co-ordinate a particular set of activities in a way that provides the basis for competitive advantage in a particular market or markets. A competitive advantage is secured behaviourally while a routine is secured evolutionally. Above all, this definition is methodologically solipsistic. A routine or a competence is also decidedly private. Core competence theorists use the governance perspective (Williamson, 1996), which is about how the internally evolved routine might govern disparate resources and different periods of production into a continuity. This cannot otherwise be secured from a market. Co-ordination, according to this theory, refers to internal co-ordination or to governance, which is the key term of transaction cost economics (TCE) (Williamson, 1985). Such a private routine would then disallow transference of any knowledge across firm boundary (solipsistically, the boundary of the firm is where knowledge fails to flow over). Each unit is not only a knowledge firm but, also, an entity that cannot know the knowledge of other units, or that fails to communicate its own knowledge.

Tacit knowledge and code

Another important dimension emerges from such constructions of cocooned knowledge. Both theories of 'core competency/routine' and the TCE are based on the idea of tacit knowledge. Tacit knowledge, in its origination (Polanyi, 1962, 1966), however, refers to two dimensions: an inarticulable aspect that appears phenomenologically (Banerjee, 1997) and that which is articulable but, often because of other incidental factors, does not get articulated. Of the two, the former – following its appearance as a known entity – gets associated with language. The latter is not intrinsically tacit. Cowan, David and Foray (2000), Dasgupta and David (1986, 1994) and David and Foray (1996)have forcefully argued how knowledge, which is of interest to economic understanding, cannot be intrinsically tacit. Also, following Arrow (1962a, 1962b), knowledge could be recognized as information, limited only by the fact of certain institutional imperfections. Institutional imperfections impose degrees of 'tacitness' or forced inarticulation on an articulable knowledge. This fact of imposition of barriers to articulation has, however, been completely overlooked by both competence and the TCE theorists.

A fact that owes its existence to governance cannot define the fact of governance. This leads to renewal of circularity. A fact of inarticulation is also not 'natural' to the 'tacit' knowledge. With institutions reshaped and incentives redrawn, an erstwhile tacit knowledge would become a codified or articulated knowledge. Further, if tacit knowledge – the bedrock of competency theory or TCE's governance approach (based on asset specificity) – loses its inarticulation and if the knowledge opens up to several forms of articulation, depending on the nature of prevailing institutions, competency, routine or transaction minimizing, governance would fail to bind the disparate resources organized together as a unit firm so far. The acceptance of this fact would deal a death blow to these theories. In fact, in contrast to accepting the contingent nature of tacit knowledge, proponents of these theories have argued that tacit characteristics be protected and trade secrecy laws be imposed more vigorously. Coming back to competency and routine, once the possibility of articulation of tacit knowledge of a firm is accepted, it cannot have or retain its core competency. The institutional marketplace can make or unmake routines of a firm provided routines are as defined.

Routines can still serve the purposes of co-ordination and exclusivity of knowledge provided the tacitness of routines is de-emphasized and it is declared that routines pertain to decisions or to certain principles, including principles of aesthetics. Decisions can be defined over the domain of psychology (or cognitive psychology, as in Kahneman and Tversky, 1979), as a pure descriptive project, or as a normative or even prescriptive project, belonging to the domain of rational reasoning (Bell, Raiffa and Tversky, 1988; Gardenfors and Sahlin, 1986; Simon, 1972, 1983a, 1983b). The rules of decision allow a firm to set agenda and co-ordinate diverse resources and knowledge. It is not necessary that such rules or principles be based on tacit, gene-like organizational deep structures. Alternatively, as in generation of utterances for achieving pragmatic communication or for realization of a pragmatic 'activity/end'-result (Castaneda, 1975; Hart, 1961), a firm might be able to generate surface sentences without sourcing the grammar of generation in a private language or in a deep genetic structure. Typically, firm-internal usages of metaphor, suggestions and rhetoric (Banerjee, 2003f) seem to say that organization of co-ordination processes inside a firm is more often than not based on non-private surface languages, while applying principles from rhetoric in the most idiosyncratic manner. Both decision-type and rhetoric-type of sentential co-ordination satisfy the requirements that routines are supposed to achieve.

Finally, if 'routine/competency' or transaction costs explain the emergence or birth and the sustainability of a firm, a natural follow-up question would be whether they can explain the demise of that firm. In the absence of such an explanation, both theories would explain a state of affairs only. TCE has often been criticized as static (Langlois, 1992; Langlois and Robertson, 1995). Langlois explains dynamic transaction costs as the costs of persuading, negotiating, co-ordinating and teaching external suppliers. Williamson (1999) counters this criticism by pointing out that TCE recognizes *ex ante* not only anticipated problems but also *ex post* both contracting problems and the inter-temporal adjustments. Williamson points out that both *ex ante* and *ex post* are inter-temporal agreements. In particular, TCE, according to Williamson, takes care of the centrality of adaptations. The understanding here is that inter-period continuity of contracts does not reflect any temporal causation in the Hicksian sense. Williamson's position that TCE is not static cannot be substantiated. A dynamic theory, in contrast to a static theory, also takes care of inter-periods but cannot or does not explain things in terms of causation. The use of parametric time by evolutionary theorists comes closest to incorporating causality. The competency and evolutionary perspective argues that it takes care of the development of firm competency (Hodgson, 1998), hence inter-temporality, path dependency (Rosenberg, 1994) and adaptations to environment take care of the temporal dimension. In both theories though, temporality is incidental only or the temporality does not causally define a transaction or a routine. Variations in transaction costs or variations in routine are not functions of time. According to the competency theory, the demise of a firm could be attributed to a mistaken shift in its core competency. Tautologically, retention of core competency ensures firm continuity for an indefinite period. A dynamic theory refers to the explanatory power of that theory to describe inter-temporal variations. This dynamic theory cannot explain, however, why even while retaining core competency a firm might vanish. An answer to this should not be located in changes in the environment of the vanishing firm but must be located in the principles that define the firm. In other words, a routine or transaction cost fails to explain dynamic instability in an economy or of a firm (Schumpeter, 1928).

Strategy for winning: theory perspectives

Rumelt, Schendel and Teece (1994: 19; italics in original) argued that 'strategic management is about co-ordination and resource allocation *inside the firm*'. Strategy research, accordingly, must strive to offer theory on effective internal co-ordination of entrepreneurship and technological progress. This internalist perspective (Mintzberg, 1979) is comparable to the externalist perspective of strategy (Porter, 1980), which emphasizes repositioning of a firm vis-à-vis other actors in the product-industry segment. Crafting strategy internally can take care of temporal shifts but an externalist approach finds it difficult to get beyond static forces of competition. Somewhat intermediate is the proposal by Winter (1987: 160) that 'an organizational strategy... is a summary account of the principal characteristics and relationships of the organization and its environment – an account developed for the purpose of informing decisions affecting the organization's success and survival'. Further, 'mere habits of thought or action, managerial or otherwise, are not strategies' (Winter, 1987: 161). This perspective of strategy is in tune with the earlier proposal by Nelson and Winter (1982: 18) that 'the core concern... is with the dynamic process by which behaviour patterns and market outcomes are jointly determined over time'. A logical analysis of strategic behaviour is emphasized in the industrial organization (IO) approach. Strategy is as rivalrous as competition. It is behavioural too. This approach demands exact and detailed specifications of a firm's strategies (since IO uses extensive form games in modelling strategic interactions) along with specifications of the timing of action. Emphasis is laid on 'dynamics of strategic actions' and 'commitment' in strategic settings. Shapiro (1989b: 127) explains the common theme running through the IO approach to business strategy as 'the timing of strategic decisions and the ability of large firms to make commitments'. The timing of action in the IO approach refers to the sequential timing: a strategic behaviour follows the sequence of the competitor's move.

The overriding concern for strategy theory, excepting in the IO approach, is about the managerial difficulty to get the organization of the firm acting in dynamic consonance with the environment. The strategy theory and practice must match the dynamics of a global market (Yano, 1993). Such approaches seem to be no different from the normative aspects of competition theory or more precisely oligopolistic competition theory. The trouble lies here. Competition is decidedly behavioural. It invokes the firm's response and the dynamism implies that the environment must respond to the response of the firm. A strategy to it, argued here, is much different. It must refer to winning. Strategy must begin from a rivalrous state of affairs and simultaneously strive to reach a state beyond rivalry achieved by the 'winning' firm. Strategy then is not a game of poker, and the firm which is 'desirous to win' does not make a competitive move as in poker. Such a firm creates situations to which others will have to respond. The active agency of the strategist firm makes a new state of affairs while simultaneously dismantling a previous state of affairs. The strategist firm does not simply respond to the provocative stimuli. The strategist firm wishes to win and hence it creates a state where it is the winner. This is the core of strategy.

Knowledge for strategic advantage

How does knowledge relate to this winning strategy? A 'competence/routine' theorist does not apparently talk about knowledge as is ordinarily universally understood. To the 'competence/routine' theorist, knowledge is operational first. This knowledge is somewhat algorithmic and prescriptive as well. In fact, knowledge for competence is without content and is like the rules of grammar. TCE has little room left for knowledge. Information, *ex ante* or *ex post* the contractual arrangements, acts as knowledge in honing to perfection the contracts already entered into. Both TCE and 'competence/routine' theories accept this view of operationalizable knowledge rules. Knowledge with content is considered as resources whose contents remain unaffected while operational rules of knowledge allocate or appropriate them. Knowledge with content is then a modular asset (Langlois and Robertson, 1995; Tripsas and Gavetti, 2000). In these theories, strategic knowledge refers to rules for connecting or disconnecting modules or, as in TCE, to remedial actions *ex post* or *ex ante* in contract forming. Evidently, they recognize a division in knowledge, of which the strategic part is without content and the resources part has content.

This knowledge of routines is conditioned by states of affairs in competition. In other words, knowledge of routines is 'framed' (Kahneman, Slovic and Tversky, 1988; Tversky and Kahneman, 1988) and is 'typical'. In a stricter sense, this is conditioned by the prevailing state of competition. Presumably, a firm might possess several routines, only a few of which in a bundle appear as 'typical' of any response to the prevailing competition situation. The firm's knowledge repertoire recognizes only this emergent knowledge of rules. The remaining rules are recognized as habit or as tacit. Further, a situation of competition (to be more precise, as in TCE or as in IO, this is a situation of equilibrium) is co-ordinative. The rules of knowledge that are known to a firm are co-ordinated with rules of knowledge of other competing firms. Schelling (1960) describes this interdependence of knowing one's rules of knowledge in a situation of co-ordination canonically. Rules of knowledge must remain consistent with one's own value system. Competitors or the 'precarious partners' who are tied up in 'incomplete antagonism' (Schelling, 1960: 15) have conflicts and common interests. They are rational and 'each participant's "best" choice of action depends on what he expects others to do and that "strategic behaviour" is concerned with influencing another's choice by working on his expectation of how one's own behaviour is related to his'. Thus the rules of knowledge about how best to deploy resources strategically are normative. A firm's knowledge about what rules it can deploy from its own repertoire, in a particular situation, is thus normatively procured.

IO theorists following Schelling have developed their theory of strategy in a particular direction. It is assumed in general that a firm is large; otherwise it cannot be effective in inducing rules of others and that it is unanimous regarding strategic decisions. This point on unanimity across several processes and even individuals inside a firm makes severe demands of this theory. A real life portrayal, however, would indicate – as admitted by the internalist perspective of evolutionary competence theorists – that a firm is highly heterogeneous. Very often, particularly in a large firm, the most difficult problem is implementation of a strategic decision. A firm is like an unorganized body with several structures disjointed and members in dissonance. A real manager takes a decision based on not only what Schelling described but after considering how far resources can be redeployed, degrees of concurrence that can be achieved in teams, business processes that can be transformed, appropriateness of incentives internal to the firm and such others. A cunning manager also looks at the burden of similar structural, systemic and human problems on its competitors. He might employ apparently irrational strategic moves often only to worsen the burden on its competitor. The 'competence/routine' theorist addresses them much better. TCE, through provisioning for redrawing of contracts, attempts this objective and thus takes care of the internal dimension of an organization.

The competence theorist, however, partitions knowledge of rules from knowledge as content. Innate rules need not be known; their computational counterparts appear in the surface rules, provided the parameters of such innate rules have interfaced with a lexicon. Surface rules do vary with the lexicon. For example, structural and technological or resources information on an industry segment provide a lexicon, as it were. The competence theory, however, has made one major assumption in this regard in overlooking that rule following and rule generation belong to two entirely different domains. Rule following must care for semantics, pragmatics and the rhetoric of discourses and conditions of power. Rule generation, if innate, could be computational and, if surface, could have several types of associations satisfying semantics. Rule following must, therefore, notice the knowledge content in the rules being followed. Thus, employees of a firm must know decision contents in order to follow a decision. The competence theory cannot specify the content of a rule while generating its routines, say, in response to a game of strategy with its counterparts. The IO theorists, for whom the firm is an integral whole, completely overlook this problem.

Importance of processes and agenda

An integrally whole firm can proffer behavioural responses that could be considered strategic in certain limited areas. The patent race is an example. Licensing, R & D rivalry or, to some extent, decisions relating to exit, belong to areas that do not require much from the internal dimensions of a firm. These, incidentally, are areas on which IO has contributed significant literature. Most other strategic decisions, including the implications of joining a patent race, for example, necessarily involve internal dimensions of the firm. Strategic decisions must be mobilizational and should be able to set agenda. Isenberg (1988: 526–8) observed that 'senior managers tend to think about two kinds of problems: how to create effective organizational processes and how to deal with one or two overriding concerns or very general goals'. Isenberg concedes further that evidence against expectations on managerial rationality is 'compelling'. Rationality, as a normative framework, is likely to guide decisions and actions. Not all of them would be successful. He further observes that 'in making their day-by-day and minute-by-minute tactical manoeuvres, senior executives tend to rely on several general thought processes such as using intuition; managing a network of interrelated problems; dealing with ambiguity, inconsistency, novelty, and surprise; and integrating action into the process of thinking' (Isenberg, 1988: 530). The rational framework or the science of decision meticulously made planning and information, derived from robust theoretical models, appear to assist the intuitive, the 'prospect'-driven or the 'typicality'-locating actual decisions of managers. There is no apparent reason to believe that junior executives take decisions or commit actions much differently. A senior manager sets up an agenda that would be in consonance with the firm strategy. The firm strategy that this senior manager chooses must recognize facts of competitive information, the likely decisions of the competitors and the firm-internal agenda. The senior manager's decisions thus clearly recognize the fact of non-homogeneity and non-singularity of the firm.

Routine or competence does not appear to be the overriding concern for managerial thinking. The split between knowledge of rules and knowledge as content does not appear to influence this thinking, which remains busy with 'organizational and interpersonal processes. By 'process' is meant the ways managers bring people and groups together to handle problems and take action' (Isenberg, 1988: 528). A typical senior executive in a Japanese corporation appears to remain preoccupied with similar business processes. The strategy of the business attracts maximum attention from such an executive, who lays down processes, respective goals and quantified and clear objectives. One might reiterate some common features: that senior managers spell out different versions of the same strategy in different languages and with different objectives as well as with different goals to each such internal process team. Members of different teams make use of inferences to apprehend and make use of discourse rhetoric or pragmatics to grasp the intended meaning of the strategy of the firm. Internal to the firm, there are then multiple versions of strategy, none of which, however, is the same as or even equivalent to the signals on strategy that this firm sends out to its competitors. An observer, using the vantage of the IO theory, for example, looks at the behavioural implications of such externally emitted signals from the firm. Such a signal cannot then narrate the complete story of strategy. The IO theory misses out strategy making and strategic acting.

An act of strategy is beyond competitive behaviour. The former busies itself with generational issues and issues relating to sustained strategic acting. Strategy cannot then treat a firm as a homunculus. It treats the actual business processes pragmatically. It has to recognize its own organizational structure and organizational systems. It should also consider the influence its strategy can have on the agenda, processes, structures and systems of its competitors. An executive, choosing strategy, therefore, considers an array of fields. The core competence theory (Hamel and Heene, 1994; Montgomery and Porter, 1991) restricts itself to recognizing only the core competencies of the firm and of its competitors. Other important elements of the array, to be described shortly, are overlooked. Also, as argued earlier, core competency assumes that certain core rules or routines are generative. As a result of this theoretical stance, core competency theory necessarily differentiates between strategy content and strategy process. A rule-based generation must differentiate between content and process, as earlier argued, drawing upon the Chomsky–Piaget debate. Apart from all the limitations pointed out, there is a further constraint in that strategy content is inseparably linked with strategy process. To different processes and actors or role-players, an apparently identical strategic agenda of the firm appears different because the strategy content appears along with its respective process through the medium of language, as argued earlier. The oral nature of the content and the process disallows the separation of the generative and content issues. To reiterate, this happens because the strategy process similar to the routine cannot be generated out of an innate 'core' (an organization has none). This generation cannot computationally consult any lexicon either. Further, a strategy process is not simply syntactic instead. Orally and situationally, interactive teams or individuals constitute a strategy process. Such surface-linguistic interactions are interactions in linguistic contents (or semantics and pragmatics). Right at its birth then, a strategy process is constituted by and is constitutive of strategy content. No such analytic separation can be logically sustained.

Strategy make-up: place of strategic knowledge

The competitive behaviours or the signals that a firm sends to its competitors cannot capture a strategy make-up. Schelling (1960) has raised strategy issues much above behavioural signals. This make-up cannot be reduced to competency, dynamic or core. Competency recognizes internal dimensions and, albeit, limits that to generative innateness that, it is argued, is attributable to conflating of theories. A strategy make-up is never innate. Following Schelling, the internal and external dimensions of a firm constitute a make-up simultaneously. External dimensions might refer more to games of co-ordination although never limited to them, as shall be argued. Internal dimensions too might refer to co-ordination, albeit with less intensity. It so happens that the boundaries between these external and internal dimensions change so often that sometimes there seems to be no organizational boundary. In a perfectly contestable market (Baumol, Panzar and Willig, 1986: 456) 'which can be viewed as a benchmark', 'no role is played by the sunk costs, pre-commitments, asymmetric information and strategic behaviour that characterize many real markets. With irreversibilities and the inducements for strategic behaviour assumed away, industry structure in perfectly contestable markets is determined by the fundamental forces of demand and of production technology'. In such a market, boundaries of firms would be less discernible. Conversely, in an oligopolistic market, a small player would find it difficult to sustain firm boundary. There appears to be several states of affairs where these two internal and external dimensions collapse and processes inside a firm become susceptible to strategic moves by an outsider firm. Can a firm have or practice a knowledge that ensures impregnability of its boundaries? Conversely, can a firm institute such knowledge practices as can allow it to overcome the boundaries of other competing firms? Similar questions raise the possibility of knowledge distinct from core competency or routines that can create strategic advantages to the firm; the one that can situate strategy as desired by the senior manager is a strategic knowledge.

A strategic knowledge is an enabler of strategy. A strategist would wish to influence processes both inside the organization and organizations belonging to the strategic array. This is the strategic objective. The strategic knowledge empowers the strategist to achieve that strategic objective. Prima facie, strategic knowledge appears to be distinct from such knowledge as is used as factors of production, as is pure content laden or as can be generated by any competent firm, by relating generational rules to a lexicon available in the market. It seems that strategic knowledge, like a negotiating tool, gives its owner a leverage over all the processes in the firm's strategic array. Strategic knowledge is then distinct, as will be closely studied in the chapters that follow.

New strategic make-up model

To recapitulate the earlier discussion on the model of a firm and that of the states of affairs in a market, a firm has five categories of business process and seven types of structure. These five processes are about: (1) sustenance of leadership by the senior managers, (2) the agenda that sets the firm as an organization, (3) structural features of the organization, (4) financial resources under the control of the firm, (5) the prospect of liability/threat (or punishment). Each firm in the strategic milieu or array of the incumbent winning strategist firm, including this strategist firm, has these five categories of process. The four types of firms principally constituting this strategic array or milieu are: winning strategist, its opponent, the follower of the middle path, and the careless firm. It has been seen earlier that the strategic milieu is defined by the domination of the winning strategist and opponent pair, and the follower of the middle path and the careless are types of firm who choose to continue on strategic courses in-between or are careless about the dominant strategic move. The other types of firms in this milieu are those who have entered into strategic alliances with the winning strategist or conversely, those that have entered into strategic commitments with the opponent, for example. These form two more groups of firm type.

With each firm in this strategic milieu having five categories of process, the strategic concern of the winning-strategist firm is about influencing all the relevant categorical processes of these four principal types of firm. This set of process categories has been defined as the strategic landscape. A strategic landscape then cares for all process categories and simultaneously so, but little for firm boundaries. Firm boundary is often not, according to this model, an important category to reckon with. The interest is in processes. Processes constitute a firm's organization, whose structure is a time-dependent manifestation of the processes in interaction with a winning strategy. *Inter alia*, it accepts a definition of influencing strategy, which seeks to influence processes in firms belonging to its strategic milieu. The firm following the middle path least wishes any influence of the dominant strategic pair on its processes while the careless firm can afford to be oblivious about the dominant strategic pair's influences on its processes. A careless firm can thus be a large corporation engaged in businesses in several industry segments. Conversely, it can be a small firm. A middle-path follower firm is one that is perhaps after some other strategic technological pursuit and would, therefore, like to maintain equidistance from the dominant pair's strategic moves. Here, the relevance of both the organization and processes of a firm are being recognized and, unlike IO, the importance of both small and large firms.

To recall the earlier discussion on strategy, a strategist plays with strategic moves. These strategic moves are not behavioural and remain unrecognized to an observer. Strategic moves can have six different modes or qualities. A strategic move can be for alliance, confrontation, fluidity, nonchalance, prevarication, and dependence. These modes are derived from the descriptive psychological states of an individual. Modes of these strategic moves reflect mental or cognitive states and are thus not observable empirically. It follows then that these modes are not normative or prescriptive rationale. Schelling's (1960) understanding is normative or prescriptive rationale because it considers strategic display in games along the singular dimension of co-ordination alone. Much co-ordination is derived in that game theoretic literature from the law of contracts. This law, in particular, disregards pragmatics and inten- tionality (von Savigny, 1988) – which are always present in common linguistic interactions – and would tend to be normative rationale and calculative of gains that are immediately foreseeable.

The six modes presented here are instead based on descriptive psychology, which takes into account 'typical' dispositions that an individual might assume in situations of which it wishes to take strategic advantage. All these modes are temporary and transient. 'Alliance' here refers to truce, achieved through payment of tribute or extraction of tribute or commitments of a varying nature. Such an alliance goes much beyond the law of contracts by clearly recognizing anthropological issues in exchanges (Polanyi, 1957). Alliance here recognizes tokens of commitments. A typical game in IO recognizes only irreversible commitment such as made through capital investments. However, this notion on alliance acknowledges the importance of token tribute or even of reversible commitment. In a perfectly contestable market, which software writing resembles closely, commitments cannot be irreversible or massive. Token-based alliances better represent such a situation.

Similarly, 'confrontation' assumes several forms, beginning with direct confrontation through deterrence to several indirect forms. 'Fluidity' refers to dynamic and continuous changes in observed strategic behaviour. The incumbent strategist has a future plan on definite strategy that is difficult to predict because of fluid strategy. 'Nonchalance' refers to a state of affairs when the incumbent does not go for either alliance or confrontation. In other words, an incumbent firm does not recognize growth or diminution in the present affairs of strategic moves by others. 'Prevarication' refers to a state of indecision. The incumbent firm does not have a degree of disbelief that can decidedly influence its decision in favour of an alliance or confrontation. 'Dependence' refers to piggybacking although achieved at a cost perhaps. A strategically dependent firm depends on the major or dominant strategy. Another point of importance in this connection is the temporal dimension of these modes.

A decidedly dominant strategy can influence the timings of strategic behaviours (this can influence behaviour alone because a junior strategist might still wait for a better time for effecting his move while behaving in a mode observationally behaviourist) of others in the strategic landscape. Most often though, each player in the strategy make-up follows a temporality punctuated by its own perception on strategic gain. The mode of a strategic move is thus decided exclusively by the perceived state of affairs. The timing of this mode is, therefore, not shared with other players in the strategic array. Each player has his own temporal sequence though the observable sequence is different from the sequence of strategic modes. An observable sequence depends on observation of a strategic action taken by a player in the strategic array. A strategic action can be observed to be an act of: appeasement, rewarding, discrimination, or punishment. The strategic mode is not observable and hence strategic behaviour can be discerned by observation on strategic actions alone.

To summarize this discussion, a strategic state of affairs comprises four types of player, each with five processes relevant to strategy, making a total of twenty in the strategic landscape. A player can move its strategy in any one of the six modes, which describe the appropriateness of the mode adopted to the percipient move-maker. These modes of strategic perceptions, however, appear in the reflections only while the observed strategic behaviours depend for their description on strategic actions that the player has committed. It follows then that decisions regarding strategic actions are based on the particular mode of a strategic move. Similarly, strategic action is undertaken on the basis of this mode of a move. Any behavioural or observational narration cannot capture this descriptive psychology of strategic thinking. The mode of a move recognizes the strategic landscape and it is this mode that searches for, collects, collates or discriminates between the information, obtained partly from observations on strategic behaviours of others and partly from other market co-ordination sources.

Manoeuvring through strategic knowledge

Knowledge is strategic when it can inform and actuate a desired mode of the strategic move. By definition, strategic knowledge can secure for the winning strategist influences over the strategic moves, possibly to be undertaken by the twenty processes in the strategic landscape of this winning strategist. The observed strategic behaviour of this player is related to strategic knowledge only indirectly. The observation on strategic behaviours of others is a source of information though. As it appears, Schelling (1960) does not differentiate between the psychology of strategizing and strategic behaviour. He does not go beyond the contractable domain of considered positions of behaviours either. Schelling (and a very large body of literature following him on strategy) does not consider influencing the internal processes of the other incumbents. It is a fact, however, that business collects information on processes internal to a firm and, in extreme cases, even uses unscrupulous methods to win over persons having a stake in those processes. IO, in general, has limited its concern to large firms (those whose decisions have impact on the market outcomes), which have been considered as unitary wholes. The resources and capability theory (Penrose, 1968) has looked at the organization of the internal processes. The emphasis on the competence or capability of a firm made this approach neglect the influences that processes internal to other firms might have on the organizing competence of the incumbent firm.

It is, therefore, doubtful that resources or competence theory can offer an explanation of strategic knowledge. The IO theory considers the firm as a unitary whole and needs to consider information necessary to take strategic decisions although it does not need knowledge of the organizing processes in order to prescribe strategic behaviour. As a result, the IO theory does not offer any explanation on strategic knowledge. What it has is strategic information. Strategic knowledge, in contrast, influences knowledge outcomes in all the processes in the strategy landscape. Strategic knowledge fiddles with the motive, is purely intentional and is causal by being a mental or cognitive state. The grammar of strategic knowledge is dramatic and is the grammar of motive, The knowledge outcomes are targeted at and dependent upon the strategy objectives. A thick description of winning-strategy objectives could be considered thus: the winning strategy is about influencing processes in the strategy landscape towards a position favourable to the winning strategist. Or, it is about creating a new turf of strategic manoeuvres, which necessarily demands that all the processes in a landscape change their states in conformity with the new states of affairs. Or, it is about framing new rules of game and so on. Strategic knowledge is about guiding, deforming, subsuming or otherwise influencing the conditions for strategic behaviours by others in the strategic landscape.

It follows then that the strategic knowledge of a firm varies with time and strategic objectives. A firm needs to switch over organizing modes of its strategic knowledge once the earlier strategic objective is replaced by a new objective. What remain unchanged in such dynamic affairs are the categories of process and the modes of perceiving or apprehending strategic modes. A categorial division of processes and mode-wise divisions of strategic moves allows one to keep undifferentiated strategy process from strategy content (or, absence of differentiation between knowledge of generative rules of competence from knowledge as content). This proposal does not need to postulate certain innate routines. Above all, this proposal acknowledges dynamism in strategy, attaches great importance to those strategies, which can influence processes internal to other firms and has little respect for boundaries of a firm. In these respects, this proposal is about strategy proper. Strategy, it is emphasized here, is beyond competition and simple rivalry; it is also beyond behavioural reactions to moves by others.

It follows from this argument that knowledge, about knowledge-generation issues, pertains to issues of strategic knowledge. However, knowledge generated appears or remains as information. The 'what' of knowledge and the 'how' of knowledge are issues that are strategic because the 'what' knowledge and the 'how' knowledge decide the influences on the strategy landscape. This knowledge, however, is different from the knowledge generated as content only. A content-only knowledge appears as a bundle of information to all, except the person who generated it. This also follows the conclusions of Arrow (1962b). Apparently, the right place to generate such bundles of information is the institution of university. Nonaka, Toyama and Nagata (2000) argue that the institution of a firm is an alternative institution of knowledge generation. Nonaka and Takeuchi (1995), however, emphasize the putative claim that most productive knowledge is tacit and the firm alone can generate as well as retain or possibly even trade in such tacit and asset specific tied-up knowledge. The corollary to such an argument – as pointed out by Cowan, David and Foray (2000) – is that an economy or a society need not spend public funding on generation of productive or economic knowledge for making it available as a public good. An extension of this view suggests that the strategic advantage of a firm is dependent upon knowledge. Public domain knowledge, according to this argument, does not promote strategic advantages of firms of a nation. It is argued then that public funding for generating information bundles be stopped or reversed to promote firm strategic advantages based, as they are, on tacit knowledge generated internally.

The point raised in this model, that knowledge is not intrinsically tacit, however, disputes such a claim. Firms make it appear tacit because economic organizations of firms have so far found it convenient to keep knowledge partly tacit. The R & D of firms does generate certain information bundles. In order that the firm-generated content-only knowledge can pass through the epistemic selection filters and can thus get recognition as valid knowledge claims, these must become public (Dasgupta and David, 1986; Nelson and Romer, 1996). A firm copyrights other forms of content-only knowledge, which do not belong to public domain. Such knowledge appears to the internal processes of a firm as bundles of information only.

Tacit characterization and asset specificity of knowledge can, as argued here, be avoided. David and Foray (1996) have argued that, given the right incentives, an articulable knowledge can be completely specified provided that the necessary nominal is available from a publicly available lexicon.

Knowledge is not intrinsically tacit. Asset specificity in the TCE framework is defined on this tacit dimension. Knowledge assets become doubly specific, the TCE framework argues, because transaction costs prevent their passage to costless imitation prevailing in public domain. The use of tacit knowledge in competency theory is not foundational. The competency theory proposed routines as foundational while the TCE accepts asset specificity as foundational to its framework. It has been argued that knowledge as content-only appears to be tacit only during its phenomenological appearance or emergence. Subsequently, its holder knows or is aware of the emerged knowledge content as an articulated or articulable complete description. Described knowledge is, however, a bundle of information and it is important to emphasize that such a content-only knowledge has the least strategic relevance.

Strategy is concerned about knowledge that can influence processes. It has little business with the content of the outcomes of the generated knowledge. The content of a generated knowledge is completely describable. Such content can influence the behaviour and the decisions. Knowledge content can be outsourced and can be utilized solely for gains in competitive performance corresponding to a given technology and a given industry structure. A firm can trade in knowledge content. It is emphasized here that a knowledge institution, such as the university, has the sole function of content creation. A firm is advantaged only if it can locate, secure, deny others the access to, or otherwise influence creation of contents. Influencing contents creation in the public domain would not privilege a firm vis-à-vis other firms. A firm would be privileged if knowledge creation and knowledge utilization in all the twenty processes in the strategic landscape can be warranted to conform to the strategic moves of this firm. A firm generates its knowledge through its processes. Strategic knowledge is that which can influence the mode and characteristics of knowledge generated in such processes.

Undoubtedly, a firm generates large contents of knowledge, some of which remains incompletely described. Incomplete descriptions are, however, warranted by the specific organization of processes both inside and outside the firm. In other words, the processes belonging to the strategic landscape warrant incomplete descriptions. Is this degree of incompleteness in knowledge description attributable to the degree of co-ordination across firms in a strategic landscape? What is the relation between the degree of incompleteness and the degree of disbelief? A degree of disbelief might refer to the modes of strategic moves, that is, to the strategizing psychology. Conversely, can the degree of completeness in description be warranted by the necessity of co-ordination? In continuation, how far should the knowledge-generating processes be opened up to conform to certain process benchmarks? Further, how is incompleteness in description related to rules and routines?

Incomplete description of knowledge

There is an acknowledged difference between knowledge by acquaintance and knowledge by description (Russell, 1984). The former refers to experience and is vague, ambiguous and fluctuating. The latter is a description and has content. Knowledge by description is propositional and can be communicated. To have cognition of experience one needs to 'notice' it or devote 'attention' to it. A problem with experience is that the status of experience is doubtful. An object of experience could be hallucinatory. Cognitive explanation of experience can be offered in terms of belief acquisition (Castaneda, 1975). A complete description of belief may not be always feasible (Stalnaker, 1987) but this belief can be rated against a second belief, which is descriptively known. This account of description and experience refers to a person. This cannot be extended to either a group of persons or to an organization. The knowledge of a person can be completely described and there is no such thing called 'tacit' knowledge except the ambiguous vacillating domain of experience, which too can be noticed through beliefs. Experience provides foundations to beliefs and idiosyncratic differences in experiences leads to revisions in individual beliefs in a somewhat idiosyncratic manner. This individuality is captured by a term called 'propositional attitude', capturing both propositional content and attitudes towards those contents. This attitude contains such things as desires, intentions, hopes, aversions and doubts. Personal knowledge is knowledge by description. One source of this knowledge is experience, which forms beliefs, which with the assistance of mental attitudes, such as intentions, in turn, pose as attitude directed not towards sentential description but towards the world.

Beliefs are mental states causally implicated in behaviour. Knowledge by description assists decision. Beliefs, although indeterminate, are implicated in behaviour. Behavioural observation cannot ascribe a particular belief to an agent though (Davidson, 1984). Such an ascription must refer to the particular linguistic context. This makes it possible, for example, for a senior manager to influence the behaviours of its employees by setting an agenda. The agenda sets the linguistic context or the 'frame', referred to by Loasby (1986, 2000). Individual knowledge by description is complete. Any incomplete description of knowledge must then be ascribed to the context of description or to the mismatches between what Davidson described as linguistic context. A description could be incomplete owing to several factors. Economists point out inappropriateness in incentives. The sociologist of knowledge points out at conventions, tradition, authority and interest but the sociology of knowledge refers to belief-led knowledge. Hence knowledge by description can have incompleteness only if attitudes (including intentions, desires, hopes and doubts), which are belief-based, prevent a complete description. The degree of incompleteness in knowledge is thus only indirectly attributable to beliefs, that is, to the facts of experience. Experience, thus, can condition the degree to which a completely describable knowledge is described. This relation between experience (and hence, belief) and knowledge sets aside the tacitness account of knowledge and the undue importance attached to incentives by the economists. Incentives cannot directly influence experience nor withhold acquisition of complete knowledge. Incentives are outcome oriented; they can influence the generation of description but they cannot influence experience.

Knowledge in relation to production is not comparable to knowledge in science. The former must refer to pragmatism. The truth here is the opinion destined to be agreed to by all and to bring in desired practical consequences. Knowledge of this kind is half way through to experience. Experience and thus belief do influence the descriptive outcome of such knowledge. Indeterminate experience and belief attitudes cannot acquire complete descriptions. Knowledge by description, when influenced strongly by such attitudes, is communicated or described (even in self-reflection) with a degree of incompleteness. The degree of incompleteness thus refers to missing parts in descriptions lost to the belief attitudes such as intentions and desires of individual holders. The degree of incompleteness is also caused by changes in the 'linguistic context': a belief ascribable to one linguistic context loses the description content when referred to another linguistic context and a description appears as incomplete to the holder of the knowledge. A degree of completeness, however, is not an antonym of this degree of incompleteness. Knowledge, by description, is completely described to the degree that the incentives and the forces of conventions, authority and other forms of social influences, bear upon it to be. The degree of completeness of knowledge can be stretched easily by effecting changes in the economic incentives and in the social modes of organization. This degree of completeness is negotiable. Often, degrees of disclosures in a group refer to the discourse situations, to the goals and interests of the members of that group, to the degree of consensus necessary to be achieved or to the economic gains or loss consequent to complete description. The degree of incompleteness is closely influenced by personal experiences and belief attitudes while the degree of completeness in descriptions refers to economic and social peculiarities prevailing in that state of affairs.

Complete knowledge description and co-ordination

The degree of incompleteness in knowledge as description is principally personal though work situations do influence one's belief attitudes. In contrast, the degree of completeness principally refers to the milieu. Issues of co-ordination are relevant then for the degree of completeness in knowledge as description. Different authors have employed the term co-ordination differently (for differences in use see Richardson, 1972, 1998; Schelling, 1960; Shackle, 1952, 1988). It will be necessary to refer to these variations.

The dominant use of the term co-ordination has been in relation to competition and equilibrium (Foss, 1999; Foss and Loasby, 1998; Hayek, 1949, 1967; Krafft and Ravix, 2000; Leijonhufvud, 1968; Loasby, 1989; Marshall, 1920). Two types of information, productive and market, have been recognized as those that can effect such co-ordination between several players in the market. Marshall emphasized the importance of a particular market. The strategic landscape or the array in this model is an extension of this idea on a particular market. A firm seeks these two types of information in order to enhance its own productive capability and to procure competitive information. Serious disequilibria might occur in the absence of such information. Co-ordination ensures transition to equilibrium. This transition or *tâtonnement* takes place through adjustments along a sequence in time for the Austrians and along a horizontal space for the Walrasians. The data required for adjustments has often been thought to be exogenous to the firm or to its strategy (Hayek, 1949; Kirzner, 1973) and a firm reacts to the new data. Others (Krafft and Ravix, 2000; Loasby, 1989, 1994; Marshall, 1920), however, recognized that such exogenously derived data could be made endogenous by way of implicating a firm as part of market institutions. In this case, the data from the market is no longer simply exogenous but can be partially located even internally, in the firm's processes. The *tâtonnement* of the firm takes place simultaneously through activities of learning, competence building (Teece, 1986) and through learning to make use of dispersed Hayckian data inside the firm (Minkler, 1993). This firm then adjusts its internal processes in co-ordination with market processes.

A strategy objective, as is understood here, goes beyond this necessity of equilibrating co-ordination. Shackle (1972: 423) noted the game theory's exclusion of tactical surprise: 'Surprise is the exploitation of the opponent's lack of knowledge or of his reliance on what he wrongly believes to be knowledge. If business is a contest instead of a universal co-ordination of action, its supreme secret is *epistemic*, the gaining and use, the denial and disguise, of knowledge' (italics original). Shackle conveys an important message for explication of what is being argued here. Business cannot limit itself to co-ordination even though it does supply some preliminary 'data', such as data on price that will obtain at equilibrium. This data is required only when a firm wishes to make an investment, for example data on the competitors' behaviour, which provide clues to say the quantity that can be produced or whether the entry barrier can be overcome with current productive technology. Data lead to higher efficiency. Data achieve better co-ordination. However, data often fail to lead to a sudden Schumpeterian discovery or a surprise as underscored by Shackle. The Cantillon profit, as explained by Shackle, appears as a surprise. Such a profit is beyond both expectation and convention. If the firm wishes to earn a Schumpeterian entrepreneurial profit or, especially, a Cantillon 'profit', it must get over the co-ordinated or pre-reconciled conventional 'profit'. A business strategy must go beyond reconciliation's boundary or the boundaries of competition. Strategy is thus about getting over the reconciled and co-ordinated arrangements. Finally a strategy must also refer to disguised actions, denial and opening up a new game or turf.

It has been argued that in launching such a strategy, a firm employs moves to control or influence the states of affairs and rules in all the processes, including those of others in the strategic landscape. The use of the term co-ordination is necessarily limited to this purpose. It follows that co-ordination, when used for strategic purposes, implies states of affairs beyond *tâtonnement* or adjustments. A winning strategy is about co-ordinating – perhaps in a disguised manner or through partial or 'premature' disclosures (Fisher, 1989) and such others – all the processes in the strategic landscape. The degree to which knowledge by description is complete or disclosed has a direct relevance to the manner in which the winning strategist firm seeks to co-ordinate firms in its strategic array. This co-ordination is distinctly different from co-ordination as used by Richardson, for example. The immediate difference between this co-ordination (in the sense of leading) and the co-ordination for adjustments is obvious. The degree of disclosure (or completeness) of knowledge by description, TCE might argue, affects the transaction cost. This degree of completeness can alter or guide business process both inside the winning firm and in the processes of firms belonging to the strategic landscape by way of increasing or reducing transaction cost. The degree of completeness can then substitute the tacit knowledge and asset specificity of the TCE.

Ordinary co-ordination provides a 'bottom-up' view of the economy, conceptualized as a network of interacting processors (Leijonhufvud, 1993), which can be characterized as a 'dynamic step-by-step problem solving process' (Krafft and Ravix, 2000). Such co-ordination is thus computationally feasible and algorithmic. Strategic co-ordination involves interacting processors but is not step-by-step problem-solving through following computationally feasible charters. Knowledge by description, when completely described, is nothing but a bundle of information. This is content-only knowledge. The algorithm-based interaction busies itself with this kind of information and such interactions are sequenced in accordance with the time of receiving such bundles of information from the processes. If firms only have completely described bundles of information (with the difference that descriptions of different processes are achieved in different time periods), there cannot be any surprise but only iterated adjustments. The degree of completeness in description breaks this sequence because even with efforts to get information and even after a time period (of production) a firm cannot access the complete description. Lack of a complete description is, therefore, a more formidable barrier to entry. The absence of a sequence of information search that is common to all also denies to the firms a sharing of a common time axis. Ignorance and consequently uncertainty rule the states of affairs.

A commonly prescribed remedy to overcome this uncertainty is for a firm to 'grow' knowledge faster. Probing data is often difficult and this remedy argues, therefore, that institutions emerge to help out firms in overcoming rigidities in the order of ignorance and in the difficulties of probing data. Knowledge competence of a firm, in alliance with institutional support to alleviate barriers of ignorance, this remedy argues (Teece, 1986), is a better solution.

In contrast, the argument here takes the strategic thrust in another direction. Knowledge competence is irrelevant here. Hastening up production of knowledge cannot be the strategy of a firm. Increase in knowledge does not ensure a complete disclosure of knowledge by description; neither does it ensure any strategic advantage. A bundle of information (which is content-only knowledge) can be purchased from the market. The knowledge strategy of a firm can only strive for strategic knowledge that is knowledge of ways and means to influence and guide processes in a strategic landscape. If the degree of description can be compared with a measure of knowledge content, the strategy is about influencing the manner in which knowledge content is directed or 'directedness'. A winning strategist seeks to influence the content but this strategist does not attempt to know the content as such. Moreover, there does not appear to be any general rule regarding the 'directedness' of contents. For example, the contents of knowledge by description can increase or decrease depending on strategic imperatives. Unlike transaction cost, where a firm is based upon a minimalist programme, a strategic imperative does not suggest that maximum disclosure is preferable. Very often, strategy takes a tortuous path and often enjoys a minimum degree of completeness in description.

A strategic co-ordination, as defined in this argument, employs this degree of completeness in description. The content of knowledge about the five processes inside the winning strategist firm, the opponent firm, the follower of the middle path firm and the careless firm is affected. Strategic co-ordination is the adjustment of disclosures and a *tâtonnement* of degrees of completeness in knowledge by description. An adjustment in prices, for example, is equilibrium seeking. An adjustment in degrees of description is, however, without such teleology and often disequilibria seeking. One comes across divisions of knowledge in disciplines and in theories, in society and in institutions that are not equilibrium seeking. Instead, these are disequilibrating. Firms do not seem to enjoy any particular rule in strategic affairs. There are instances of both equilibrating and disequilibrating departures. The winning strategist makes a strategic move towards influencing the desired 'directedness', which is situation specific.

Gaps in knowledge by description

The five categories of process in the organization of a firm are about: sustenance of leadership by the senior managers; the agenda that sets the firm as an organization; structural features of the organization; the financial resources the firm has control over; and aspects that relate to the prospect of 'liability/threat' (or punishment). Each firm in the strategic landscape or the strategic array of the incumbent strategist firm has them. Extensive literature on management related issues of firms has identified their relevance and importance. Perhaps the fifth process on the prospect of liability or threat has been noticed the least. Firm-related legal theories and linguistic issues have, however, noted the importance of tort and the threat of punishment consequent to non-fulfilment of obligation. This threat is considered more fundamentally operative than the four other processes in this argument. In fact, the four other processes will cease to be operational if the threat of punishment or tort liability (where applicable) is withdrawn. The threat of punishment is a better representation because tort liability is limited to the context of specifiable contract only, while, internal to a firm, very little can be contractually specific. The threat of punishment, however, is not causally linked to these other processes but provides the ambient condition or maintains the state of affairs where the four processes can be operationalized. Threat takes up various culture and convention specific forms, such as excommunication, loss of status, loss of job, loss of incentives, loss of reputation and voice and relegation to silence and similar others. Threat's *a*-causal linkages with the four other processes allows autonomy to all the processes, making the five processes accordingly important. These processes are organization-wide and unlike a business process, as described in the literature on business process re-engineering. A business process can be outsourced while a process from these categories cannot be outsourced or alienated.

These processes suffer from a large degree of incompleteness in knowledge by description though. Leadership, for instance, would be rendered irrelevant if knowledge about business, current and prospective, is described. Leadership manoeuvres the twilight zone between knowledge and 'unknowledge'. This twilight zone is the realm of belief. Similarly, agenda-setting refers to directing the organizational discourse which is otherwise loaded with subterfuges, silences, rhetoric and metaphoric suggestions (Banerjee, 2003f). These categorial processes are about operations in the realm of beliefs. Beliefs, following the previous account, are not completely describable. When attention is focused on describing a belief, the belief holder takes recourse to 'translation' or secures the assistance of another belief in order that the belief of attention is described in the languages of belief of translation. It may also be recalled that a belief is not tacit or phenomenal but is cognitive. However, a cognitive belief (which is causally implicated in the mental states of belief holders) is not knowledge by description. The latter is 'undubious', unambiguous and tradable and is the bedrock of decisive decisions. Belief, in contrast, provides the 'typicality' in a decision situation and belongs to descriptive psychology.

Belief is thus arguably at the core of the incompleteness in knowledge by description. Belief attitudes, such as intentions, desires, hopes and doubts, are based on cognitive accounts. Such attitudes can even have an information content (Barwise and Perry, 1983; Jacob, 1996) and such information can be transmitted. Unlike a completely described knowledge by description, however – which is absolutely informational – a belief attitude requires support of another belief to be only incompletely described and transmitted. Such attitudes are the most important parameters that make organizational processes operational. Economic incentives have been proposed as instrumentalities that can actuate belief attitudes in the right direction but seem to be limited in scope. An incentive system can work in the desired manner only when the provided parameters are completely describable. In the absence of complete description, the incentive system suffers from ignorance. The responses of belief attitudes to economic incentives cannot be completely known in advance. Economic incentives thus cannot substitute the function of agenda or that of leadership. Processes can be compared to state space descriptions and processes are necessarily incomplete.

Strategic moves attempt to influence this degree of incompleteness. Influencing can be attempted at two levels. The first level of belief attitude is with the individual. There is, however, another belief attitude belonging to a group of individuals. This is the second level of belief attitude. Sociologists and anthropologists explain the specific facts of emergence of this second level of attitude. A strategic move is concerned with influencing this second level but is not readable. The strategist deploys such moves at the belief attitude levels. People belonging to the process cannot read a move and, behaviourally, people cannot situate them vis-à-vis a move. Behaviourally, a process reacts to a readable fact that is offered by strategic actions. The contemporary game theory offers accounts of conjectural co-ordination that are beyond the immediate ken of behaviours but can be described in this theory only when rationality and rules or structures of the game are either common knowledge or mutual knowledge to the parties engaged in the game.

The observation on strategic actions provides causal input to the belief-led behaviours of processes. Threat and liability, as discussed earlier, form the most potent process and sustain the ambient condition in which beliefs lead to behaviour in the direction desired by the strategist. The ambient condition of threat forces attitudes to recognize the exemplar of threat provided by strategic action. The exemplar is the causal factor. Similarly, of the four types of strategic actions, threat (of punishment) is the most potent. Overall, threat provides the maximum strategic force to take a process to the direction desired by the strategist. A strategic action alone can be an exemplar. The mode of strategic move being unreadable cannot influence behaviours of a process. A strategic action, as discussed earlier, can be observed to be an act of: appeasement, retribution, discrimination, or punishment. The winning strategist can easily act on processes internal to the organization and, with some difficulty, on processes internal to other firms belonging to the strategic array.

Strategic moves and beliefs

Six categories of strategic moves influence the conditions of believing. Belief holders are individuals or collectives in the processes. Strategic moves attempt to alter the conditions of belief consequent to which the process-based holders of beliefs formed their respective beliefs. The new belief condition on offer must appear credible and this credibility of a belief condition offers scope for belief revisions (Gardenfors, 1988) or at least for a new 'translation'. A 'translation' refers to a reading of one's own belief in terms of another belief. A credible belief situation then need not replace an old belief; a revised belief might as well be a translation of an old belief expressed in a new language. Process owners (individuals and collectives) make inferences on the credibility of a new condition of belief by observations of strategic actions of the winning strategist. A strategic move cannot be observed. It has to be inferred. Strategic actions, in contrast, are observable facts and, as stated before, can be observed as acts of appeasement, rewarding, discrimination or threat or punishment. The strategic mode is not observable and hence strategic behaviour can be discerned by observations on strategic actions alone. Belief holders who are participants in processes observe strategic acts and attribute causal relationships between strategic acts and process behaviour. The strategic act of threat or punishment provides the final determinate relation of causality because, as an exemplar, this act of punishment sustains a threat. A threat is as yet unexecuted but powers causal determination of behaviours.

Strategic moves, it may be recalled, can have six different modes or qualities: alliance, confrontation, fluidity, nonchalance, prevarication, and dependence. These are derived from the descriptive psychological states of an individual or a collective. A strategic state of affair of a process is a quality or a state of mind or a psychological state, which is descriptive in nature and causally implicated (Fodor, 1981; Stalnaker, 1987). This strategic state of psychology of a process (its collective mind) is causally implicated in the next and subsequent strategic behaviours of that process. A strategic move of the winning strategist is not visibly displayed in general. Processes in the strategy landscape cannot, therefore, observe a mode of the winning strategist. The behaviours of the processes are caused by direct observation on strategic acts of the winning strategist. However, strategic modes of the processes are not caused by such observations alone. Strategic modes of the processes make inferences and judgements on possible strategic mode(s) of the winning strategist. Consequently, on the basis of such judgements and their own beliefs, processes consider revising their beliefs on strategic modes. These exchanges between processes in a strategic landscape are not conditioned by behaviours nor caused by them. They are between states of 'minds', as it were. Such exchanges are thus distinctly different from incentives-based or behaviour-based affairs. Attempts to influence strategic behaviour by providing prospective desserts or through a system of incentives act on the causal principle. They influence behaviour alone.

From the earlier discussion on belief as the condition of knowledge it would appear that different belief holders arrive at different knowledge states with the same input information content or knowledge content. Belief provides the conditions of knowledge. The argument here is that strategic modes are specifically deployed to influence and possibly govern the conditions of knowledge for all the processes in the strategic landscape. The strategic mode is not concerned about the knowledge content in the processes. The argument here is that the knowledge content is unimportant for strategy. Knowledge content determines static behaviour: a response to one strategic action by the winning strategist is determined causally by the current knowledge content of the responding process. Behaviour cannot tell anything about intention. A strategic behaviour, often being a subterfuge and evasive or deceptive, cannot describe the strategic intention. To overcome this behavioural limitation, a series of behaviours is observed and a reading made on the behavioural responses to a prospective dessert or an existing incentive. However, circularity is involved here and intention has been substituted in this schema by a linear continuation of behaviour pattern. Surprise cannot be accommodated in these behavioural games. The argument here is that strategy is precisely about bringing in surprises. Possible surprise cannot be inferred unless strategic intentions are accommodated and behavioural games would fail to make room for that.

Knowledge and rule following

The strategic mode causally implicates the belief holder's conditions of knowledge in the processes in the strategic landscape. Conditions and not the content of knowledge determine the content of intentions. A strategy is for governing the content of intentions of the processes. This content of intentions of the processes determines the strategic responses of these processes to the strategic actions of the winning strategist. The present departure from behavioural theory is significant on this score. Processes, it is argued, do not intend to respond behaviourally to a strategic act of the winning strategist. All the players in the strategic landscape observe strategic acts of the others and no one responds only behaviourally. Each searches for the other's intentions. Then, based on his own content of intention, displays a particular strategic act. The content of intention is not at all the content of knowledge of a belief holder. Strategic moves causally implicate these contents of intentions and achieve another feat of warranting a certain rule following. Rule following, in terms of the earlier discussion, is not based on innate characteristics. Theorists of routine and of core competencies mistook this point. Rule following is fallible and following rules that are almost always unwritten is the outcome of contents of intentions. Rules are followed often even without any conscious effort because a primitive intention warrants their following.

Rules are followed intentionally. Conformity to rules, in contrast to following a rule, does not require presence of intention. The rules of a game are then, in the absence of intention, not followed but players conform to the rules. Conformity does not require the agent to know the rule or to know that the rule has been followed. Obviously, it does not also require that the agent need have a desire to follow the rule. Only behaviourally, does an observer relate a certain strategic situation in a game to a behaviour on the part of an agent. Such a behavioural relation has been described in the IO literature as rule following. Moreover, rules in IO are derived from structural features of the industry segment in which the players are present. Naturally, a rule of this kind is no rule. An IO rule is a normative prescription, which a rational player must conform to.

Rules and routines in competency or evolutionary theory are comparatively well founded. These theories situate rule only in the context of the internal affairs of a firm. Other strategic players cannot directly participate in the formation of rules and in the following of such rules inside the organizational black box. These theories have, moreover, failed to differentiate between conforming to rule and following rules. Evolutionary theory fails to be dynamic, for instance, if there are no rules or routines. Yet instances of rule following – that these theories provide as examples – are often instances of conforming to rules. Further, one is not shown how rules are formed and what these rules are.

The point here is that a rule can be followed only intentionally. A rule must also be applicable to an indefinitely large number of situations. It must be, or must fix, a normative condition on all the relevant decisions or judgements of an agent. This is an objective condition. In order for a rule to be followed it must satisfy subjective conditions simultaneously; it must satisfy the intentional content of the agent who is following the rule. Satisfying these two conditions together is a near impossibility. Pettit (1992) identifies three subdivisions of the subjective condition: the rule must be identifiable as a rule; it must be capable of instructing an agent what it requires of him; and finally, a rule must be clearly readable. Understanding how a rule can both satisfy the objective normative criterion and the three subjective conditions together leads to irresolvable issues (Kripke, 1982). There is also the question of how the identification of a rule begins. If it is an actual example of the application of a rule, extending this to indefinite situations leads either to ambiguity or to possibilities of several contending rules. Also, the finite mind of an agent cannot unambiguously identify a normative constraint, which can be called a rule, over an indefinite array of situations. This leads to scepticism – that following rules is illusory.

An organizational context makes rules simpler, however. The argument here is that rules are not present objectively in the form of a specific normative constraint. On the contrary, the context of organization and that of the strategic landscape present a threat. A strategic act of threat of punishment and of liability serves as an exemplar and guides all the anticipatory strategic moves of the processes in a landscape. Threat indirectly causes future strategic moves to fall in line. A threat is real but not a normative constraint because the latter needs to be specific either in extension or in intention. In contrast, a threat specifies nothing other than that certain things are prohibited. A list of negatives, which are not allowed, therefore, entitles enough freedom to those following processes to follow rules, which are subjectively present in ambiguous manner. It is argued here that the ambiguity in apprehending a rule, presented to the follower in varieties of semantics, conforms to the intention of strategic actions. Intention demands that rule following be strategically advantageous. The content of intention, from the earlier discussion, is belief driven. Belief, therefore, guides rule following of the processes or of an individual in a process.

Following rules cannot then be a routine affair and must be a part of strategy. A routine affair, such as maintaining a business in exact identity with the mode it has so far followed, is a myth and only happens by default. A business and, thus, rule following in a business, is an ever changing and ever strategizing process. Rules are followed because intentions perceive strategic advantage in following a rule. Further, rules can be followed because there is a real threat. A strategy fails to perform if there is no threat. This threat alone provides scope to imaginative intentions (Banerjee and Richter, 2001), which seek to source from each following of a rule a certain novel strategic advantage. A winning strategist, as argued earlier, seeks to guide these intentions in processes belonging to the strategic landscape. Such a desire is feasible because beliefs of those processes can be guided through employment of strategic moves. To recall, strategic moves attempt to influence the beliefs in processes. *Inter alia*, they seek to influence intentions in processes and hence, through influences brought upon intentions, a strategic move can determine how far and what rules are followed or not followed in a strategic landscape. Once rule following can be controlled in this manner, a strategist fulfills his objectives.

Controlling or guiding rule following is, it is argued here, a substantive strategic objective. On the basis of the earlier argument, this cannot be achieved simply through provisioning for economic incentives in a system. Again, influencing rule following is not co-ordinating a system of rule following. Further, rules discussed here are not structurally derived as in IO. This reference is to an extended version of what evolutionary theory presents as rules. Evolutionary theory has collapsed rules to an organization internal domain. This has been extended to the strategic landscape, which includes processes belonging to all the firms in a strategic milieu. It has been shown how beliefs and intentions matter for following rules, and how strategic moves might influence warranting a rule or recognizing that there is a rule or in what manner a rule can be read as well as acted upon.

Strategic knowledge, intention and co-ordination: reconciliation, co-ordination, knowledge content

It has been emphasized here that knowledge content has little significance for strategy and what is significant is the difference between content and conditions of knowledge. The latter is related to strategic knowledge, which is directly relevant to strategy, and influences, controls or guides conditions of knowledge. This perspective on the irrelevance of knowledge content is acutely aware of the unseemly emphasis on content of knowledge by several theorists of organizational knowledge and its management (Hodgson, 1993). In an attempt to appreciate knowledge content, it was found that knowledge by description provides most of the content. Propositional attitudes, including hopes and despair, desires and aversions, can largely be addressed through this informational account of knowledge content. Knowledge by description is an informational account of knowledge. It can be communicated, stored and processed further. This perspective helped in getting over the tacit account of knowledge barrier. A tacit account holds knowledge privy to private quarters while the informational account makes the knowledge free.

It has been argued here that knowledge must be public because unsupported by public testimonials and public scrutiny, knowledge loses much of its claim to validity. More than that, private knowledge, unless made to stand against public scrutiny, cannot claim to have any economic worth. It cannot be exchanged not because it is tacit but simply because of a non-existent market. This economic worth refers to the content of knowledge. A new art of manufacturing or a novel algorithm provides its possessor with an efficiency which its competitors do not possess, but such a possession cannot be strategic. The economic worth of knowledge content comes from it being publicly noticed. Knowledge content loses its strategic worth right there.

Knowledge content, as shown by Baumol, Panzar and Willig (1986), is efficiency and competition related, with its benchmark provided by a perfectly contestable market. Institutions in an economy can or do set up several exchanges that link up the discrete contents of knowledge to the repository of knowledge lexicon. In turn, the previously discrete piece of knowledge assumes a new relational significance and thus gets known or marketed as a new content of knowledge. There have been such markets and exchanges of knowledge contents in every economy and perhaps at all times. The present perhaps has accentuated the traffic of knowledge contents. Even so, a hastened traffic in contents does not alter the irrelevance of content for making strategic moves based on knowledge. On the contrary, as has happened through extensive benchmarking based on best practices and through workflow-based mapping of business processes, individual firms have lost out on individualities of firm-based processes. A firm, under the circumstances, cannot boast of peculiarities. Instead, it attempts to become more efficient. An efficient firm is not necessarily a strategist firm. An efficient firm needs knowledge contents to be both procured and related to knowledge lexicons. All rational firms in a competitive milieu will perform the same rites and all firms will be equally efficient provided they all undertake identical acts of piecing together contents of varied knowledge. Equality amongst the firms' efficiencies implies that competitive advantage can be secured by one of these firms through resorting to better quality of resources and by employing better quality of decisions.

The contents of knowledge exhibit true co-ordination. Knowledge contents will be procured from the market or through firm-internal mechanisms and will often be related to lexicons only in order to adjust the efficiency of this firm to the benchmark efficiency. Benchmark efficiency has to be a common knowledge. Adjustments or the *tâtonnement* bring firms in a competitive milieu to the same or similar status of knowledge-content holding. Knowledge content is a factor of production (Arrow, 2000) and similar to equalization of factor efficiencies. Equalization in knowledge-content driven efficiencies appears as the goal of competition. A market driven by equalization of efficiency of knowledge content is dynamic because any equilibrium reached will be surpassed immediately by the disequilibria generated by a new combination of knowledge contents. However, no firm can have a strategic advantage from such combinations of knowledge contents. A combination of knowledge content must, in order to be competition generative, offer the combination as a benchmark or as a public knowledge. This, in turn, through the disequilibria set up, generates a co-ordinative process amongst the competitors. A knowledge combination thus, while proving its economic worth, simultaneously must set in motion a co-ordination that ultimately results in a diffusion of that particular combination of knowledge. Finally, content of knowledge is not accepted as veridical truth till this content is adjusted against or co-ordinated with other contents of knowledge that have been in existence.

A belief, in contrast, is free from such constraints. One believes things, the truth of which one is not sure about. Truth demands co-ordination. Belief is not constrained by co-ordination. However, it might happen that the contents of one's beliefs are partly co-ordinated with the contents of knowledge and even with contents of beliefs of others. Even so, conditions of believing are largely free from the demands of co-ordination. Co-ordination is a current process, a *tâtonnement* undertaken dynamically by interacting parties in order to reach any equilibrium. Pre-reconciliation refers to the past, to situations and states that have already occurred. One pre-reconciles one's decision with mutual knowledge (Brandenburger and Dekel, 1989), which is a mutually known fact, while 'a common knowledge is knowledge about other knows my knowledge about' and so on (Geanakoplos, 1992). Aumann (1976) has shown, through the impossibility of 'agreeing to disagree', that with a 'common prior' and with common knowledge about some event, one's belief content must be equal to the belief content of the contending party. From Brandenburger (1992), one knows that a particular equilibrium follows if belief-based conjectures are mutual knowledge and even if conjectures are common knowledge, another equilibrium in conjectures follows. In all these cases, however, structure of the game and the rationality of the players are mutual knowledge. In the language of Brandenburger (1992: 95), an 'interactive belief system is in some sense "transparent" to the players themselves. This is not, in fact, a formal assumption; rather, it is a tautology, reflecting the fact that the interactive system already describes any ignorance on the part of the players.'

This ignorance or its converse, the mutual knowledge, is about the content of the beliefs or conjectures. These are not about the conditions of beliefs. There is also a strict initial condition regarding mutual knowledge (and about common knowledge) on rationality and on rules or structure of the game. The conditions of belief, which in these discussions appeared as the supremely important element in strategic moves, reflect intention and imaginative as well as emotional states of mind. Belief content, even under normative or prescriptive conditions on rationality and structure of game, is reconciled only partially, that is, to the extent of conjectural reconciliation. A conjectural reconciliation is not about reconciliation of strategic acts. Strategic acts would get reconciled only if players are rational by prescription. In contrast, it is argued that one acts on 'momentary' emotion, driven by intention deeply seated in one's Hobbesian 'passion'. Actions are decided, according to Hobbes, by the passions at the moments of actions. Mere conjectural reconciliation does not ensure either reconciliation of conditions of belief (the strategic move) or of strategic acts. Conjectural or content-wise reconciliation is a mutually known fact while belief conditions are not. They are believed only. Hence one attaches not a probability but a possibility (Shackle, 1972) to one's belief about the relevance of belief conditions in the processes in the strategic landscape.

Strategy, emotion and violation of rationality

Assumptions regarding rationality miss out the fact that a strategist gains by skipping rationality. It is argued here that one is not a 'bounded' rationalist or an intended rationalist (Simon, 1983a, 1983b). A 'bounded' rational is unable to cope up with complexities of computation. While giving up computation in the face of stupendously challenging computation could be agreed to, one would stress more the fact that one does not often wish to enter the vicious cycle of computation. One gains by doing so: through imagining and by intentionally rejecting either rationality or a stance of rationality. Radner (2000) refers to the Savage paradigm, which specifies rationality as the normative prescriptive limits of almost every conceivable economic action and calculation. Simon's procedural rationalist does not challenge the central Cartesian claims of rationality as reflected in the Savage paradigm. One is not only referring to a certain vagueness or ambiguity in the confronting situations but simultaneously insisting on the intention of giving up rationality. This implies that rationality appears as a stance till such time that the structure of a game remains inviolate. However, every strategic act of winning sets up a new structure of game and for every strategic act of winning to be accomplished, both the common and mutual knowledge about one's rationality get violated by oneself: one can win through violence on rationality. It is not known whether a descriptive psychology of this intended violation is based on a second-order rationality. A second order or higher rationality is unacceptable. A higher knowledge will require an even higher rationality and will thus involve circularity. Violation of rationality is most likely to be based on imagination and emotion.

To be a winner is not a rational goal. Passion dictates the intention to win. Passion or emotion, however, can be defended on grounds of epistemic validity or on grounds of pragmatism. In either case, a substantive outcome, instead of a rationalist procedure, dictates the intention. March (1991) defines this outcome dependence of an action as the intelligence of that action. The choice of an action against an ambiguous past and an unknowable future can be guided by a 'sensemaking' (Weick, 1995), through acts of imagination and intention. 'We will need to continue to discover useful expectations about ambiguous possible futures and to construct imaginative reinterpretations of dubious pasts' (March, 1975: 368). These intelligent actions are, however, trapped in the legacies of organizational or situational history (March, 1999) or in the frames of belief, riddled with existing paradigms, such as on normative rationality. Emotion is needed to overcome such trappings. Emotion pays attention to the constraints of norms and prescriptions of rationality (Elster, 1998), while looking for the opportune moment when such constraints of rationality and rule-based playing can be violated. 'There ... are ... degrees in which imagination can be constrained. Mere fictions and fantasies are no concern of the decision-maker. The imagined outcomes must pass a test imposed by *practical conscience*, the test of *seeming possible*. In short ... they must be *expectations*' (Shackle, 1988: 107; italics original).

Shackle proceeds from this grounding in constrained imagination to the 'surprise' that a 'profit' might offer the entrepreneur. 'To rank as profit in the decision-eliciting sense which I have adopted, the outcomes must fall *outside* a range of envisaged possibilities. Not necessarily wholly rejected in expectation, profit must be something *surprising*' (Shackle, 1988: 122; italics original). This is the Cantillon perspective on profit. Surprise in strategy is unlike this. A strategic act by the winning strategist comes as a surprise to all the processes in the strategic landscape but surely cannot be a surprise to the protagonist – the winning strategist. Other processes consider acts by the winning strategist as those that 'fall outside a range of envisaged possibilities' as a surprise strategic act. Surprise is subjective in profit. In strategy, surprise belongs to the inter-subjective or objective domain. Failure to apprehend the winning strategist's strategic moves leads other processes to believe that the surprise strategic act did not have a causal link. This appearance of *a*-causality, which gets interpreted in the timeless system of 'kaleidic economics' of choices (Shackle, 1972) as 'outside a range of envisaged possibilities', is the source of surprise. Subjectively and unlike in the case of surprise-profit, *a*-causality appears not in the mind of the strategist subject but in the inter-subjective domain of strategic behaviours.

The difference with Shackle here lies in the fact that the strategist knows subjectively the causal links between his intentions and states of mind – his strategic moves and his strategic acts. To the subject there is no surprise. For Shackle, 'refusal to set out explicitly any formal frame of ideas about time, amounts to a belief that we mainly need, and are best able, to study the *texture* of economic affairs... rather than try to see it as a matter of exact, stable quantitative relationships' (Shackle, 1972: 439; italics original). Shackle calls this *a*-temporal relational texture a kaleidics. A timeless system can pre-reconcile all the choices, as in games; choices are 'formally simultaneous'. This is the ideal timeless market but it cannot have any room for strategy.

A strategy is aimed at influencing, guiding and leading the courses of possible future actions that all strategically relevant processes might undertake. In the language of March, a strategy aims at a substantive outcome. A strategic move is employed precisely for influencing belief conditions and hence even of abductions. A strategic move based on what is defined as strategic knowledge deforms conditions of knowledge for all the processes in the strategic landscape. Abduction, it may be recalled, is a jump in the selection and formation of hypothesis in inductive reasoning based upon experience. Shackle argues that a detailed description of experience, which includes an account of originary expectations and such others, is impossible. Consequently, experience and consequently belief content, is not completely known even to the subject. Belief conditions, propelled by intentions and passions, are known only in the instant of their appearance. Abduction and other conditions of knowledge (including conditions of epistemic justification) are not descriptively known. In other words, these are not knowledge by representations. A strategic move by the winning strategist is targeted to deforming these conditions of knowledge. By definition, a strategic move and a strategic knowledge are intentional and 'intended causal'. Strategic knowledge is 'intended causal' because not all strategic moves (based as these are upon strategic knowledge) succeed in achieving the intended outcome. However, a strategic move must entail an outcome in the reciprocating strategy processes. Strategic knowledge is then 'intended causal'.

Intention and strategic knowledge

This account of strategic knowledge and move differs substantially from the kaleidic explanation of Shackle. Shackle observes the loss of causality. IO theorists offer in lieu of causality a normative guide and a kaleidic texture of choices, conjectures and such others. The evolutionary theorists offer (Nelson and Winter, 2002) an *a*-causal account of routine-based learning which, only by default, transforms temporality into an evolutionary parameter. Choice kaleidics is replaced in evolutionary theory by routines and accidents. Causality and intention are lost. The TCE account is blatantly *a*-temporal and *a*-causal. Shackle, following Keynes and unlike other post-Keynesians (Davidson, 1991), along with March, Radner and others, offers an account that incorporates surprise and novelty, imagination and intelligence but only as accidents. A profit, to Shackle, is an accidental outcome. Shackle and other are close to IO, bereft of normative and prescriptive conditionality of IO. The argument here is that strategic move and strategic knowledge are 'intended causal' and are thus definitely inscribed in time.

This account, *inter alia*, gives a different narration on commitment. An act undertaken is a commitment, 'one, which by its nature irreversibly alters the essential conditions which constitute it' (Shackle, 1972: 404). This committed strategic act alters the previous texture of beliefs of others in the strategic landscape. Shackle invokes a new term, 'disbelief', to describe the change in texture. This is not in terms of the distributional characteristics or in terms of other Ramseyan variants, such as degrees of belief. This is through the 'unlistableness and the rivalry of suggested answers to a question about the sequel to a contemplated course of conduct, and the crucialness of the experiment consisting in the adoption of such a course' (Shackle, 1972: 404). Surprise, according to Shackle, is a feeling about 'emotion which springing directly from the combination of some formal kind or source of disbelief, and is an actual taking-place which belies that disbelief'. Surprise, as this difference between emotional and formal disbelief, it is argued here, springs from the emotional or the intentional. A strategic move is based on a reading of the conditions of belief of others in the strategic processes. This reading is defined as strategic knowledge. The formal part of this strategic knowledge is a formal disbelief about the existence of intention in other processes. The intentional or emotional part of this strategic knowledge is about disbelief in certain intentions in others. A formal disbelief can partake of histories of intentional acts by others. The intentional disbelief cannot or does not recognize these histories. This is a pure act of intention or, to be precise, of strategic intention.

Strategic knowledge or the knowledge about conditions of belief of others (that is the processes in a strategic landscape) is not amenable to co-ordination or pre-reconciliation. Uncertainties or ignorance facing the winning strategist and other strategists in a strategic landscape need not be considered as disadvantageous. A strategist can hide his intention behind the veil of ignorance. Strategic acts are known as facts. Ordinary business decisions depend on the knowledge content of such facts and of other facts of business and of technology. A statistical account of strategic and other acts could then act as a nice veil behind which intents can be hidden. An act becomes strategic when it is undertaken purposefully for influencing or eliciting conditions of belief, or strategic knowledge or the strategic moves of others.

Strategic knowledge is 'intended causal'. Some aspects of 'intended causality' prohibit strategic knowledge to be pre-reconciled or co-ordinated. The knowledge content, in contrast, is co-ordinated. 'Intended causality' allows one undertaking a strategy a structure that is uniquely one's own because such a uniquely individualistic structure alone can enjoy a unique temporality and, thereby, generate a unique intended causality. The acquisition of strategic knowledge and deployment of strategic moves are 'intended causal'. Hence they presume a prior existence of a unique structure based upon a unique temporal category. Such a strategic firm, by being strategic, exhibits a distinctiveness, standing not on certain routines or knowledge contents or distinctive competence but on 'intended causal' and hence temporal strategic knowledge. Being 'intended causal' demands a structure that is not imitable by others. This implies that other firms in the strategic landscape of the winning strategist also acquire similar uniqueness in their structures by virtue of their unique strategic moves. In other words, a firm exhibits a unique structure in so far as it employs strategy.

The fundament on which such a distinctive structure can be erected is the 'intended causal' strategic knowledge that is different from knowledge content according to this account. This strategic knowledge and its owner strategist is unique not through its engagements with competition, competitiveness or competence. The structure of a firm is thus absolutely essential to deploy strategic moves. Conversely, strategic moves through their distinct features retain and keep alive a firm structure. This implies that in so far as strategic moves are deployed, uniqueness in structure is retained and, upon the ceasing of strategic moves, this uniqueness is lost. A firm that has lost its uniqueness is, for all purposes, a dead firm. It is dead because then its structure inheres through co-ordination only. A dead firm is an exemplar of the benchmark possibility of transaction cost minimizing or resources optimizing entity belonging to an industry segment. This chapter began with a discussion on the necessity of a theory of death of a firm's organization. This argument brings a possible sketch of the introduction to such a theory. It has been seen that a firm is living as long as it is strategic or as long as it acquires strategic knowledge and deploys that intended knowledge exclusively for its own strategic moves. The absence of these aspects or the death of a strategist firm might, however, allow a structure to be retained, as is retained by a firm in a pure equilibrium.

4
Knowledge Wealth: An Indian Software Profile

Knowledge as wealth is a constituent of the structural sort of a firm. A structural sort, in terms of the earlier discussion, is a manner of describing several structural aspects of an organization. A sort is larger in scope than the scaffolding perspective, which is a description of structure in terms of hierarchy and divisions or units. A structural sort has seven constituents, one of which is knowledge as wealth and finance. Knowledge as wealth, as argued earlier, is different from the two other types of knowledge: as a factor of production and as strategic knowledge. Of these, the former is descriptive knowledge and is publicly available or tradable and can be accessed by an organization, a group or an individual. Strategic knowledge is not descriptive and is held in non-descriptive attitudinal or intentional form by the individuals, including the chief and process groups of an organization. The structure of an organization cannot be the residence of strategic knowledge. Knowledge as wealth is thus only partly descriptive and largely attitudinal. This knowledge, like strategic knowledge, cannot be publicly generated or traded. Knowledge wealth constitutes the structure and, therefore, is resident in the structural sort. It cannot reside in single individuals such as the chief. Limitations to trading or public generation of knowledge wealth make it appear to be tacit but, as argued earlier, it cannot be a tacit knowledge.

Knowledge wealth again is not merely descriptive. Descriptive knowledge can have a complete informational account, which can be subject to public scrutiny, tested and can, therefore, be valued and traded. Only a fragment of the knowledge wealth of a firm can appear in the public domain and most parts of this knowledge cannot be completely described informationally. As a result, a behavioural description of content of knowledge wealth will necessarily remain incomplete. Observations on Indian software firms are surely limited by this boundary of behavioural description. This intrinsic limitation would render any data-based description of these software firms inappropriate and insufficient, if employed to narrate their knowledge wealth. In the absence of data-based description though, this narration would remain subjective and qualitative only. A middle path is, therefore, followed: qualitative and theoretical assertions and analyses are not rejected while depending partly on data for imagining the knowledge wealth of Indian software firms.

An additional difficulty in this narration is in the proposed division of knowledge in three categories, one of which is knowledge wealth. The claim here that knowledge wealth is a structural constituent is partially novel because received literature has not recognized this (though it has touched upon it), partially developed it or hinted at this possibility. A pragmatic, theoretical stance with models or arguments from putatively alternative theoretical accounts, it has been argued, should be unhesitatingly accepted only if this improved comprehension. This piecemeal engineering is both sound and robust. The novelty of this account, therefore, often resides in such borrowings.

An advantage that a putative wholesome theoretical account enjoys is its global claims to truth. Those claims empower this theory to reject other adversarial claims. A global theory is polemical, which this model cannot be. It has transgressed boundaries and thereby reduced claims of all such theories from the global to a local status. Theory building is thoroughly local. This account, however, does not have the aspirations that a theory-building route has, namely that the built theory will slowly approach a global explanatory and predictive power. It is not slow but fast and does not ever aspire to claim the status of a global theory. This limitation of this account prevents a novel account of knowledge wealth of these software firms. Other claims to description are not rejected but what is emphasized is that other theories did not recognize a category called knowledge wealth. Other theories have often narrated that some knowledge was tacit or constitutive of distinctive competence or even, while the knowledge was actually a market-based resource, it acquired uniqueness inside a firm, owing to the recombinations undertaken internally on those resources.

Not only is knowledge wealth denied all tacitness, it is simultaneously denied that this claim is sourced from the market. There will be attempts to locate a few structural characteristics in association with aspects of knowledge wealth, including aspects of knowledge employees. This is not necessarily a causal account. The association between knowledge wealth and structural sort is *a*-causal, which is why knowledge wealth is not a cause of structure but a reason for a structural sort. Given this background, the present narration on knowledge wealth can never attempt to have predictive powers though the structural robustness or weakness of software firms in this account can be associated with their knowledge wealth. It follows also that this account cannot claim certain aspects of knowledge wealth as either the 'best practice' or a benchmark. The theoretical stance forces the acceptance of variability and since what is narrated can never have a reach of global theory, one cannot compare this with other 'global' knowledge practices in order to adjudge what practice proved to be the 'causal' best or causal benchmark.

Salience of Indian software enterprise

Having established knowledge as wealth that is only partly descriptive, which cannot be publicly generated or traded and comprising the structural sort, it is emphasized that only a fragment of the knowledge wealth can appear in the public domain. While descriptive knowledge can have a complete informational account and be valued and traded, observations on Indian software firms based on the intrinsically limited data-based descriptions are rendered inappropriate and insufficient if employed to narrate knowledge wealth. The *a*-causal association between knowledge wealth and structural sort makes it the reason for the latter and not a cause of structure, thus depriving this account of predictive powers. Competency, we argue, is an epistemic capability. Competency is neither 'knowledge about', nor a capability 'about'.

Managers and entrepreneurs of software firms suggested that an indicator of competence (IOC) be defined. Discussions on IOC and related issues on knowledge wealth avoided the alignment thesis or the thesis about the strategic fit. The alignment with respect to the strategic intent was assumed. A firm aligns resources or wealth in accordance with the mismatch between the strategic intentions and current outcomes. The respondent executives or entrepreneurs suggested several possible modes of combining resources and knowledge wealth in order to secure high organizational or structural competence.

Knowledge wealth in those structural features received the least weight. Notably, however, greater emphasis on research experience did ensure the attractiveness of certain aspects of the factor of production. Knowledge wealth, being different from this factor available in the public domain, is a structural feature. There was evidence of executives and entrepreneurs holding different opinions on structural sorts relating to knowledge wealth. These differences in relative importance or relative arrangements of the constituents of a structural sort indicate differences in the strategic intentions of the firms.

Informational knowledge about the market and its application to the other constituents of the structural sort generate structural robustness. The nature of market matters and outsourced businesses must remain dependent on the path dependencies of the customer firms. Competence must then refer not only to firm-internal structural coherence but also to aspects of co-ordination with structures of outsourcing customers. The umbrella cover as a strategy takes care of this aspect of correspondence. The data indicates that firms were almost evenly distributed over structural compulsions. The competence in knowledge wealth captured through the IOC or market competence refers to competence in yielding a structural sort. This competence to reshape is the ability to take umbrella cover. An organization changes the structural sort whenever necessary and resource allocàtion takes place as a result of the variations in structural constituents.

The investments that firms make are deeply embedded in the inter-structure relationships of co-ordination. The fluidity and prevarication types of strategic moves require an Indian software firm to hold enough assets in liquidity. Typical financial ratios are not indicative of investment in durable assets or commitments to asset specificities but are indicative of choice for a particular liquidity. Liquidity acts as an insurance against lack of knowledge about another's structural sort.

This fluidity cannot be appreciated in terms of the Schumpeterian innov-ator's profit. Such profit is not entirely counter-expected but reflects an expectation being fulfilled. This is the first understanding of a profit that forms the basis of an action and requires co-ordination with existing knowledge. We refer to Shackle and Keynes' reference to Cantillon's ideas on profit, that is based on speculative valuation of the current states of affairs and leads to a counter-expected outcome in the form of windfall trading revenue surplus. This counter-expected surplus emerges from a state of ignorance and from a novel recognition of reality. Structural liquidity is the expression of ignorance. Knowledge is scarce and expensive. Lack of knowledge, around choices that could be made and on the durable asset or committed action on which the liquid asset can be spent, results in holding on to both deferments of decisions and liquidity. The precise strategic moves or structural appearances that would induce others to invest more in liquidity, strengthened with social investment vis-à-vis investment in durability, are therefore the concerns of the strategy of Indian software firms.

Managerial perception of knowledge wealth: indicators of organizational competence

A holder of knowledge wealth perceives that he has knowledge but, initially, this is not 'knowledge about'. Upon questioning the holder, as in a problem-solving situation (Newell and Simon, 1972), the 'knowledge about' is generated in a descriptive mode. This, as pointed out earlier, is not descriptive about the knowledge content but of the 'knowledge about'. Responses to several questions would then generate several facets of the knowledge content. All the facets put together would still remain an approximation of the content. It follows then that the holder's knowledge appears more as an epistemic generator, which responds to queries by generating knowledge descriptions or several informational accounts. The epistemic generator refers to a capability or a competency. However, the competency theorist's (Cohen and Levinthal, 1990; Teece and Pisano, 1994) understanding is greatly different from this account. It generally refers to a recombination of resources whose dimensions have been variously described (Leonard-Barton, 1992; Zajac, Kraatz and Bresser, 2000) as employee knowledge and skill, technical systems, managerial systems and the system of values and norms. The reference to competency here is about an epistemic capability and not about a problem-solving skill that recombines given resource dimensions dynamically and in response to the problems thrown up by the environment. An epistemic capability is neither 'knowledge about' nor capability 'about'.

Epistemic generators are a significant component of the knowledge wealth, which otherwise has several other components, such as the lexicon of listed names and situations. Knowledge wealth has both descriptive and non-descriptive contents. A query generates descriptive knowledge and this response can be observed to be principally descriptive in content. The query then first generates and thereafter aligns the observed knowledge content. This process is greatly dissimilar to the strategy-alignment process described by competency theorists. Moreover, what is being aligned is not a resource at hand but a resource generated by the query itself. This query, following the earlier discussion, is the strategic intention of the incumbent. In other words, a query is not objectively given. In received theories (such as for IO and game theoretic versions, resources theory, competency theory and evolutionary theory), a query is often objective, given by the environment (as 'variations', for example). The environment is not disregarded because it is argued that a strategist does not respond behaviourally to the environmental query but realigns its strategic intentions in response to which a query gets reformulated or perceived by the incumbent. Generated knowledge in response to this query is thus a response to strategic demands.

Knowledge wealth is a structural feature, coexisting with several other constituents of that structure. This wealth can be approximated through looking at the interrelations between some structural constituents. It can otherwise be approximated through eliciting managerial responses to questions such as what they believe constitutes their knowledge wealth. In order to appreciate these aspects, several senior executives and entrepreneurs were asked questions, both structured and unstructured, through workshop meetings and long interviews. Most respondents were from small firms. Interviews and questions related to the multiple dimensions of a structural sort that could be linked to knowledge wealth. A pivotal concept in these discussions was the 'Indicator of Organizational Competence', which referred to competence or capability of the structural sort to muster the organizational knowledge wealth. The competence theorist's indicator would have attempted to capture the capability to align or realign resources contingent to an environmental demand. The IOC, in contrast, does not probe so much into the capability to realign resources but looks into the structural aspects, to appreciate the extent to which knowledge wealth matters for a structure.

The resource alignment thesis has another problem. A firm in need of aligning its resources would require prior knowledge of an alignment benchmark, which should exist to begin with. Such a benchmark, however, cannot exist at a global level; it can only exist at a local level, provided locality is defined by commonality in information and technological platform. The knowledge of a benchmark often fails to diffuse even inside an organization, across its multiple processes. A firm, therefore, might have data on underperformance of its current resources allocation but cannot possibly have data mismatches between what is required by a potential benchmark and its current allocations. The IOC and related discussions on knowledge wealth avoid discussing the alignment thesis and it is assumed here that benchmarking is done with respect to the strategic intent. That is, the firm aligns resources or wealth in accordance with the mismatch between its strategic intentions and current outcomes. On the basis of guidance, an understanding of the views of some senior software executives and entrepreneurs on the relationship of knowledge wealth to the firm structural sort is attempted.

Managerial perception

IOC refers to the structural sort in several modes. The workshop meetings and unstructured interviews with the entrepreneurs suggested (Banerjee, 2003c) that certain structured questions needed to be asked. Alongside this suggestion, the respondent executives or entrepreneurs were asked what mode of combining resources and knowledge wealth – available either internally or external to the organization – the respondent would follow in order to secure high organizational or structural competence. The question recognized several kinds of wealth such as 'generating start-ups or entrepreneurs from within', 'using R & D community outside the firm', 'using novel ideas from incubators or science parks', 'using rating agencies for evaluating intangible assets' and 'rewarding stakeholders, including important employees'. Respondents were also asked what preferred weights they would attach to each and the responses showed that the five options were nearly equally valued, although the first and the last items received maximum weights. The third and fourth items were accorded minimum weights as shown in Figure 4.1. The first and fifth items refer to elements that are part of the structural sort. Start-up from within is an epistemic generator and stakeholders are either an organization's allies or its knowledge employees, both belonging to the structural sort.

Respondents similarly rated the relative importance of types of epistemic generative capability of the firm's knowledge employees or their groups working together in a process. Executives and entrepreneurs were asked about

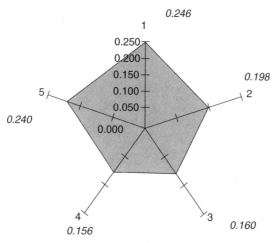

1: start-up/entrepreneurs from within; 2: R & D community from outside; 3: ideas from incubators; 4: rating of intangible assets; 5: values to stakeholders.

Figure 4.1   Choice of structural elements for organizational competence

the strategic goals of R & D in software; they were provided with a few epistemic categories and were asked to give percentage weights to each according to their strategic relevance. These epistemic types were for

- acquiring mathematical/logical/linguistic-advanced techniques;
- applying computer technology to domain problems;
- translating visionary future software into a reality;
- optimizing software projects.

'Translating visionary future software into reality' as a strategic thrust of R & D received the maximum weight, followed by application of computer technology to domain problems as shown in Figure 4.2. Business pragmatism defines what could be a 'relevant' epistemic generator. Both these types of epistemic competence are relevant for knowledge wealth. These can be used for both product strategy and a value-added software projects or services strategy. Moreover, these choices refer to interrelations between elements of a structural sort. The first parameter, namely 'mathematical etc. ability-raising' epistemic received the least weight. Optimization of software projects, including its cost-reducing aspects, too received lower estimate and ranked as the third important parameter.

Similar views were expressed when respondents ranked the importance of epistemic capabilities, captured in terms of skills that get expressed through the educational background and the academic degrees of the firm employees. Undeniably, academic degrees cannot capture the epistemic generative

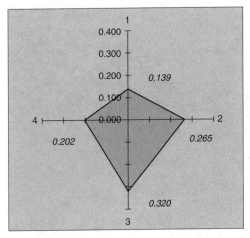

1: mathematical, logical, linguistic techniques; 2: domain knowledge; 3: futuristic software into reality; 4: optimizing software projects.

Figure 4.2   Thrust of knowledge wealth

competence. Degrees have often been used as a surrogate indicator, however. Firms, while inducting fresh recruits, also take decisions on employability by considering factors, one of which is this degree. Further, knowledge wealth and knowledge employees are two distinct constituents of a structural sort. Qualifications and the experience, as well as the knowledge acquired on the job, relate these two constituents. The respondents were asked to rank in order of importance the epistemic qualities exhibited by

- a basic degree in computer science or engineering highly specialized knowledge;
- a basic degree in sciences or engineering highly skilled domain knowledge;
- any degree with good analytical and communicative power;
- a PhD or post-doctorals in engineering or sciences;
- any basic degree with long and varied international experience.

The third factor received the highest score, followed by the second and the first factors (Figure 4.3). The last factor received much less importance. The highest degree represented in the fourth factor received the minimum importance. This ranking reinforces the previous observation regarding business pragmatism. The highest degree without relevant experience exhibits an epistemic capability that would be less desired when compared to a capability derived more from experience.

Similar evidence was collected from a few surveys undertaken in 2001–02 (Banerjee, 2003e). A few firms had employed a very large number of personnel

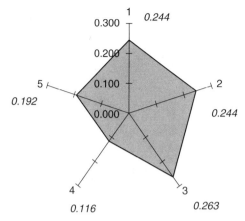

1: basic degree in computer skills; 2: basic degree in sciences or engineering; 3: any degree with analytical and communicative power; 4: PhD or post-doctoral; 5: any degree with international experience.

Figure 4.3 Importance of manpower qualification
Source: Banerjee (2003e), *Global Business Review*, 4(2), p. 246, fig. 1.

with a doctorate in computer science or engineering, who at times constituted 25 per cent of the total employees. In general, product centric firms emphasized more of a computer science background while projects and services centric firms employed persons from other streams of engineering. Firms with consultancy as the key driver of business generally opted for a higher proportion of persons from a management background (see Table 4.1).

Workshops and interviews with software managers and entrepreneurs suggested that their firms accorded priority to certain structural features that characterized knowledge wealth. These features were pointed out to the managers and the respondents were asked to rank relative weights of eight items influencing the IOC of the firm. These structural features were:

(1) R & D as percentage of turnover;
(2) foreign exchange earning as percentage of turnover;
(3) total PhDs and MTechs as percentage of total manpower;
(4) earning from own product as percentage of total turnover;
(5) per capita value of patents, copyrights and research publications;
(6) number of collaborations, partnerships and acquisitions per turnover;
(7) earnings from new projects as more than 80 per cent of the total earnings excluding earnings from own products;
(8) earnings from system software as percentage of earning from application software.

Table 4.1 Profile of eleven software firms

Business type	Manpower percentage with PhD or MTech in (Comp.) / (other disciplines)	Manpower percentage with BE in (Comp.) / (other disciplines)	Manpower percentage with Diploma or B.A. etc. in (Comp.) / (other disciplines)	Manpower percentage with (MBA) / (other from arts & commerce)
Product	1/3	50/29	8/1	8/0
Project/services	7/6	36/29	11/2	6/3
Consultancy	1/0	7/13	0/13	54/12

Source: Banerjee (2003e), *Global Business Review,* 4(2), p. 252, table 3.

The question sought to determine the opinions of executives on the relative weights of each of these eight items in the indicator of organizational competence of the firm. Two types of measures were then computed. The first measured the average value of weights indicated by the respondents and the second, in terms of the difference between the numbers of managers who considered it as most important and those who considered it as of least significance. The structural type indicated by 'earning from own product as percentage of total turnover' received the highest weight, in terms of both the aforementioned measures. The next most important item was 'earning from new projects as more than 80 per cent of total earnings (excluding earnings from own products)' when reckoned in terms of both the above-mentioned measures. 'Foreign exchange earning as percentage of turnover' received the third highest weight and a significant number of respondents gave this factor the least weight as well. Both structural features captured through 'earning from system software' and 'PhDs and MTechs' were given the least average weight and the largest number of respondents considered these as of least importance.

The knowledge wealth in those structural features which contribute to innovations in products or projects and services were attributed maximum weights. In this attribution, the academic background of an employee, especially if considered in terms of higher degrees and grounding in research, received the least weight. Significantly, the higher degrees representing experience in such research as a doctoral or post-doctoral, can ensure that a firm can secure from such an employee only knowledge that amounts to that as a factor of production. It may be recalled that knowledge as a factor of production was differentiated from knowledge wealth. Knowledge wealth, it was argued, is a structural feature. A higher degree and research in public bodies endows a prospective employee with knowledge that can be secured from public places, from the market of knowledge. A firm structural sort amasses knowledge wealth over the firm's life. This knowledge wealth values more the experience and the knowledge that is structurally gained. No wonder that executives accord highest importance to earning from own products. For firms earning from projects, executives thought they earn more from new projects. This is shown in terms of a simple arithmetic (Figure 4.4). Measures shown here are formed by multiplying the 'average weight given to a parameter' by the 'difference between numbers of managers who considered it as most important and those who considered it as of least significance'.

An important dimension of this discussion that must not be overlooked refers to divergences in perceptions. The discussion pointed out the average propensities and the generally shared trends but the differences remained poignant. They indicate that executives and entrepreneurs held different opinions on structural sorts relating to knowledge wealth. A structural sort, to recall the earlier discussion, is an outcome of the incumbent's strategy.

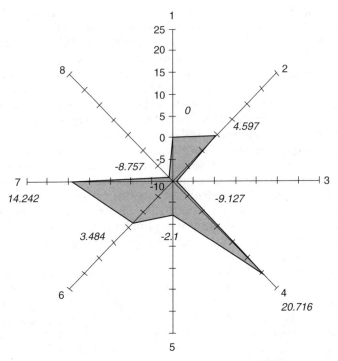

1: R & D to turnover percentage; 2: foreign exchange to turnover; 3: higher degrees to total manpower; 4: earning from own product; 5: per capita research output ; 6: alliances to turnover; 7: new project earning more than 80 per cent; 8: system software earning

Figure 4.4   Choices on knowledge wealth
Source: Banerjee (2003) *Technovation* p. 597, fig. 1.

Differences in perceptions of relative importance or relative arrangements of the constituents of a structural sort, therefore, indicate differences in strategies or, more properly, in strategic intentions. Benchmarking, it was argued, cannot be done with respect to an objective benchmark. Instead, a benchmarking must refer back to mismatches with strategic intent. These differences in opinion refer to perceptions of executives on the limited role that an objective benchmark could play. Respondents were asked whether an IOC should be benchmarked (1) only globally, (2) first globally and then domestically, (3) first domestically and then globally. Divergences in perceptions were significant and responses were nearly equally divided. Benchmarking relates to both the structural patterns of the partial market that the firm is serving and the strategic intent of the incumbent firm in taking up a position in that partial market. In other words, firms responded by saying that they would prefer to benchmark differently, suiting respective strategic intents.

Of market, knowledge wealth and structure

The alignment thesis refers to the alignment of resources to environmental variations. The argument here has been that structural constituents are readjusted in correspondence with any perceived difference between strategic intent and strategic outcomes. In order to readjust these constituents, firms, therefore, reallocate such resources as knowledge employees, or readjust such other constituents as its allies or its knowledge wealth. These readjustments are to overcome failures in strategies. It is often difficult to locate the partial market and the particular strategic landscape a firm is seeking to manoeuvre strategically. This difficulty arises particularly because software firms keep changing their alliances, strategic landscapes and their partial markets. A partial market or a strategic milieu, it may be recalled, is not objectively given but constructed around the strategic goal of the incumbent. A close watch on a firm alone can mitigate this difficulty. Since firms differ in their dynamic positioning, tracking the paths of all the separate movements in this single narrative would be difficult and only certain stable patterns of the firm's strategic behaviours are considered here. Amongst such behaviours must be considered marketing and strategies on software products or projects and services.

Knowledge from marketing is important. Von Hippel (1988) described this as sticky. A sticky knowledge cannot be described completely outside its original context and, since a complete description provides an informational account, this knowledge fails to transfer its informational content, even if it wishes to. The context of this sticky or idiosyncratic knowledge is the structure of a firm. In other words, sticky knowledge transforms into an informational account only in the context of the firm's structural constituents. Sticky knowledge is thus readable, internal to firm structure. Behaviourally speaking, a firm would align its marketing resources in accordance with its strategies on products or projects and services, or in accord with the identified domain knowledge. To an outsider, partial information on distribution of resources such as its marketing manpower would be available. However, such information can never disclose details of either marketing knowledge or the structural sorts. Given this limitation, only certain behavioural implications can be studied.

In 2001–02, a second series of surveys was undertaken with 27 firms studied on their marketing related behaviours. Table 4.2 indicates certain marketing features of 13 firms. An overwhelmingly large number of them own their marketing outfits. Nine of these 13 firms are large and are primarily in the projects or services area or in consultancies. Their marketing staff comprises between a minimum of 0.3 per cent and a maximum of 7 per cent to 8 per cent of the total employees. In another small survey of the same group of surveys, 14 firms reported on their marketing staff strength that was observed to be between 1 per cent and 12 per cent. It appears

Table 4.2 Structure and marketing strategy

Firm	Revenue ratio, product to service	Product superiority strategy for new items	Through existing client strategy for new items	Other strategies for new items	Ownership of marketing outfit	Number of clients who provide 80 per cent revenue	Contractual relation with customer	Type of customer base
1	7/93		Yes		Owned	10	Offshore development centre	Very stable
2	15/85	Yes		Brand building	Owned	30	Fixed cost; man-hours	Dynamic
3	20/80		Yes	Rely on current large clients	Owned			Dynamic
4	50/50	Yes	Yes	R & D, repeat order, maintenance	Owned		Long term and one time	Dynamic
5	Only service		Yes		Owned	3	First and long term	Very stable
6	N.A.	Yes	Yes		Owned	15–20		Dynamic
7	8/92		Yes	Word of mouth, reputation	Owned	Top 30%	Upgradation and maintenance	Very stable
8	4/96	Yes			Owned	20		Dynamic
9	30/70				Owned			Dynamic
10	30/70		Yes	Value proposition	Domestic-own; Export-partner	25	Partnership; Profit loss sharing; value	Dynamic
11	Only service		Yes	Large customer	Own	4	Long term contracts	Dynamic
12	10/90	Yes	Yes	Technical expertise	Mix of own and others	2	Long term contracts	Very stable
13	Only service	Yes			Own	1		Very stable

that firms with more earnings from products tend to employ more marketing people and firms with small marketing teams tend to earn most of their revenue from repeat customers, with whom the incumbent firms in general entered into long-term contracts. Only one firm, marketing abroad through its partner and which offered value-added engineering services entered into value-based contracts (Lacity and Wilcocks, 2001) involving profit and loss-sharing arrangement. The customer bases of a large number of firms, however, are dynamic. The dynamics and instability of the customer base do not seem to deter firms from undertaking 'long-term and one-time' or 'long-term' types of contracts. In other cases, even when the customer base is highly stable, a firm entered into several types of contractual arrangements, 'fixed and long-term' to 'upgradable', including acting as an 'offshore development centre'. Only a few firms are building up a brand presence. A few others are building up technological expertise especially through R & D. Banerjee and Dufflo pointed out the importance of reputation and of dependability in the designing of contracts. This small survey extends and supports their argument.

A structural sort, to recall the earlier discussion, comprises allies, knowledge wealth and knowledge employees. A long-term marketing arrangement indicates an alliance type of a relationship. In fact, all the customer relationship types from Table 4.2 indicate formation of alliances, which are sometimes explicit, as in the 'offshore development centre', or in 'long-term and one-time' types or are somewhat less explicit as in profit-and-loss sharing, value-based contracts. Firms abroad, who are outsourcing some of their information systems components to Indian software firms, are often large (typically belonging to Fortune 500). They can influence not only the types of contractual relations but – as discussed earlier, through strategic moves – the strategic intents of the comparatively smaller and dependent software firms from India. Strategic moves, to recall the earlier discussion, are not behavioural to an observer but remain unrecognized. They can have six modes or qualities and can be for alliance, confrontation, fluidity, nonchalance, prevarication and dependence. Most marketing agreements discussed here fall under the types 'fluidity', 'prevarication' or 'dependence'. The constituents of the structural sort are influenced by these strategic moves. Knowledge wealth pertaining to different types of agreements is different, for example. The absence of marketing alliance partners or of allies, with whom strategic technology development can be undertaken, as revealed in this part of the survey, is indicative of a specific type of knowledge wealth. It seems that Indian firms, often protected by dependency type long-term contractual obligations, fail to muster the sticky knowledge they learn from marketing and transform it into knowledge wealth. Information from marketing is a description available to the structural constituents of the incumbent firm and this informational knowledge wealth needs to be related to the strategic actions and strategic moves by the incumbent.

Typical to strategic acts would be pushing the products or projects as an adversary to or complementing existing or likely future products or projects from firms in the strategic landscape or the partial market. Surely, strategic acts and strategic moves are employed for such purposes. However, acts and moves of strategy demand more of strategic knowledge than of knowledge as wealth. The latter is a constituent of the structural sort and is a partially described or partially informational account of knowledge held idiosyncratically by the firm; information from and about the market influence strategic acts and moves. This information, it is being argued, is structural and sticky and it is a component of a firm's structure. It is also being argued that this knowledge wealth as a structural constituent must get related to other structural constituents, such as knowledge employees, allies, and even the umbrella cover. It is argued that knowledge wealth can be appreciated from looking at the inter-constituent structural features. Decisions pertaining to resource allocations or finance and information on market are important facets of this knowledge wealth.

Data from Table 4.2 indicates that firms depended on existing clients as the most dependable ally for a product launch or for project concepts. This has been followed by a strategy on enhancing or innovating upon product or service superiority. Brand and reputation building has not been the frequented mode, perhaps because Indian software firms have not often been able to muster enough finance and other resources, in general, being small. This data indicates further that technological achievements, R & D and value propositions are well-accepted modes of strategy. In short, the most preferred strategic mode appears to be to depend on the large customer as a quasi-ally and forge with it long-term contracts. It also emphasized product and service superiority, helped by R & D where necessary. Importantly, the markets being served by these firms are often very dynamic. The structural proposition that they seem to have opted for is, therefore, an umbrella cover, enabling the incumbent firm to be technologically poised and capable of taking up market challenges while taking refuge under long-term contracts with large customers. As will be seen later, these firms, therefore, often took up strategic moves corresponding to fluidity, prevarication or dependence.

Why could domestic firms not form alliances, especially with other domestic firms, as the data indicated? Most firms cater to all market sectors, leaving them with little scope to specialize. Nor is there much by way of division of labour across domestic firms because there are few complementarities among them. A likely major reason appears to be the path dependence of the small domestic software market, relatively less dynamic and underdeveloped and under-specialized. Indian software firms grew in the market of outsourced information systems or outsourced business processes. As explained, the outsourced market necessarily remains underdeveloped in so far as division of labour is concerned. Again, Indian firms did not initially have the wherewithal of reputation, brand or finance to back them in the global market. Searching for opportunity became the most frequented approach for growth, and domestic firms became more dependent on the path of techniques. They avoided manufacturing or providing variegated and divided services. Division of labour has historically been most propitious to manufacturing and even to services while techniques have provided little differentiation in the labour. This path of a typical Indian software firm led it to specialize in techniques, which could offer few complementarities to other domestic firms. The natural corollary to that is that domestic firms could find little advantage in domestically forged alliances.

A small number of Indian firms have global alliances, which understandably seek complementing capabilities that Indian firms can hardly offer, limited as they are by their techniques dependency. Further, hurdles to the global alliances came from the problems of cultural mismatch and absence of trust (which a cultural togetherness can provide easily and comfortably). Table 4.3 presents data from another part of this same series of surveys undertaken in 2001–02. Most of the represented firms are large, some are foreign-owned and only firm no. 2 is a medium-sized one, while firm no. 3 is small. Almost all the firms are exclusively dependent on their own marketing set-up, frequently earning only about 10 per cent of their revenue through the collaborator's distribution channel. In some cases, other modes of distribution, such as franchising, are dominant. The dependence on collaboration or alliance for marketing of projects is also minimal and is partially explained by the revenue percentage earned through repeat customers. This is more than 60 per cent in most cases. Market information is yet another aspect of these operations and sources of information on market opportunities are market agents and direct talks with interested companies. Following agents closely received priority over several other modes of direct information while information from collaborators or alliances were not considered important. Further, several firms offer products only with their own brand names and few develop products carrying the collaborator's brand name. In all the cases cited, the number of own brands is more than the collaborator's brands. Small and medium firms often have to develop brands for collaborators or develop products for a buyer in order that they can then go for own products.

Knowledge wealth and structure co-ordination

It has been argued here that market competence is a reflection on structural competence. The knowledge of the market and its application by a firm to the other constituents in the structural sort generates structural robustness, which can be measured through certain definitions of market competence. Competence in a market is also simultaneously a function of the characteristics of the market. The software market, at least the market

Table 4.3 Structural pattern of marketing

Firm	Rev. % by own distr.	Rev. % by parent's distr.	Rev. % by colla. distr.	Rev. % by others	Proj. mktd. by own	Proj. mktd. by coll.	Proj. mktd. by parent	Proj. mktd. by others	Rev. % through repeat customer	Info. source on mkt. opportunity
1	57		25	18	45		25	30	70	A, IC
2	30		70		2		4	17	60	A, IC
3					60			40	55	IC
4									60	IC
5	100				100				90	Direct BDM, A
6					100				60	Direct, A, IC
7	80		5	15	80				75	Direct, IC
8	80			20	100	20			80	Conf., Exhibition, Sales leads
9	5		5	90	80	10		10	40	A, IC, Sales leads
10	64	36			100				75	IC
11	80		10	10	85		15		70	IC, Sales leads
12	100				100				85	IC
13						30	70		45	Parent
14					100				90	IC, A

Logo: IC = interested company; A = agent.

generating growth for Indian firms, is the outsourced IS (information system). Outsourced IS bears characteristics of the path dependencies of the customer firms (such as 'migration', necessary for most US-based firms that switch from mainframe devices, or from legacy systems, or wish to co-ordinate several discordant pieces of software). Even more important is the aspect of co-ordination (Richardson, 1997) of products – such as amongst those who develop upon Windows or work on alternatives or co-ordination of products with novel technologies, chips or communications protocols and such like. To recall the earlier argument on co-ordination, software needs to be co-ordinated with either existing systems or expected 'futuristic' systems. Competence must then refer not only to internal structural coherence or robustness but also to aspects of co-ordination with structures of outsourcing customers and with existing or expected groups of products or services or techniques. This argument takes one back to the earlier thinking on structure. A structural sort, it was argued, results from strategy and, as with strategy, a structure must, while remaining robust, resort to structural correspondence with other structures in the firm's strategic milieu or landscape. The strategy on umbrella cover takes care of this aspect of correspondence. External structural correspondence must, following our previous argument, also appear in the internal structure of a firm as correspondences across several internal constituents, namely, across knowledge wealth, knowledge employees and allies.

Market competence of an incumbent firm ought to reflect both aspects of structural robustness, looked at internally and as aspects of external correspondences. Of these two correspondences, the former refers to co-ordination between some internal constituents of a structural sort and the latter to co-ordination with other external structures or strategies of other firms. An example of market competence is presented here. The purpose of the definition is to capture these two types of co-ordination and the definition is applied to a small set of data obtained from the first survey undertaken during 1999–2000. The data being limited, a rigorous definition of competence is not attempted.

This defined competence has nine modules, each a simple ratio of which market competence is the sum. These modules are ratios reflecting on several constituents of the structural sort and a few other ratios reflecting on external co-ordination across structures. The market competence profile of 33 firms, reporting only one-year data, is presented in Figure 4.5. The number of modules was large because several respondents did not report on all relevant data items and certain data did not exist in some firms, such as start-ups. The objective of the competence profile here is to compare competencies of several firms and not measure absolute competence of a firm. The picture of comparative profile must, therefore, be considered as only indicative because of this limitation. Also, values close to zero do not indicate an absolute value of zero competence. Contrarily, a lower value indicates lack of

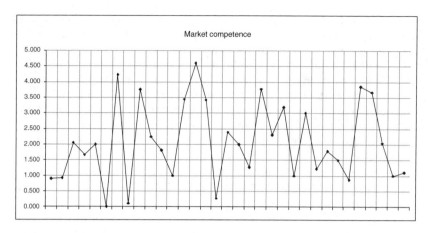

Figure 4.5 Market competence of select firms

specialization because all the modules are ratios. This profile compares such aspects of co-ordination as might indicate variations over specializations.

The first module refers to the ratio between 'employees sent to the USA for both offshore and joint development of a product or project' to 'total number of employees sent abroad for a similar purpose'. The second module refers to the ratio between 'experience-years weighted total number of employees having global experience' to 'experience-years weighted total number of employees'. The third module refers to the ratio between 'numbers of products with own brand' to 'total number of products developed for all purposes'. The fourth module is about the percentage of total revenue earned through own distribution or marketing channel. The fifth refers to the ratio between two modes of presence, by the firm itself or in collaboration or alliance or as subsidiary, in the markets categorized in the three types: geographic, current product and expected product. This fifth module takes care of inter-firm co-ordination. The sixth module takes care of co-ordination in product market but from a different perspective. It is a ratio between the 'number of products that complement an existing product, that compete with an existing product, that serve customized demand, that complement an expected product and finally that create a new market in the USA' to the total number of products. The seventh module is about internal structural aspects compared to the co-ordinated externality. This utilized the ratio between occurrences of products or projects development funded through 'internal accrual and/or customer support' to all instances of funding, which includes bank or venture capital support. The eighth module then reports percentages of projects won through competitive bidding in the USA to the total of such projects. The final module reports on the percentage of total projects developed that get marketed by the firm.

Market competence, accordingly, reflects the competence mustered by the firm. Ratios take care of features of structural sorts devoted to competence mustered alone by a firm against features representing the firm's modes of dependence, alliance and collaboration. A lower value of these ratios thus indicates a structure which has taken an umbrella cover strategy; this means that the structure of the referred firm has reshaped itself in accordance with the structures of other firms in the strategic landscape. Similarly, other strategy issues – on marketing, product development and such others – refer to ratios between two types of strategic acts. The first of these two types is about overcoming the constraints of co-ordination and the second is about remaining with co-ordination. The lower value indicates greater reliance on co-ordination by a firm. The profile of these 33 firms indicates that they are nearly equally and evenly distributed over all structural compulsions. Firms at the zenith have opted for minimal co-ordination and those at the nadir opted for maximal co-ordination. There are equally greater numbers of firms who have chosen paths intermediate between these two extremes.

Information held by knowledge employees, in the form of experiences or joint development of projects or products abroad, is necessarily sticky. Structural constituents of a firm translate sticky information of this kind into its knowledge wealth as an informational account. This knowledge wealth held in the structure is re-employed in such strategies as development of products, which can co-ordinate with products existing, expected or which can compete with a current product or else can create a product market. Re-employment of initially sticky information for structural generation of informational knowledge thus generates situations that call for reshaping the structure. Demands on reshaping the structural sort are generated when a firm markets these products or projects alone or in alliances. Competence in knowledge wealth, captured severally in the form of IOC or market competence, refers then to the competence of a firm in yielding its structural sort. Such competence to reshape the structural constituents is the ability to take umbrella cover and it is a constituent of the structure. This departure from the resources allocation perspective must be recognized. For the present account, resources allocation appears as a subsidiary function of an organization's attempt to translate sticky information into organizational knowledge wealth. Translating sticky information involves the firm reshaping the structural sort whenever necessary. The resources allocation appears as a result of this yielding of structural constituents.

Structural characteristics

A structure results from the strategy and, as argued earlier, does not stand in the form of a scaffolding of divisions, departments, information flows or systems. Strategy insists that structure evolves and is reshaped several times in accordance with strategic intent, strategic achievements as well as demands on co-ordination or threats from the strategic milieu of the incumbent. This landscape or milieu exists in the background of an institutional environment. For example, financial holding (which is a constituent of the structure) depends on several such environmental or institutional aspects, including taxation policies, technological opportunities, opportunities for employment of cash and reserves in hand in the market, and others. Similarly, accounting legacies and disclosure legacies determine the extent to which a firm would disclose its expenditure on R & D or its investments in intangible assets. For a given institutional or environmental legacy to which all the firms under consideration belong though, a comparison across such similarly situated firms could reasonably place a profile independent of that legacy. Comparison across such similarly situated firms on disclosures of R & D expenditures or of other intangible assets, or keeping afloat a large reserves and surplus, provide an intelligent reading on comparative structural policies pursued in the industry. *Inter alia*, finance being a constituent of the structural sort and deft handling of finance being as much an outcome of knowledge wealth as the writing of innovative software, one might compare profiles of software firms to discern structurally implicated knowledge wealth in relation to other constituents of the structural sort. Some examples of such comparative aspects relating to finance and other structural constituents are being examined here.

Capital investment by a firm is generally considered to be a feature that strengthens its structure. In the Chandlerian (1990) argument, for example, capital intensification is attributed as the cause (and not a reason) of corporate structural scaffolding. Capital is invested exclusively in the structure, including its machinery. The control over the invested capital, the Chandlerian paradigm argues, demands an evolution of the structural scaffolding. This paradigm seems to have no answer when the nature of capital investment gets beyond the domain of exclusivity in property rights claims, whose framework had been provided by Berle and Means (1932). Investment by software companies is rather different as will be argued in detail. Briefly, a software firm invests little in fixed capital. Most of its investments are in the nature of human capital and in the infrastructure. Agents, other than the equity participants in the software firm, invest in human capital and in infrastructure. A software firm ordinarily limits its investment to several constituents of the structural sort, such as in skill upgradation, communications and computing equipment and land and buildings. This, however, remains much below the average capital intensity of manufacturing. The other problem is that since the investment in human capital or in communications, for example, also represents the working capital requirement, it may be legitimately asked if such investments can be brought under capital investment.

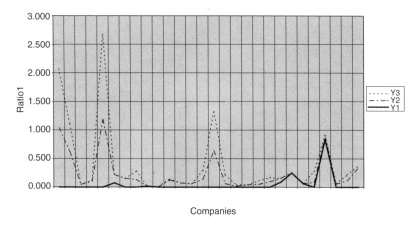

Companies

Figure 4.6   Profile of ratio investment to total funds

Figure 4.6 shows the profile of the ratios of investment to total funds of 29 software firms for the period 1997 (as Y1) to 1999 (as Y3). Term investments and total funds are as defined in the accounting procedure and the data has been collected from their respective annual reports. Not all firms reported all the data, so a few ratios could not be computed. This profile shows that except for a few firms, most firms ordinarily depended on internal accruals for investment and, in general, kept such investments below one quarter of the available total funds. Only four firms (three of which were from the USA entering India), setting up new establishments, had to borrow and invest a great deal. The accounting definition of investments refers to capital market investments but one must consider investment in fixed capital as well, which is not disclosed by the accounting figures. Investments have been interpreted as those made in fixed assets or in capital market investments. This is reconfirmed in Figure 4.7, depicting uses of funds by 17 large software firms for three years 1999, 2000 and 2001. Increasing investments in two categories, namely, 'fixed assets' and 'investments', characterize behaviours of these firms. The working capital requirement has often increased as corroborated by Figure 4.8. The source of funds for the same 17 large firms indicates that revenue-earning has contributed most, followed by capital proceeds. This latter source of funds is naturally applicable to only large firms that are registered with stock exchanges with shares attracting a premium. Naturally, small and start-up firms cannot enjoy this premium-earning. The sources of funds for such firms are exclusively dominated by revenue-earning. Similarly, the use of funds by the non-large firms in fixed assets is rare and virtually never in 'investments'.

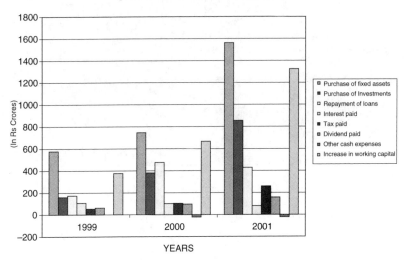

Figure 4.7   Use of funds by large software firms

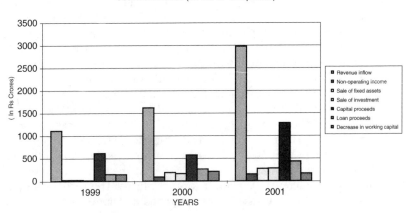

Figure 4.8   Sources of funds for large software firms

The nature and source of investment reconfirms the argument that software firms belong to a domain excluded by the Chandlerian scaffolding-structure paradigm. Investments in lands and buildings and in the capital market need not demand structural scaffolding where capital intensification demands command and authority structure and clearly delineated flow of information. Contrarily, investments by software firms generate what has been described here as the structural sort, a key constituent of which is finance. Most importantly, the value of such investments is deeply implicated in the functioning of inter-firm structural co-ordination. The dependence of asset values on the functioning of a partial market (and not a global 'market') takes one away from the stationery and undisputed property rights claim provided by the Berle and Means framework. Invested capital appears to be moving away from the domain of undisputed authority and control of the firm's structure. In order to maximize the value of its investment, a firm would, therefore, be less restricted to its own structural aspects. The growth of assets of a software firm thus get related to strategy-interdependencies in a partial market. This is a very significant shift and marks a departure towards a social venue. This shift points to the increasing importance that a software firm must attach to issues of strategy. Strategy, as defined and argued here, enables an incumbent firm to modulate structural sorts of other firms in its milieu of partial market. In other words, an incumbent often gains by warranting such situations where potential competitors make investments on items that do not contribute to the competitive and strategic strength (such as, technological or marketing superiority) of that investor, for example. Investing in lands and buildings or in the inter-corporate market or in equities of unrelated companies and in such market instruments transforms the firm into a typical portfolio investor of the capital market. This loss of strategic and structural strength of firms in the milieu of an incumbent strategist ensures the incumbent a strategic leverage on the assets of other firms. It follows then that the knowledge wealth of the incumbent includes this knowledge on the structural sorts of other firms in its strategic landscape or milieu.

The investment behaviour of most Indian software firms is indeed unenviable. It is argued here that personnel cost and cost of communications could be considered as investments. Figure 4.8 shows that for some large firms, the decrease in working capital has remained positive or has never been negative. Most of the working capital requirement is on the grounds of costs of sales and on personnel and communications. It appears then that firms often did not increase these apparent costs while their revenues-earnings surged ahead. The relationship between these three types of apparent costs is profiled in Figure 4.9 for 14 firms, mostly large and a few medium-sized, for the years 1997 (Y1), 1998 (Y2) and 1999 (Y3). This profile is about the ratios between personnel cost to the cost of sales plus cost of communications. Recalling that only about 3 per cent to 8 per cent of personnel remain engaged in marketing, this profile indicates the overwhelming dominance of personnel cost. The communication cost of a software firm is a significant attribute of its real capital investment. The personnel cost does not include such costs as are incurred on direct training. This cost reflects the salary and

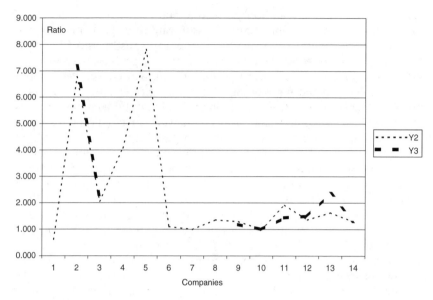

Figure 4.9   Personnel cost with relevance to the costs of sales and communications

wages. The value of this ratio has almost always remained above 1, close to 2 and sometimes approaching 7.

The profile of ratios between R & D expenditure to the pre-tax and pre-depreciation profit (PBDIT) is presented in Figure 4.10. It is observed that interest cost to a software firm is insignificant and is decreasing over the years. The PBDIT then represents cash that will be modulated by the depreciation policy of the firm and by the declared expenditure on R & D. Few firms in Indian software disclose figures to suggest that any R & D at all is undertaken by them. Thoughtlessly, the Indian government considered R & D

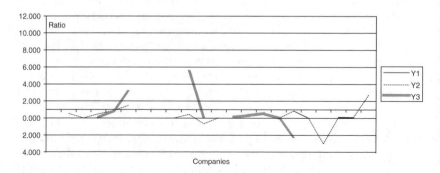

Figure 4.10   Ratio of R & D to the PBDIT for eleven companies

disclosure a function of tax benefits and this was reflected in its policies. Most often, however, declared information on R & D and on other intangibles is a function of firm strategies and the market. Very low values of R & D thus suggest several possible states of affairs. These include firms doing R & D but not declaring actual R & D expenditure – respondents chose to avoid responding to the question on what constitutes R & D in the software firm – or firms not doing R & D or declaring only a part of the information, thereby understating expenditure. Figure 4.10 shows a few firms with the value of this ratio approaching 3. All firms reporting a ratio value greater than 1 in this profile are from the USA and the reports are on their subsidiaries. Others, such as a public sector firm, show the ratio value at about 0.8. Yet others report far lower value, often around 0.001.

This understatement or non-disclosure may be attributed to two facts not causally linked perhaps: the Indian market's institutional rigidity and its subservience to very large customers in the USA. Institutional rigidity refers to the absence of domestic partial markets linking strategies of a few local firms through a strategic landscape. This rigidity also refers to a resultant absence of competition in the domestic partial markets and the absence of a domestic strategic milieu for the software firms. The strategic milieu of an Indian software service or solutions provider firm includes the customer firm (typically a large firm in the USA) and the service or solutions provider in that market. A domestic firm thus belongs to a global partial market. There can be little competition between the domestic firms and even this needs external mediation. The second point is about subservience or, as described here, a strategic move of dependence. Other relevant strategic moves are fluidity and prevarication. An Indian firm trying to get a foothold in the US market or repeat orders from its large customers (such as Microsoft) would be reluctant to disclose R & D because such a disclosure could present it as a potential competitor to the customer. In fact, stringent legal clauses in contracts with the customer often prohibit an incumbent service provider to undertake or disclose its R & D expenditure. In reality, an incumbent service provider, as the field observation suggests, does often undertake R & D, without which it would fail to provide a technologically better solution to its customer. A public sector firm could publicly talk about its R & D while most private sector firms could not possibly declare theirs.

Asset liquidity and structure

Knowledge about the structural sorts of other firms in the strategic milieu of the incumbent cannot be secured from simple accounting ratios divulged in the annual reports or from their other public communications. A firm may follow different modes of data presentation. Data on investment in knowledge, mostly held in employees, for example, is not shown as investment but reported as costs. A comparative profile based on a few compound ratios might partly alleviate this problem. A group of ratios considered together could indicate features of firms that remain otherwise hidden. One major difficulty cannot be overcome though. Indian firms suffer from institutional rigidity and, even when belonging to the same segment of business or the same territory, most often do not belong to the same strategic milieu or to the same partial market. As a result, a profile comparing firms not belonging to the same strategic milieu misses out the hidden agenda. Here poor access to data acts as a limitation.

It appears from these discussions that strategic considerations warrant an Indian software firm holding enough assets in liquidity. One such profile, presented in Figure 4.11, shows data for nine software firms between 1997 and 1999 providing a ratio indicating the relative apportionment of liquid assets by these firms. This ratio is defined as: the ratio between [(Personnel cost/Total revenue) + (Depreciation/Profit before tax, etc. PBDIT) + (R & D expenditure /PBDIT)] and [Interest/Reserves and surplus]. The numerator and denominator of this grand ratio are pure numbers, indicative of liquidity profiles. Personnel cost and expenditure on R & D represent investments on entities that are not durable. Moreover, increased expenditure on both cannot be considered as strategic commitments (emphasized so much by the IO/game theorists) because personnel mobility in software firms is very high. Therefore, the ratio between personnel cost and total revenue (or R & D expenditure to PBDIT) is not indicative of investment in durable assets or

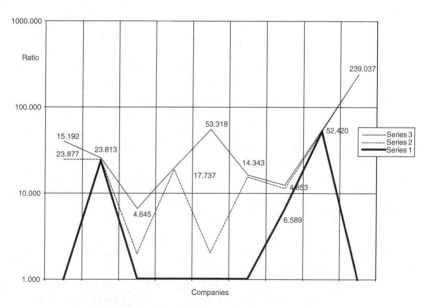

Figure 4.11   Asset liquidity profile of nine software firms

commitments to asset specificities. Instead, it indicates a choice of a particular mode of liquidity. Similarly, the depreciation policy reflects the disposition of a firm to exhibit certain amount of an otherwise liquid asset as a cash liquid asset. The denominator ratio again indicates the liquidity choice of a firm. This profile indicates wide variations amongst firms. The ratio value for a firm sometimes jumped tenfold from an initial value of one. Values otherwise varied widely. Higher values indicate higher reserves and surplus and lower burden of interest. Conversely, higher values indicate the higher values of personnel cost, depreciation and the like. Significantly, values here indicate not simply gross liquidity but modes of liquidities. Liquidity is an insurance as it were against lack of knowledge of others' structural sorts. Liquidity is also an enabler of fluidity and an enabler of growth in the direction of scope.

Figure 4.6 (p. 123) can also be represented as a dummy that represents competence of firms in the scope dimension, expanding whenever there is an opportunity and in the scope direction would demand that the firm keeps a substantial liquid finance. Liquidity represents what has been described here as fluidity under the strategic moves types. In fact, if one wishes to treat holding of liquid assets as a means of earning interest income, as is provided by the Keynesian General Theory, one will have to 'debase' the speculative aspect (as argued by Shackle, 1972). Moreover, one can employ insights from Keynes on the possible employment of liquid assets by a firm in 'demand management' problems. This discussion is being reserved for a later chapter. In contrast, structural fluidity and holding of assets in several fluid modes in the context of an industry, which thrives on shortest product life cycles and quickest innovative surprises, appear to justify the contention here that Indian firms are opportunity seeking. Shackle argued that 'durability engenders non-rational conduct' (1972: 158). The liquid assets include, beyond the cash that a firm holds, its most important resource: manpower assets. Manpower liquidity is discussed in another chapter. It is suggested here that assumptions of resources theory cannot hold for the behaviours of these Indian firms. Firms hold liquidity and put up a fluid structure.

The resources theory, however, assumes a resources market in equilibrium and the managerial decision behaviour as rational or 'bounded rational'. Accordingly, this theory argues that, firms would differ in performances in proportion to the resources that they can amass. In contrast, it is suggested here that firms do not consider the resources market at equilibrium. Firms hold liquidity because they are speculative. By keeping assets liquid and the structure fluid, firms can defer their choices. The deferment of choices is undertaken with a view to gaining speculative profit. This speculative profit, it must be observed, is not a Schumpeterian innovator's profit (Hanusch, 1988), which is close to what Keynes described as the windfall profit in *A Treatise on Money*. In fact, there are also differences between the two ideas on profit. Schumpeterian profit is not entirely counter-expected but an expectation fulfilled. In Shackle's language, this is the first understanding of a profit that forms the basis of an action. It is also speculative, though only partly. It requires co-ordination with existing knowledge and the Schumpeterian innovator searches for an alternative explanation or route that might bring him an additional earning in the background of the existing knowledge. He knows for sure that his technology is beyond the ken of normal domain that any average inference from existing knowledge could bring to notice. This certainty of the innovator is, however, confronted with the uncertainties of market outcomes. Therefore, Schumpeterian profit is not thoroughly speculative.

Shackle and Keynes also offered two notions on profit in the light of Cantillon's ideas on profit. The first profit is based on speculative valuation of the current states of affairs. This conjecture on speculative profit initiates economic actions. Shackle calls this conjecture a focus hypothesis. Working on this hypothesis often leads to a counter-expected outcome, in the form of windfall trading revenue surplus. This counter-expected surplus is the windfall profit of Keynes or the resolutional profit of Shackle. 'Whereas profit in its first guise appears as part of the incentive to action, to choice of a practical conduct, in its second guise, as resolutional profit, it appears as an incentive to thought. The unity... for our frame of profit ideas rests partly on their involvement of uncertainty, and partly on their character of incentives to some *demarche*. Where there is profit,... there is an impulse to activity: to enterprise or to strategic re-thinking' (Shackle, 1972: 420–1). Speculative profit emerges from a state of ignorance. Resolutional profit emerges from a novel recognition of reality.

Liquidity is the expression of ignorance. Knowledge is scarce and expensive. The lack of knowledge on choices that could be made or on the durable asset or the committed action the liquid asset can be spent on results in holding on to both deferment of decisions and liquidity. 'Liquidity is, in some sense and degree, a *substitute* for knowledge' (Shackle, 1972: 216). Liquidity is about the ignorance of the circumstances in the strategic milieu. How the structural knowledge and structural sorts of the others are going to behave is only partly known. Demand management, as will be argued later, partly alleviates this problem of ignorance. In fact, the dynamism in the demands, it may be recalled from the above data, called for entering into long-term contracts. The other mode through which this ignorance can be alleviated is to have knowledge on the durability of assets and on commitment to actions that other strategist firms in the milieu have undertaken. The asset durability of other firms is thus convenient for an incumbent strategist. Asset durability alone can ensure a proper Richardsonian co-ordination, which is achieved amongst firms through the exchange of two types of information – economic and technical. Both these information types are definable when firms have committed actions and durable assets. The asset specificity of the TCE framework, it may be noticed, is one such durable asset. Durable assets, such as land, buildings, hardware, asset specificities, immobile employees and such others complete a structural sort that is bereft of an umbrella cover. Such structural sorts can attempt to co-ordinate commitments because the co-ordinating parties have near complete information on others.

The liquidity of assets makes co-ordination impossible. In other words, voicing Keynes, liquidity is indefinable. Knowledge that can 'substitute' liquidity is the structural knowledge. It appears then that higher liquidity is indicative of a larger ignorance of the incumbent regarding the composition of structural knowledge of others. As a corollary, an incumbent's strategy should be to induce others in the strategic milieu to invest more in durable assets. What precise strategic moves or what structural appearance of the incumbent could induce others to invest more in durability is the subject matter of strategy. Durability would enjoin its holder to a relatively higher immobility.

There is another dimension to this structural and asset liquidity. Sticky information from the market, as argued earlier, is rendered into an informational account inside the structure. An informational account is illiquid. The structure had to interpret sticky information in a definite manner in order to arrive at this informational account of knowledge. Therefore, in order that not all sticky information on the environment is translated into a definitive informational account, a firm would strike a balance between its ignorance about others in the environment with its definitive informational account about them. It follows then that the incumbent strategist would encourage the holders of sticky information, namely its employees, to retain in part that private knowledge. Such private knowledge, retained by the employee (since strategy allowed retention) appears as tacit with qualities of asset specificity. However, by definition these cannot be tacit since complete transformation of privately-held knowledge into informational account is possible. A firm gives up translating private knowledge because strategy has demanded that the firm held assets in liquidity.

Finance apart, the constituents of relevance to the structural sort are knowledge wealth, knowledge employees and the umbrella cover. Allies too have entered in the discussions here. The endeavour was to map out the linkages between these constituents. The vicissitudes of interrelations indicated the importance of liquidity to Indian firms, which are small compared to their customers or to their competitors abroad. Accounting measures of growth rely on larger investments in durability and in commitment. It was observed that Indian software firms face a serious dilemma because in order to appear attractive they must show higher accounting-based growth or invest in durability. This, however, portends possible loss of Cantillon profit. The fluidity of strategic moves and liquidity of assets promise an umbrella cover to the structure of this fledgling firm. The durability of assets, deep commitment and the rigid structure with a rigid baggage of knowledge specific assets, portend a possible loss of strategic and even possibly technological dynamism in the not too distant future. However, small size and small technological or weak strategic threats from current Indian software firms appear to be faceless. To make the strategic threat effective, the current size of the structure and wealth would have to be much enlarged. That would portend rigidity.

5
Value Addition Strategy

The Indian software dilemma has been elaborated in the previous chapter. An Indian firm needs to become large and use a strong marketing network to present its products in the global market through a forceful strategy. Such a firm must make strong commitments and substantial investments in durable assets, including manpower. However, if the firm invests in durability and makes strong commitments and, by doing so, grows large in the current market, it would possibly lose its ability to make fluid strategic moves, its asset liquidity, and strategic umbrella cover for its structure. Durability and commitments, especially for the competition in the current product markets, would demand from this incumbent firm that it grow structural knowledge wealth. Knowledge wealth is enhanced through vigorous acquisition of sticky information on both the current and potential structures of the competitors and transforming that sticky information into organizational knowledge wealth. This commitment to durability, products, current market and competition alone ensures that this firm can offer currently forceful strategic moves and acts. A strong commitment to the current competition, products and such like, however, *severely limits ignorance* (because ignorance is liquidity), which proves to be an asset to the speculative innovator and to the maker of an apparently insignificant yet potentially significant strategic move. Critics point out this weakness and argue that Indian software firms ought to move in the direction of making strong commitments, bring out products, seize the market by entering competition and enhance their structural knowledge wealth. This position of the critic overlooks the dilemma though. It is suggested here that Indian firms have lower commitments to the current competition, hold proportionately higher liquidity and are less committed to the growth in structure, structural knowledge and product portfolio. These firms have comfortably positioned them on the services and solutions track. They appear to have chosen not to be big and to be pervasively present in very dynamic and volatile frontiers of software demands. This chapter looks into this choice of services.

Critics have adopted a prescriptive mode. They have made a couple of commitments to certain theoretical positions and their prescriptions follow those often unstated commitments. Influential prescriptions have most often followed tenets of resources theory and capability competency theory. They define competency in terms of use of resources. Core competency has been projected as the key issue and defined as 'capabilities... [that]... differentiate a company strategically' (Leonard-Barton, 1992:619). This definition involves circularity. Core competency has often been defined in terms of the capability to recombine resources. The dependence on resources and on the manners or modes of usage differentiates firms and their capabilities accordingly.

Strangely, these perspectives have almost completely ignored structural aspects. The Chandlerian paradigm, in contrast, has highlighted the importance of structure. The competency perspective has also largely overlooked the decision perspective. A competency, as argued earlier, cannot refer to any innate qualities and must largely be derived from structural features. In fact, competency is reckoned to be the switching competence, that is, the ability to assume an appropriate structure as a strategic umbrella cover. In the case of choice between product and services, competency should reflect this switching competence. In this analysis, the resources usage takes a back seat and decisions relating to use of resources appear important. Moreover, resources usage reflects both structural characteristics and the process characteristics of a firm. Processes are amenable (in terms of the earlier discussion) manoeuvrings of the strategic moves. In other words, strategy, which conditions structure and strategic moves and processes, also influences the extent and modes of resources and its usage. This position on the relation of resources to strategy is the converse of what resources theorists argue.

Strategies on products or services are, accordingly, more a reason, if not a cause, for the use of resources by a software firm. Competency based on resources would thus be doubly circumspect. Moreover, strategy choice must also refer to speculative profits and to limitations that might arise owing to constraints imposed by the demands of co-ordination. A firm can speculate when it retains fluidity in strategic moves and liquidity in its structural composition. *Inter alia*, ignorance that refers to states of affairs in firm-internal processes and firm-external markets engenders speculation. A near complete structure possesses enough knowledge on these states of affairs. Thus, to remain speculative and, therefore, innovative, a firm must, by strategic intent, keep its structure unfulfilled along with incomplete structural knowledge wealth and its strategic knowledge pertaining to processes. It follows that maximization of current knowledge on the states of affairs ensuring acute efficacy of current strategy (and consequently of structure, resources and processes) simultaneously undermines the foundation necessary to remain innovative and speculative. Structural and process incompleteness would appear prima facie as weaknesses. A services strategy supported by warranted ignorance might, however, prove useful.

Dealing with the Indian dilemma

The Indian software dilemma, as encapsulated, revolves around growth that – if fuelled by major structural commitments and investments in durable assets to market its products – would hamper its ability to make fluid strategic moves, its asset liquidity and umbrella cover. At present, Indian firms have lower commitments to the current competition, hold proportionately higher liquidity and are less committed to current structural sorts, deriving their competency, instead, from the ability of their structural sort to assume an appropriate umbrella cover. It is argued that competency to switch across product and services refers to speculative profits and to the limitations that might arise owing to constraints imposed by demands of co-ordination as well. An Indian software firm could assume structural liquidity because speculation, engendered by ignorance, is possible with fluidity in strategic moves.

Received literature concedes that an organization's routines include higher orders that govern learning itself and that make it possible for a firm to maintain behavioural continuity. Past learning and its accumulation help behavioural continuity and received theorists argue that competency is defined through this unimaginative accumulation. This continuity denies scope to acts of insights, speculative inventions and innovations. The early Schumpeterian approach recognized an individual innovator with a drive for profit and supported by credit as the source of process of innovation. Received theorists have neglected this process of innovation and the importance of speculative insights. Usher (1954, 1955), however, talked about a 'cumulative' process and a Gestaltic synthesis. Following Usher, it is argued that conscious attempts at cumulative syntheses bring about acts of insights, which do not result from learning or competencies or through accumulations of such knowledge. Acts of innovation must search for disequilibria. An innovation is guided by the desire to bring about strategic surprise. Learning and cumulative knowledge adjusted to behavioural continuity cannot bring about strategic surprise.

A structure evolves through strategic acts, not through strategic moves. Innovation refers to the competency of structure as its ability to transform or adapt itself to another structure. Switching a structure is thus not a simple structural change made through accumulation of knowledge but results from strategic acts that are different from strategic moves. Switching competence involves both firm-internal and firm-external aspects and refers to a partial market that is often identifiable in terms of peers or closest rivals.

The dilemma of the Indian software firm regarding whether it should develop a product or deliver sophisticated project solutions, is, however, not derived from considerations on its three tiers of structural competencies alone. The 'product/services' strategy is dependent on the problem of demand management, which is a novel idea. The structural transition of a software firm is undertaken in response to the expectations on management of demands. The joint production of demand implies that the software firm is no longer simply a supplier and the client firm is no longer a customer and this is achieved through a new mode of co-ordination. Vertical integration proves to be uneconomic and joint authority is impossible too. Joint production of demand implies that customers' structural sort remain in dynamic co-ordination with the supplier's structural sort.

It is strange that this demand is generated by the dynamics of structure. This aspect was captured in the framework of structural sorts. Demand can be generated only by structural changes and can be managed only interactively and through mutual co-ordination. The product strategy of a software firm fails here. A service is suited to that objective through speculative destabilization of its customer's structure. The absence of a strong strategy on product cannot then be described as weakness on the part of Indian software firms. The software supplier's reliance on switching between proto-products and services appears to be sound. A proto-product is a non-dominant product for non-global market with a short life cycle and for a specific strategic milieu.

A software firm often takes on product development as a supplementary act that sustains its principal occupation with providing services. The structural competence to switch from product to services is somewhat different. Competence to switch across several services can be reckoned in terms either of a *'service-product-service'* strategy or without intermediation of a reigning meta-product platform. Structural switching in this latter case is necessarily simpler. A switching coefficient must reflect the structural ease with which a firm can switch its structural sorts.

Competency and structure: structure, processes and core competency

There are several perspectives on competency: in some, structure is important; in a few, organizational processes seem to be important. In many others, structure and processes both appear to enjoy equal status, and, in yet a few others, firm-external market characteristics enjoy the precedence. Firm competence (as pointed out earlier) also appears as equivalent to biological evolutionary or linguistic generative competence. Again, in such analogical referencing, firm competency has been defined variously, sometimes as routines, at other times as a capability to use resources, or knowledge learned and honed in different contexts. Analogies often appear compelling but the earlier argument pointed out several simple flaws in such analogy making. A linguistic generative competence never refers to structures or even processes of surface linguistic utterances. An evolutionary competence can never refer to an individual in a species and can refer even less, therefore, to the physical structure of an individual. The analogical reasoning on the competency of a firm can thus barely refer to the linguistic or evolutionary species competency.

Firms differ and there is compelling evidence in support of a firm's unique and individual traits. Common sense then prevails in hypothesizing certain deeper than surface level ability as at work and as generating individuating characteristics. This is the first ground on which the competency hypothesis rests. The second ground is provided by conditions of rapid dynamism that a contemporary high-technology firm, such as software firm, faces. Competency arguably can guide this firm through the vicissitudes of rapid changes. The third ground is provided by the logic of retention. It is argued that a firm must have certain sets of endowments, which need to be updated and honed continuously in order that this firm retain its advantages. As Chandler argued (1990: 594), 'capabilities, of course, had to be created, and once established they had to be maintained. Their maintenance was as great a challenge as their creation, for facilities depreciate and skills atrophy.' The creation and maintenance of capabilities, Chandler (1990) and Lazonic (1991, 1992) argued, were the result of competitive engagement of the firm's structure with its competitors. Porter (1985, 1994) raised similar issues. Competency has been explored on these three grounds: uniqueness of a firm (Nelson, 1991); rapid changes in market and technology (Breschi, Malerba and Orsenigo, 2000; Klepper, 1996; Marsili, 2001); consequent demands made on 'co-evolution' of scientific knowledge and firm structure and industrial competition affecting size, structure and diversification of a firm (Chandler, 1992; Montgomery and Porter, 1991) vis-à-vis achieving competitive advantage.

The running theme across these diverse approaches seems to be 'behavioural continuity' (Nelson and Winter, 2002). They argue that 'if the economy is undergoing continuing exogenous change, and particularly if it is changing in unanticipated ways, then there really is no "long run" in a substantive sense. Rather, the selection process is always in a transient phase, groping toward its temporary target' (Nelson and Winter, 2002: 26). Further, 'the *behavioural continuity* assumption reflects the point that it does matter whether the firm behaviour arises from systematic and persistent causes or merely reflects "random chance or what not". Behavioural continuity might take the form of persistence in actions, in rules of action or something else' (Nelson and Winter, 2002: 27; italics original). The long run trend can condition the long run behaviours of firms, such as argued by the theorists from the structure, conduct, performance paradigm (SCPP) (Porter, 1980). Exogenous, unanticipated changes call for adjustments with changes and break from behaviours conditioned by history. Gibrat's law (Sutton, 1997) on adjustment of a firm's structure to random 'errors' recognized the size of the structure as an important variable influencing the outcome. Access to information (Jovanovich and Rob, 1987) can reduce the impact of randomness and small firms, especially those from high technologies with complementary assets, in contrast to Gibrat's anticipation, might grow more (Henderson, Orsenigo and Pisano, 1999). In fact, if the complementary assets (Bogaert, Martens and Cauwenbergh, 1994) prove to be anticipating forthcoming changes or if they are complementary to new changes, the apparent randomness might reinforce and strengthen the incumbent firms (Tripsas, 1997; Christensen, 1997). Coping with 'random' changes is possible (evolutionary and competence theorists argue) owing to the existence of 'organizational routine', which does not reflect persistent behaviours but reflects a deeper capability to align behaviours. Nelson and Winter say that routine is the organizational analogue of individual skill: 'routines provide a focal point for a learning-based answer to the competence puzzle. Most fundamentally, routines are the basis of the characterization of behavioural continuity' (2002: 30).

Nelson and Winter go beyond the typical behaviourist's 'simple rule' of behaviours. Henderson and Clark (1990) talked about higher 'architecture' of the system (Winter, 1987). Leonard-Barton (1992) defined this higher order as the core capability. Teece, Pisano and Shuen (1997) defined this behaviourally continuing asset-based aspect as dynamic competency. Such higher order rule, Nelson and Winter argue, is not the 'simple' rule of conditioned behaviour but simple when compared to 'infeasibly large optimization calculation'. They refer to aspects of an organization that go into making rules, which are broadly represented by structural and systemic, organizational processes, assets, and learning. They concede that 'when an organization's "routines" include higher-order routines that govern learning itself, the evolution of behaviour at the level of the organization becomes a complex matter in which the structure of the problems faced, the structure of the organization and the historical path of the system are all intertwined'. (Nelson and Winter, 2002: 30, note 6) This argument on competency or routines points to a complex of behaviourally interacting structures (of the problem and that of the organization) that learns from past performances. This learning by the structure and systems of a firm is behaviourally conditioned. Behavioural learning leaves little scope for inventive and speculative insights. A relatively higher mode of learning is recognized in the discussions on path dependency. Path dependency refers to history, its interpretation and the accesses that it affords through discourses by individuals, groups and systems of a firm (Rosenberg, 1982). However, data to be stored in memory that any learning recognizes is derived from the behaviourally implicated structures of a firm and from external situations of competitive strategy.

This approach on defining core competency and the routine does not differentiate sufficiently between the roles of structure systems and organizational processes. Moreover, assets or resources have very often been considered as constituents of structures and systems. Rather often, competence (or core competence) has been defined as a set of skills or their combinations. For example, Nelson and Winter (1982, 2002) draw an analogy with skills, Hamel (1991) and Prahalad and Hamel (1990) define competency as a set of recombined skills. Core competency is recognized as different from assets, though assets – rather strategic assets (Amit and Schoemaker, 1993), that is assets that have potential for 'strategic competitive advantage' (Barney,

1991) – go into the making of this core competency (Bogaert, Martens and Cauwenbergh, 1994; Dierickx and Cool, 1989; Teece, Pisano and Shuen, 1997). These assets are several and comprise the resources (Rumelt, 1984; Teece, 1980, 1986; Wernerfelt, 1984). This dependence on resources severely limited the scope of the competency theory. How could content of competency of a routine be the same as that of the content of resources? Chandler (1992: 99) asked what 'the contents of routines developed to evaluate and capture new markets and move out of old ones' were. Reed and DeFillippi (1990) asked what causal linkages were noticed between strategic assets and competencies. Overall, resources, assets and organizational processes transformed understanding of competency, which was no longer determined by a behaviourally interacting structure.

A departure from the resources-perspectives based assets to assets that are formed through 'managerial and organizational processes' (Teece, Pisano and Shuen, 1997: 518; also Garvin, 1994) identified the path of inquiry established previously by Penrose (1968) and Simon (1961, 1991). The recognized processes were 'co-ordination/integration', 'learning', and 'reconfiguration and transformation'. Simon (1991) recognized a set of different processes though. Simon and Penrose emphasized authority-driven processes as well as those that go beyond behavioural learning. Sociological studies and organizational approaches (Mintzberg, 1979) identified this dependence of competence on processes inside a firm even earlier. Strategic assets thus could not be procured from the market (Teece and Pisano, 1994) and the processes transformed a market resource into an asset of strategic relevance, capable of making the dynamic capability of a firm. This theory also claims that these reconfigured or reinterpreted assets are of several types, such as 'technological assets', 'complementary assets', 'financial assets', 'reputational assets', 'structural assets', 'institutional assets' and 'market (structure) assets'. The dynamic capability theory named these assets as positions.

This recognition of the importance of processes could not, however, shift core competency and its routines from out of their 'embeddings' in the thesis of behavioural continuity. In fact, Nelson and Winter (2002) clearly noted the importance of process in the continuation of behaviours. Dutrenit (2000), Narduzzo, Rocco and Warglien (2000), Szulanski (2000), Tripsas and Gavetti (2000), Zander and Kogut (1995) and other have all drawn attention to processes that build learning and knowledge and transform assets into routines and core competencies. These theorists (Klepper, 1996; Mowery and Nelson, 1999) claim that processes are intertwined with both internal firm structure and systems and the external structure of industry or technology, and, that the relationship of this intertwined complex with the Schumpeterian industrial 'life cycle' implicates innovative behaviours as well as the behavioural continuity (Christensen, 1997; Shane, 2001). It follows that considerations on the structure of a firm could not be swept aside while looking into and emphasizing the importance of internal and non-structural processes.

Schumpeterian exogenous and apparently randomized signals cause behavioural responses and learning and make it possible for the firm to retain behavioural continuity. This, to the understanding here, is the major limitation of recent formulations of competency and routine. It seems to have underemphasized the differentiated places and roles of firm structure, inventive or speculative insights and different genres of knowledge.

Processes, inventive and speculative insights

Usher (1954, 1955) drew attention to three different types of actions: innate activities, acts of skill and inventive acts of insight. He studied inventions in mechanical artefacts and related capital formation to technical change understood in the light of such acts of inventions. Usher's argument rested largely on insights into Gestalt psychology on one hand and the century old experience on accreditation of individual acts of inventions on the other. The three divisions pointed out by Usher can be immediately observed in terms of their contemporary relevance, particularly their relevance to the critical issues raised here. One strand of objection could be that Usher studied inventive acts of individuals whereas contemporary society has largely relegated these individuals and substituted them by corporations. Schumpeter's departure from the early study (1934) on the individual entrepreneur to the later (1950) study on corporations as the site of innovative acts is often cited as the supporting argument. The Chandlerian paradigm has led to the belief in the virtues of largeness (Galambos, 1988; Hovenkamp, 1988). Several recent studies have, however, pointed out the failures of large size to cope with changes (Haveman, 1993) brought about particularly by Schumpeterian unanticipated technological or market changes (Orsenigo, 1995) or where largeness is a liability, or of even small or start-up firms diversifying (Bothner, n.d.). Nelson and Winter concede that 'in the quarter century after World War II, most readers of Schumpeter, ourselves included, believed that the regime supporting the large corporate R & D lab was the modern regime, while the individual entrepreneur with a new firm was largely a thing of the past. The history of the last few decades clearly indicates that the judgment was premature. Today, a number of industries are experiencing rapid technological advance where entrepreneurial start-ups whose innovations are based largely on the work of one or a few individuals play a prominent role and offer significant competitive threats to large firms' (Nelson and Winter 2002: 37).

Usher agrees that 'Novelty is to be found the more complex acts of skill, but it is of a lower order than at the level of invention' (1955: 43). 'Such acts of insight frequently emerge in the course of performing acts of skill, though characteristically the act of insight is induced by the conscious perception of an unsatisfactory gap in knowledge or mode of action' (*ibid*: 44). In differentiating between the three modes of the aforementioned actions, Usher points out that innate activities develop as 'responses to the structure of the organism', while acts of skill are based on all learned activities. 'Inventive acts of insight are unlearned activities that result in new organizations of prior knowledge and experience' (Usher, 1955: 46). Acts of skill occasionally exhibit spurts of insights, which are not the outcomes of learning reorganization such as are seen in higher orders, even involving theoretical reversals. He pointed out in his study on mechanical inventions that acts of insights involved four steps: perception of an unsatisfactory pattern, setting of the stage, primary act of insight and critical revision and development. Further, 'Entrepreneurs... invent new concepts of social ends and new procedures in social action. They discover new meanings in motivations and new modes of reconciling authority with individual freedom. But these acts of insight are dispersed through a highly diversified array of acts of skill' (Usher, 1955: 49). Acts of skill and acts of learning are important, involving often-higher capabilities though at higher levels 'Virtuosity in performance becomes an essential requirement' (*ibid*: 50).

Usher concludes his observations by pointing out that at higher levels, acts of skill and insights are not distinguishable. Banerjee (1997) argued on similar lines. It was argued that skilled engagement at the pure phenomenal level opens up the phenomenological strata of the object of engagement. The object then loses its external shapes and forms. At that level, skilled engagement, as an artist enjoying his or her work of art, generates unanticipated and unforeseen forms and modes of the previously known distinct object of skilled engagement. As argued earlier, this phenomenological level of engagement is purely private and words, when they are employed to express that flight of imagination (Bachelard, 1971; Banerjee and Richter, 2001), fail to express that state. That words cannot reach that ferment of imagination is, however, different from both Polanyi's (1962, 1966) understanding and the contemporary interpretations on what constitutes tacit knowledge. Tacit knowledge, as argued earlier, is wilful non-disclosure while the phenomenological imaginative ferment is beyond the ken of words. This ferment is private and is attained by few individuals who are masters of their skills. This is not a transcendentalist account. Moreover, this is a step forward from the accounts of Sternberg, O'Hara and Lubert (1997) and Simon (1979a) and differs from what was argued by Usher.

Contemporary theorists from several theoretical belief systems, especially those from the TCE account, have grounded their theory on this weak foundation of tacit knowledge and on the consequent asset specificities (Englander, 1988 and Williamson's reply, 1988). The trouble is not just with underemphasizing the role of technology, as Englander argues. Competency theorists, in particular those from evolutionary accounts, have in fact studied contributions of technology in very great detail. However, the contribution of technology has been framed under the phenomenon of learning, development of routines and in continuing with the behaviours. This continuity denies the scope to speculative inventions that, it is argued here, are drivers of innovations. The trouble with a large number of competency theorists is that they remained ensconced within the boundaries of production function approach to innovations, as proposed by Schumpeter in his *Business Cycles*. A change in the form of production function was understood as an innovation. This version of innovation, much different from the early Schumpeterian perspective, took into cognition only three 'simplifying assumptions' (Ruttan, 1959: 76): construction of new plants and equipment, introduction by new firms, and association with the rise to leadership by new men. The Schumpeterian definition rested on innovation process and an innovator, credit mechanism and drive for profit maximization. Ruttan remarked, 'neither Schumpeter nor the growth economists have given explicit attention to the *process* by which innovation – technological and organizational change – is generated' (Ruttan, 1959: 76; italics original).

Evolutionary theorists have recognized this process explicitly but unfortunately remained within the boundary set by Schumpeter. This boundary is set by the environment, by the ability to learn, by the ability to frame a 'routinized process' (a term used by Schumpeter) and the likes. Usher shares only certain similarity with this evolutionary perspective. Usher talked about a 'cumulative' process – an accumulation and a Gestaltic synthesis. Ruttan suggested that Usher had argued that such an innovation should be considered as an innovation. Acts of insights, according to Usher, do not emerge out of environmental or historical necessity. Instead, they emerge through sudden but conscious attempts at cumulative syntheses and do not result from learning or the competencies or accumulations of such knowledge.

The argument here is close to Usher's position though he depended on insights from the Gestalt theory. What is suggested here is a line of argument that borrows from Husserl, Bachelard, Sternberg, Simon and above all, Shackle. Here, innovation, including invention, is not so much a result of simple accumulation through stages: on the contrary, accumulation could often prove to be a burden. Innovation is speculative and brings in strategic surprise. Innovation here is necessarily out of disequilibria. An innovation is guided by the desire to bring about strategic surprise. Learning and cumulative knowledge, including memory (for example, organizational memory), cannot accordingly bring about strategic surprise. Learning must remain ensconced within the boundary allowed by co-ordination. Surprise is lost when co-ordination arranges an efficient arrangement. Much argument of the competency and evolutionist theorists hinges on this efficiency doctrine and its attainment through iterated generations of organizational and technological processes. Such generations alone can claim to have behavioural continuity. Co-ordination is definitely necessary to guide the behavioural continuity because only through co-ordination of norms or routines can continuity be maintained. It is argued that normative co-ordination is achieved through structural realignments and innovation is beyond the co-ordination of norms or routines.

The discussions on competency reveal a sense of unease amongst the theoreticians, reflected in their attempts to locate the site of competency: is it in structure or in the organizational processes? Is the site based on assets of several types? In Nelson and Winter one could locate an undifferentiated choice spectrum spanning over both structure and process. In Teece, Pisano and Shuen (1997), the choice was clearly in favour of processes that rested on several assets. To recall the earlier discussion, a structure is different from the organizational processes; the latter owes its existence to the undertaking of strategic moves. A structure also evolves but through strategic acts and not through strategic moves. Moreover, here the important constituents of structure are considered to include knowledge as wealth (a term synonymous with assets), knowledge employees and umbrella cover (that is, structural forms to which the present structure can adapt at almost no cost). Therefore, attempts were made first to implicate structure as resulting from strategy and secondly to implicate competency of structure to the latter's ability to transform or adapt itself to another structure. However, one tried to argue that this knowledge wealth is different from strategic knowledge, which is implicated in strategic moves. Strategic moves cause surprise, are uncoordinated and influence organizational processes of the incumbent firm and of other firms belonging to a strategic landscape. Organizational processes are warranted only when one is concerned about aspects of mobilizations, influences, subterfuges and such like that bring in strategic surprises. Strategic knowledge and associated competencies cannot be captured in the form of routines. Structural aspects, however, can refer to routines and competencies because these are resident on the organization.

This differentiation between strategic knowledge and knowledge wealth (the latter depending on the structural sort, the former depending on strategic moves) helped in better navigating the speculative dimensions of strategy and the surprise dimensions of innovations. This departure took strategy beyond the territory of co-ordination. Usher's reference to acts of insight is not resident on the organization but on the individual that impacts an organization and is close to strategic knowledge, as has been suggested here. Schumpeter's reference appears closer to structural aspects. It is, therefore, proposed that routines and competencies are viewed in the light of the earlier discussion on structural sorts and its constituent knowledge wealth. Schumpeter's early reference is, however, closer to strategic knowledge that, it may be recalled, embraces closely Shackle's ideas. Routines and competencies from the evolutionary perspective (or its variant, the dynamic perspective) can be better addressed through the lens of structural sort.

Resources and competency

Knowledge wealth, finance, knowledge employees, allies, and transitional structures described as umbrella cover are constituents of a structural sort in this account. Teece, Pisano and Shuen (1997) present a systemic account of dynamic competency based on three types, namely, processes, positions and paths. Processes, in terms of the earlier argument, may be disregarded. Paths, adumbrated under path dependencies, technological opportunities and such like, provide interpretative and hermeneutic dimension or the dimension of organizational memory as well as the limitations imposed by self-reference and reflexivity. Teece *et al.*'s second systemic component is a position that gets adumbrated under several types of assets, such as technological, financial, reputational, structural and such others. These position components are the typical assets described by others (Dierickx and Cool, 1989; Peteraf, 1993). These are simultaneously the resources as proposed by the resources theorist (Barney, 1991; Wernerfelt, 1984). Some resources theorists (Amit and Schoemaker, 1993; Prahalad and Hamel, 1990) included under these resources such types as skills and metaskills, competencies, strategic architecture and several other process capabilities. In comparison, Teece *et al.* have unambiguously differentiated between resources captured under assets belonging to positions and processes as well as paths. Teece *et al.*'s 'positions', however, are similar to the resource theorists' assets which are also closely similar to the argued position here regarding some constituents of the structural sort such as knowledge wealth, finance, knowledge employees, and allies.

Barney (1986) and Foss and Robertson (1999), and others, present a resources perspective of strategy wherein a firm competes for resources from a resources market in equilibrium. Barney's argument depends largely on this fact of equilibrium in the resources market, a critique of which is offered by Bromiley and Fleming (2002). Barney's assumptions regarding the equilibrium remain unclear and unsupportable though. He assumes resources to be untradable and the resources market at equilibrium. Barney's equilibrium apparently refers to the firm. Moreover, he restricts resources only to those that can raise 'efficiency and effectiveness' (1986). Barney (1991), however, accepts resources as those attributes of a firm that allow it to 'exploit opportunities or neutralize threats in its environment'. This second definition, however, positions resources as resulting from strategy. If resources are to be tangible, tradable and able to yield rents (Peteraf, 1993), equilibrium in the resources market might appear as an attractive ground. If, in contrast, resources are the outcomes of strategy and dependent on strategic purpose and environment, surely resources cannot be in equilibrium and should be treated as outcomes of organizational processes, as argued by Teece, Pisano and Shuen (1997). Bromiley and Fleming (2002) critique the resource theory's inability to specify those processes whose outcome can be considered as resources. Amit and Schoemaker (1993), while offering resources as tradable assets, simultaneously consider their internal generation (Galunic and Rodan, 1998) and their strategic upgradation through firm-internal recombinations (Henderson and Clark, 1990). Dierickx and Cool (1989) have hinted at this process view of tiers of resources in terms of flows and stocks.

First resources are necessarily procured from a market. There has to be, thus, a preliminary market of resources, which, however, need not be in equilibrium. Markets, it is further argued here, are predefined by the incumbent's strategy. Theorists of 'strategic groups' hinted at similar possibilities while limiting their speculations to similarity in performances alone as characterizing a local market. On the other hand, there are 'local maxima' (March, 1991) defined markets to which local equilibrium a firm, if displaced, would be unable to come back. White (1981, 2001) defines a market as limited by differentiated products and inimitable firm specializations. Distinct turfs otherwise share the so-called factor markets. It is argued here that the severalties in markets are further differentiated into strategic landscape or milieu-determined partial markets. Sociological studies have indicated how markets get fractured along managerial beliefs regarding who their peers are (Porac and Rosa, 1996). Burt and Carlton (1989) differentiated markets in structurally equivalent sections. Structural equivalence has been computed on measures of similarities in buying and selling from or with other sectors, for example. Bothner (n.d.) similarly identifies markets in terms of strategic relevance, especially regarding a firm's closest rivals, as defined in terms of patterns of transactions across market segments, geographies, technologies and such like.

A market is thus identifiable in terms of peers or closest rivals. This is very similar to the argument in this account regarding the strategic make-up of a market and the relevance of the strategic milieu in determining the market of resources that the incumbent firm draws upon. The resources market is identified, even if in local equilibrium, with the strategic milieu and hence the choice on strategy process made by an incumbent defines its market. Therefore, the first resources that this firm draws from the market are dependent on the firm's strategy. Corresponding to this first choice of strategy and consequent to the first choice on resources, a firm exhibits a first-order competency or simple competency (Banerjee, 2003d). The strategic milieu, it may be recalled, has four major types of constituent. Structural sorts of a firm reciprocate this strategic milieu. This implies that the first-order competency referred to is a component of the structural competency defined in the earlier chapter.

The incumbent firm thereafter, following resources acquisition, undertakes recombination of these resources to generate new quality resources internally. Obviously both the structure and the organizational processes influence the outcome of these second-order resources. The discussions in this chapter are limited to the structural variations. The incumbent firm has possibly honed its routine (Cohen *et al.*, 1996) or has learnt from its experience on effectiveness in recombining. Henderson and Clark (1990) have described these second-order resources as architectural resources. The arrival at the appropriate form of second-order resources (which again, are constituents of the structural sort) is dependent on another form of structural competence that is of a higher order compared to the simple competence. This is the second-order competence, which refers to the structural aspect of knowledge, defined in this account as knowledge wealth.

Knowledge wealth, however, has the freedom to be reflexive. Unlike the lower order competency determining first strategy, the architecture of resources and its corresponding second-order competency must refer to its own acts of recombination in the light of what Teece *et al.*, (1997) described as the 'path' or its history. The architecture, therefore, must reflect on the formal aspects of assets architecture. This reflexivity cannot, however, remain at the level of tangible (or even intangible) second-order architectural resources. It must, while reflecting on formal aspects shed its tangible attributes and appear as a resource of even higher order. This is described as the third-order resource, which does not have attributes and it is reflective knowledge. Knowledge wealth, discussed earlier, is the content of this reflexive practice and must be equivalent to decisions. This highest order of resources is being called the third-order resource and the competency of a firm structure that determines such an outcome, is the third-order competency, which can be considered as the core or the dynamic competency. Behavioural continuity, which Nelson and Winter constructed as the pillar of their argument, can be maintained only by a non-behavioural yet structural constituent – and this third-order competency fulfils that.

Structure and competency orders

Divisions in competencies are then the result of strategy. Strategy shapes up structural constituents that in turn influence the competencies of the firm. Strategy shapes up organizational processes as well though these processes contribute to the strategic knowledge alone. Strategic knowledge affects competencies of individuals and cannot be supervenient to the organization as a whole. Structure, in contrast, has knowledge wealth as one of its constituents and this knowledge wealth by being resident on the structure affects competencies more directly and succinctly. These competencies are thus structural competencies. The first-order transformation of resources bears the mark of idiosyncrasy. A firm alone can supply this idiosyncrasy (Chandler, 1992; Nelson, 1991), which gets reflected in structural principles and systems in directing resources combinations or shaping architectural knowledge (Henderson and Clark, 1990). It may also get reflected through invisible assets (Itami and Roehl, 1987) and routines to direct project staffing (Clark and Fujimoto, 1991) or the level of education attained by the firm employees (Leiponen, 2000). First order competency reflects simple organizing principles or first-order rules, as it were, along with the contents of organization. The content of a simple competency as a rule cannot be distinguished from the formal rule. Simple competency appears undifferentiated and the structure can reckon its strategic behavioural response as this competency. This response, simply put, is unable to differentiate between rule content and rule form. Hence, simple competency directly reflects the strategic behavioural responses to resources appropriation.

Nelson (1991) identified three aspects as an adequate description of a firm – strategy, structure and core capabilities. Nelson, following Chandler, identified the relationship between structure and strategy and yet fell short of ascribing causality to the strategy. In the present framework, strategy causes the structure. A cause is far more direct than a reason. Moreover, as it appears in Nelson, capability or the routine is an independent or quasi-independent entity. These three, namely strategy, structure and capability enjoy quasi independence and there is no implicating cause. It is, however, argued that strategy is the causal agent and, being so, implicates capability as well. Core capability, according to Nelson, is based on hierarchy of 'practiced organizational routines', which organize through 'higher order decision procedures' the practice of 'lower order' organizational skills. Lower and higher order rules (Chandler, 1990; March and Simon, 1958) are implicitly accepted. The higher order rule is warranted in the dynamic context faced by lower order rules. Grant (1996) describes a combination of input resources and knowledge in a 'hierarchy of integration'. Galunic and Rodan (1998) integrate the lower order 'highly specialized capabilities' into some form of 'higher order systems or clusters of resources' based on the previous work of Henderson and Clark (1990). Teece, Pisano and Shuen (1997) recognize higher order as the dynamic capability and implicate dynamic capability as the process response of current positions that are inscribed by the paths traversed by a firm. Leonard-Barton (1992) recognizes a higher order as the core capability. Core or dynamic capability has been variously described as a knowledge set that differentiates a firm from its competitors.

Strategic differentiation between firms, however, according to this account, takes place at the initial level. The response to a particular strategic milieu shapes the incumbent's choice of structural sorts that includes the incumbent's processes. The initial response is simple and differentiating. Higher order competencies differentiate the incumbent from not just the current strategic milieu but from potential strategic milieus as well. Higher order competencies thus necessarily refer to less and less of the content of structure and this abstraction alone, it is argued, can render competencies a core or the dynamic profile. Leonard-Barton (1992), in contrast, argues that core capability has a content embodied in employee knowledge and skills, technical systems, managerial systems and values and norms.

A simple competency, as defined earlier, can respond to a particular environment or is milieu-specific. A firm having responded to the current context through a set of simple competencies would now be asked to respond to a potential environment. This new environment demands that a firm gather up second-order competency that alone can attempt a recombination of knowledge acquired on its own past performances. This is what Teece and Pisano (1994) describe as the path. In the first order, a rule and its content were inseparable while in the second-order competency, only the abstract contents are retained. Abstract contents cannot be tangible resources but must remain tied to concrete resources, as attributes remain tied to concrete-notions. Scholars have often equated this type of competency to the problem-solving activities undertaken by a firm. Iansiti and Clark (1994) frame the 'knowledge base' of a firm in the context of its problem-solving activities. Dosi and Marengo (1994) too recognize that problem-solving cannot be reduced to simple information gathering and processing. Since this abstraction grapples with problem-solving, the second-order competency cannot be free of tangible content or of a strategic context. It must have an intermediate status. It cannot surely be free to undertake speculative and imaginative acts of insights and its strategic innovations must remain tied to the problem-solving context. The second-order competence can thus have an abstract content of resources that are undifferentiated from formal aspects of routines.

A core competency is, however, a pure rule devoid even of abstract resources. Core competency or third-order competency that enables a firm to be a creative innovator looks for potential and imagined or speculated strategic milieus. The incumbent firm generates this milieu that is often observed as market creation. Such a milieu cannot be extrapolated from the current strategic milieu through linear extension. Problem-solving necessarily remains tied up with generating higher efficiencies. Second-order competency thus refers to efficiency of strategic acts. The third-order competency looks beyond this immediacy of context. It creates its own strategic milieu where it can set novel rules of game. A second-order competency is still about resources that are abstract and yet undifferentiated from the formal properties of routines. In order to overcome context dependency, second-order competency must be reflexive and must be guided by logic or by a set of decision rules.

Third-order or core competency is a set of pure decision rules (March and Simon, 1958). Such decision rules alert a firm to the potential changes in the environment or to the potential in the milieu that this incumbent can create. These formal rules allow the incumbent to switch its ensemble of second-order competencies. Simple competency referred to constituents of structural sorts such as finance, knowledge employees and allies; second-order competencies referred to the reasons through which these first-order assets enrich another structural constituent, namely 'knowledge wealth'. Third-order competency refers to the reflexive reasons and speculative imaginations through which knowledge wealth can generate several novel umbrella covers or structural possibilities that the incumbent might assume. An umbrella cover is both a ploy for defence against strategic attacks and a structural form that can assume novel attacks. The structural transition is the reflection on strategy. The third-order competency in the form of formal routine enables a firm to design second-order competencies in such a manner as to demand the lowest structural transition or switching cost. All these three types of competencies are structural and refer to several layers of relations and interdependence between the constituents of a structural sort. Simple competency refers to the interdependence between knowledge employees, finance and strategic allies. Second-order competency refers to the relation between the wealth or assets to the knowledge wealth, another constituent of the structural sort. Finally, the third-order competency is derived from the relation between knowledge wealth and the umbrella cover. It is argued that these competencies are structurally derived.

Nelson (1991) and March and Simon (1958) seem to characterize a core competency as decision rules without a content. In contrast, an ordinary competence has decisions or rules loaded with contents. Typically such contents are either resource procured from the market such as manpower, or resources-architecture, such as the system of skill enhancement. A training system or a system to deploy or identify skills are examples of such rules built upon resources. This training system takes care of problem-solving and is built on the edifice of the accumulated stock of knowledge. Even so, the third-order competency reflexively indulges in acts of insight and takes its departure from the learning-based behaviourally adaptive route. This route spoke of path dependency. The third-order competency is absolutely free from reference to history, path or strategic milieu. This competency is proactively seeking to establish its own strategic milieu. The ease with which a structure can switch over to a potential and speculatively attractive structural sort and a corresponding strategy is determined by this third-order competency. A typical skills organization or a typical training system reflecting simple competency of a firm indeed is a knowledge resource. Changes in current competition or present demands ask the firm to reconfigure the architecture of such a knowledge base. The current strategic environment makes demands on the incumbent to reconfigure simple competencies. The possible future market, however, asks for highest free-wheeling competencies that can, with ease, transform the present structure. This highest competence is the core competence and it is akin to pure rules or decisions capabilities.

Structural competency: managing demand

The decision problem of a typical Indian software firm regarding whether it should develop a product or deliver sophisticated project solutions, is, however, not derived from considerations of these three structural competencies. This decision is riveted to the problem of demand management. Demand management is a novel idea. The structural transition of a software firm, it is argued, takes place in response to the possibility or potentiality of management of demands. Explanation on competencies, as provided in the received literature, neglects the demand aspect altogether. Competency in their reckoning is purely internal. In fact, software production is not much characterized by the stage of development (Tessler and Barr, 1997), as exhibited in a typical manufacturing-based production process. A manufacturing set-up learns significantly through mastering the 'process' (Utterback and Abernathy, 1975). New product development practices in manufacturing (Balbontin *et al.*, 2000) depend on the learning from process and these are reflected in reduction of lead time and other similar parameters of production. There is, therefore, a positive relation between the age of the firm and its launching of new products. Product conceptualization (Orihata and Watanabe, 2000a, 2000b), however, has the potential of innovating new products. A conceptual development takes a leap, based on insights and on speculations regarding the manifold of demand management.

The discussion here should integrate aspects of demand management with the structurally derived aspects of competency. Demand in IS/IT (information system, information technology) is manifold. The two major divisions in demand are product, and process or custom solutions. Further subdivisions, such as in the product 'Windows', represent a generic platform product while off-the-shelf retail applications are generated products (often dependent on the choice of product platform) (see *Journal of Economic Perspectives*, 2001 Issue). The market for process solutions is very large. Over the years, there has been an upward shift and corporates are moving more towards the custom-built software solutions space. A major part of this market is based on what gets outsourced (Lacity and Willcocks, 2001). Lacity and Willcocks (2000: 18) found that information activities that lean towards infrastructure and technology space (such as, disaster recovery, client/server and PCs, mainframe, networks, help desk, etc.) are outsourced oftener than what is core and internal to the organizational processes (such as systems analysis, systems design, systems architecture, procurement, IT strategy). The latter tend to remain internally sourced.

Sauer and Willcocks (2002) point out that such divisions often lead to a 'patchwork' of point solutions that is more flexible than a fragmented technology platform but suffers still from inflexibilities. 'Organizational architect' is the term used by Sauer and Willcocks to capture organizational capability that allows the firm to respond immediately to unpredictable changes in the environment. 'The organizational architect has to balance between sticking with a reactive approach based on technology that becomes increasingly complex and inflexible and riding the risk-return potential of a new platform' (Sauer and Willcocks, 2002: 48). An active 'architecture' is then required to maintain consistency in business (Earl and Fenny, 2000). A dependent strategy (such as on ERP) on activation of architecture through updated supplies from vendor, however, proves inflexible to structural switching. What has been described here as the structural switching (or the umbrella cover) has been captured in this vision as activated architecture, which is based on custom-built consistent and flexible infrastructure. Literature on strategy, structure, processes and technology (Boynton and Victor, 1991; Hsiao and Ormerod, 1998; Miles and Snow, 1984, 1992; Scott-Morton, 1991; Yetton, Johnson and Craig, 1994) has broadly agreed on the strangeness of IS-based or IS-driven organizational transitions. This strangeness follows from the fact that while in ordinary organizational transformations the change agent and the changed organization are distinct, temporally sequential and causally related, in IS-related organizational transformation, temporal sequence, causal order and the distinct separation between these two become elusive.

This mode is strange because information is pervasive over organizational structure and processes. No transaction can be conceived without transactions in information. Technology for the business is represented in the structure, processes, systems and embodied artifacts of an organization. Technology for information is represented in information systems, documentation and the IS/IT. These two technologies cannot surely remain distinct and separate. Change in one would demand corresponding change in the other. Such changes are represented through speech acts and through several contemporary approaches to change management. Little of such inseparable and indistinct co relation between the two modes of technologies can thus be logically and physically separated in different embodied media. However, each technology in its abstract aspects, such as in the algorithmic aspects or in computability aspects, is driven by a discipline-internal dynamism. A single firm cannot specialize in all conceivable disciplines. A firm would necessarily depend on a supplier who has specialized in the respective component technology. It follows then that a firm cannot distinguish between changes in information and changes in business, and a firm must receive the fillip to organizational transformation from information-specialist firms with whom the incumbent firm must remain in dynamic structural co-ordination.

Earlier, when technologies were thought to be separate, as with a capital goods manufacturer who could treat its technology in separation from the organizational processes of a customer, a firm could adopt arms-length transactions as in auctions. The inseparability between the dynamics of IT and that of organizational IS implies that auctions be replaced by interdependence and co-ordination. This co-ordination is remarkably different from what Clower and Leijonhufvud (1975), Krafft and Ravix (2000), Leijonhufvud (1968), Loasby (1994), Richardson (1960) and others have argued. Co-ordination in this received literature refers to firms that are competitors and belong to the same industrial sector. Another extant literature on strategic alliance, also from game-theoretic IO, refers to co-ordination between firms that specialize in complementary sectors, for example. IS-related changes refer to co-ordination not just between complementing, substituting or competing firms but more precisely between two firms that are jointly producing a demand.

Joint production of demand implies that the software firm is no longer simply a supplier and the business firm no longer a customer. Co-ordination in the received literature recognized interdependence between suppliers and customers and this literature discussed strategic leverage through vertical integration in the event co-ordination transactions prove costlier to govern. Large corporations had emerged between the late nineteenth and late twentieth centuries, this theory argues, to economize on these transaction costs of governance and thus to leverage vertical integration. What this argument failed to distinguish is that leveraging could prove feasible only when the entities being integrated had been distinct both before and following the integration. Marketing thus remained a distinct department or a function in a vertically-integrated corporation. Departments, strategic business units (SBUs) and such others retained a quasi-distinct status even after their integration. This quasi-autonomous status (Williamson, 1990a) alone could guarantee the economy achieved in a vertical integration.

The argument in this account is that joint production of demand by a software solutions provider and its customer would remain elusive and unachieved if vertical integration has taken place under the common authority. The vertical integration literature forgets to mention the supreme importance of joint authority that must logically remain distinct and separate from entities that are getting integrated. Simon recognized its importance and repeatedly harped on this theme. A joint commanding authority in a vertically-integrated corporation commands co-ordination while remaining – and this it must – independent of both co-ordination and the entities being co-ordinated. However, IS-related dynamics cannot leave the authority as an outsider to the changes. On the contrary, it is precisely the authorities (as the principal constituent of the structural sort) that must first change. The joint production of demand implies that authority and, subsequently, other constituents of the customer's structural sort undergoes transformations that are in tandem with the changes in the supplier's structural sort that includes the authority of the supplier. If a customer and supplier get integrated (even horizontally), the agency for change has to be sought out either in the environment or in an authority that stands as the causal agency outside the changes. The first type of change initiated by the necessity for alignment with the environment has spawned a large literature around the strategic fit. Authority-driven change is typically exhibited by commonly observed corporate transformations.

Demand management is achieved, therefore, through a structural trans-formation of the customer corporate first and then reciprocally of the solutions provider software firm. It is strange that this demand is generated by the dynamics of interdependence between two structures. These aspects are captured excellently in this structural sort framework and its dependence on the incumbent's strategy. The umbrella cover is the residence of the third type of competency and it represents, as a structural constituent, the ease with which a structure can switch over its form. To recall, a structure results from the strategy or, in other words, a structure is not given a priori but evolves from the incumbent's strategy to influence the structural sorts of all the firms in its strategic milieu. The structure instead of being given a priori is an interdependent or co-ordinated outcome. The umbrella cover being a constituent of this structure is thus an outcome of co-ordinated interplay of strategy as well.

Demand management is thus a particular strategic device. Through demand management, a software solutions and services provider strategically influences and co-ordinates the structural outcome of its customer, ordinarily a large corporation. In the course of this co-ordination, the structural sort of the supplier too is transformed. Demand management is such a strategic device that transforms the structural sorts of both the supplier and the customer. This management happens through the interaction of two structures and is the result of strategic interdependence. To recall, the umbrella cover is the residence of core competency or the third type of competency. The changes in structural sorts appear as the umbrella cover. Demand management offers two striking aspects: (1) demand can be generated only by structural changes and can be managed only interactively and through mutual co-ordination; and (2) co-ordination of structural changes cannot lead to vertical integration because the demand that is being managed is not given beforehand. Instead, this demand gets speculatively generated, and bringing the supplier under the same authority as of the customer would destroy the scope on speculative changes in structures.

It follows that structural competency is a product of the abilities of two parties, customer and supplier, to conform and to co-ordinate changes in structural sorts. Structural competency is, therefore, not internal to an organization. It results from the management of possible and future demands. The second point that follows then is that typically co-ordination implies – as observed by Shackle – a loss in surprise and a loss of speculation. According to this understanding, co-ordination often results in vertical integration. If the futures and the speculative moves were to be co-ordinated, however, a vertical integration would prove negative. The parties, it is argued, therefore remain quasi-autonomous, tied together through severalties of relational contracts that take into account possibilities and futures. They thus keep changing or switching respective structural sorts in dynamic co-ordination with each other. Another important feature of demand management is that in order to keep structural sorts in dynamic co-ordination, the parties must exchange a new type of information. Richardson (1972) talked about exchange of only two types of information, namely, on structural aspects of the current market and on technology. However, it is argued here that the parties must exchange information on their respective current organizational structural sorts and their present strategic moves on structural transformation. This present move by customer would be followed by a possible structural move in the immediate future that would depend on the present outcome at the customer's end and the possible structural moves in the customer organization. The exchange of such structural information constitutes a new type of information for co-ordination.

Products, services and structural competencies

Structural competency, as proposed in the earlier discussion, is sharply different from several competing theories on competency. Kern and Wilcocks (2000) drew out a comparative chart on the relationship between customer and supplier in IS/IT. None from a set of researches appeared to have developed upon contractual relations. Kern and Wilcocks develop a customer–client interaction framework that recognizes the importance of context, contract and structure. The context they refer to is the path and objectives and expectations. This context formulates the relational contract (Macneil, 1985), which in turn influences structure of interactions between the two parties. This perspective too then falls short of the expected. This does not get into structural changes as shaped by futuristic and relational contracts and by moves on demand management. Other approaches taking into account structural changes in the context of strategy, technology, management processes and individuals (with their roles and skills) either took a static view (Scott-Morton, 1991) or considered a limited dynamics (Yetton, Johnson and Craig, 1994). Sauer (1997) extended this latter approach and analysed the strategy dynamics in terms of new competencies (built up but different from the old) developed bottom up from available management processes and individuals with their roles and skills and through technology. This new competency demands repositioning of strategy and structure. In this model then, the historical path, intra-organizational negotiations and learning (as in evolutionary models) prove crucial. All intra-organizational issues, although influenced by the supplier and such like, retain their independence. Strategic milieu, speculative demand management and structural interactions cannot be incorporated even in this model.

Iansiti and Clark (1994) followed Dosi and Marengo (1994) by emphasizing the problem-solving dimension of routines. Iansiti and Clark defined dynamic performance in terms of consistency of achievement of positive performance by an organization. Capability, they argued, could be measured by this perfor-mance, which depends on consistency in performance, consistent improvement, external integration through dynamic sampling of external information sources and through internal integration of this information with the skills and systems. In this model and in some previous models (Clark and Fujimoto, 1991) on product development several modes of integration, such as customer integration and technology integration, took care of some structural aspects, some aspects of demand and aspects of internal processes. Competency, accordingly, has been conceived as internally generated while external information remains as input. Strategy and speculative moves, particularly structural switching in correspondence with demand management, have little relevance in these models. Miles and Snow (1992) conceptualized a network of organizations dynamically allocating the risks though the competence of an organization in that network that is structurally interacting remained outside the scope of that model. Leiponen (2000) measured competency based on first-order resources, such as educational backgrounds. Henderson and Cockburn (1994) utilized data on patenting by an organization to relate with the organizational measures undertaken towards the enhancement of publications that was accepted as a measure of competence. Ichinowski *et al.* (1997) emphasized complementarities amongst organizational practices or structural elements that raise competency. Such perspectives harp on measurement of competency at several levels of an organization.

One crucial difference as pointed out earlier appears to be the insistence on product (or project execution) related competence. This approach, based on the initial formulation by Utterback and Abernathy (1975), cannot recognize the aspects of demand management in particular as it is derived from structural interactions. In software-related services or solutions, an absence of product is remarkable. A product, even while based on sampled information from prospective customers as in Iansiti and Clark (1994), fails to derive demand from changes in structural sorts brought through mutual interactions and through mutually sustained structural switching. A service in contrast is suited to that objective. In other words, a software services or solutions provider can engage in speculative destabilization of its customer's structure. The supplier aligns with selective constituents of the structural sorts of the customer and aggrandizes the possibilities of further structural switching. Each service is individual in lieu of standardized products and draws upon a specific strategic milieu. A product, such as available on ERP, addresses a global milieu of operations. An operational level that also strives to be independent of strategic and technological milieu seems to be non-existent. In contrast to the strategy based on the mass marketing of a product, a software service hones a specific local strategic context and destabilizes the existing structural orders of a particular strategic milieu. By doing this, a software service achieves its future market as well.

Even so, a product concept is dependent more on institutional inducement (Orihata and Watanabe, 2000a) than on the particular experience learned by a firm. Heeks (1998), for example, following the product paradigm approach has argued that a software product adds more value while a project adds less value. Such a belief in the product superiority is borrowed from the

Fordistic paradigm. A product might promise a platform of products (Muffatto and Roveda, 2000), several upgrades as in most ERP products, or a champion product as such Microsoft. Software solutions developed on high technology offer a similar advantage to their users on several counts. Further, a service requires very little capital cost. Most of the cost of a service is on current manpower and hence a start-up software firm with product concepts or with high skills and knowledge of the domain can supply high-quality, low-cost projects with the least lead time, supported only by cash flow. A project then is technologically attractive and prima facie ensures the same return on investment as would be provided by a product. The depiction of the Indian software scenario in terms of providers of simple services (Arora *et al.*, 2001) would thus amount to simplification and possible under-representation.

A typical software product defies the logic of scale economy. Copying a product costs virtually nothing and the marginal theory breaks down in this instance. However, a copied product cannot offer custom-specific features and once such features are added to an existing product, there is no longer any difference between a product and a solution. The potential brand-name build-up and possibilities of market-making induce a product to generate firm competence in brand building and market making. In contrast, a project-based firm would remain satisfied with a reputation that it has novel generic competence. Further, a product-based firm is very reactive and seeks cover under a very strict intellectual property rights regime. It must seek to protect its current financial investment. This reactive nature makes a product firm resist changes in a strategic milieu. A milieu, it may be recalled, takes care of the structural sorts of firms that are strategically tied through such objects as an existing and dominant product. A supplier strategy must strive to destabilize the dominance of this product. The protection previously secured through copyrights and now replaced largely (as in the USA) by patents rights, acts as a barrier to strategic innovations. Instances of this reactive stance are plentiful in the drugs and pharmaceuticals business. In the USA, software patents have now offered a typical product firm such barriers to strategic moves.

Product strategy resists changes. Building a product requires comparatively large capital investment, especially in the marketing of the product. Switching from a one-product platform to another not only requires a large capital base but, as argued by Drucker (1988), a new organizational set-up. Switching a structure, which is the key to demand management and to the innovations in strategy, becomes difficult for a firm that has remained strongly committed to a dominant or champion product. Moreover, a product can bring about changes that are fewer and insignificant compared to the changes that custom software solutions can bring about in the customer firm. A typical product cares for global strategy. A concurrently developed product cares less for such a global strategy. The global strategy of a product fails to attend to strategic niceties in the customer firm. Finally, without the support of venture funding or of the IPO, it is nearly impossible for a start-up software firm to launch products. Entrepreneurs suffused with product ideas but not supported by an IPO or venture market are then often forced to supply high-technology projects. The conclusion here is that a services or solutions strategy is more pointed, of least cost and more effective. Indian software firms have adopted the services and solutions track. Few Indian firms offer products. This absence of a strong strategy on product cannot then be described as weak.

Another point that must not be overlooked in this regard is that structural competence as argued above is derived from interactions between the structural sorts of both the customer and the supplier. The structural switching in the customer, it has been observed, affects structural switching in the supplier. The competence to switch structure is co-ordinated between the customer and the supplier. Further, from the above argument it appears that the product strategy inhibits structural switching in both the supplier and the customer. It follows then that supplier's competence to switch structure is a reflection of both the customer's competence in structural switching and supplier's competence in switching between proto-products and services or solutions. A proto-product is defined here as a non-dominant product with a non-global market and a short life cycle. A proto-product is specific to a particular strategic milieu. An Indian software firm suffers from the dilemma regarding the types of competencies it should build up. Should its goal be product competence or services competence? Or, should it follow a common competence which would allow switching from existing solutions-competence to a proto-product competence at the least cost?

Software firm managers, it may be recalled from our discussion in the earlier chapter, indicated that they often referred to a set of competencies, and these are 'domain thrust competence', 'domain knowledge competence', 'product competence' and 'project competence'. These competencies are the second-order competencies because they refer to the capability in utilizing knowledge or resources architecture to improve upon dynamic performances. A typical software firm operates its business in accordance with these systems of knowledge bases. A domain refers to a knowledge specialization. Examples of domain could be an expertise in banking software or in insurance software. A domain might as well refer to a skill. Sometimes a domain refers to a pattern of market demand. Domain competence refers to the ability to continue with a behavioural response pattern that a firm displays to its environment. This is the first type of competence.

The next type is the domain thrust competence. This competence is about a firm's decision to deploy the generic competence of its employees that they picked up in the firm on development of products or services belonging to a domain. Providing formal training in a domain can provide domain thrust competence. This provides a generic capability. A firm insisting on domain thrust thus adds generic internal knowledge resources in the area of a domain over and above what domain resources this firm secured from the market. Domain thrust competence is not a simple combination of resources. It is a second-order competence developed through the internal generation of resources although it behaves as a first-order simple competence because the internally generated resources are organized in a certain architecture by this competence.

Contrastingly, the third type, namely the domain knowledge competence, does not represent the generation of resources inside the firm. It reflects upon the choice made by a firm and the general states of affairs in the market as well. The general states of affairs raise the profiles of commonly available technical knowledge and that of the profiles of experiences in domains. Domain knowledge competence represents the extent of experience that higher degree holders have compared to the total experience of all the personnel of the firm. This is a quality of the structural sort. It represents the quality of knowledge employees that is a constituent of the structural sort. Domain knowledge competence thus represents the deliberate choice of a firm in procuring resources from the market. It is, therefore, a simple first-order competence. Both domain competence and the domain knowledge competence are simple first-order competence of a firm's structure. The domain thrust competence is a second-order competence since it is derived and is a structural competence as well. These competencies reflect the extent to which resources of a firm are organized around achieving superiority in product or services. A simple structure allows a firm to employ both first-order simple organization of resources and second-order architecture of such organizations of resources. It follows then, as argued earlier, that there must be a competency higher than even the second order, which organizes both these first and second-order competencies together. This third-order is the core competency.

The differences between competencies to provide products and services are thin indeed. Strong domain competencies enable a firm to switch from a service to product or vice versa with little additional effort. A firm dependent primarily upon first-order simple competency will, however, find it difficult. It has little flexibility. It can transform its structure along only one dimension – that of the simple resources. Consequently, this firm will be constrained to switch its own structure as well as the structure of its customer. It will be rather rigid, failing to manage demand. Such a firm will have to first organize the first-order resources as architecture. A combination of architectures of resources that provide this firm with a second-order competency allows it to enjoy two degrees of freedom: along simple resources and along architectures of resources. Along one dimension of structural change, this firm can recombine simple resources while retaining the old order of architectures. On the other dimension of structural change, this firm can retain proportions of simple resources as constant while changing the architectures. Hence a domain thrust competency enjoys two degrees of structural change.

The fourth type of competency, previously discussed, is about rules and abstract resources. Domain competence is about contents. This is of the first order and has only one degree of freedom. The domain thrust competence is about architectures of resources. It has simple rules about the content as architecture and has two degrees of freedom. The fourth type of competency does not refer to any content: it refers to the qualities of content. It is a set of rules about abstract contents. It thus enjoys three degrees of freedom and can direct the organization of resources towards restructuring. Or, it can seek a reorganization of architectures of resources for bringing about structural switching in the second dimension. Finally, on the third dimension, it can redirect quality of resources, such as knowledge, towards structural switching. This fourth type of competence is thus the most versatile and most potent. It can bring about structural switching in the most significant manner and with the maximum ease. It has been observed that barriers between product competencies and services competencies are thin and can be broken. The ease with which a firm can cross this barrier would thus indicate the degree of competency the firm enjoys. The fourth type of competency will afford maximum ease of switching while the least ease will be observed in the case of simple competency. Moreover, the ease of switching refers to the structural changes of both the supplier and consequently of the customer. If the structural changes in the customer cannot be observed, this switching coefficient of the supplier would be an indicator of the switching ease of the customer.

The products–services basket

Software firms in India are mostly start-ups. These young firms cannot provide time-series data and being small they often do not maintain detailed databases either. This account, thus, had to depend on long interviews eliciting mostly qualitative data. Also, because these firms are mostly privately held, the accounting data on their operations is not public. The internal resources of these firms are often widely divergent and classifying such resources under a few types has proved difficult. Qualitative data has thus been the primary wherewithal here. As indicated earlier, there were two rounds of investigations, first in 1999 and second in 2001–02. During the second round, diverse inquiries were solicited with several questionnaires. The examples of several such small and medium-sized software firms will be discussed in two parts. The first will be a narrative on thirteen firms drawn from the second round of the survey that will observe their products–services mix. The second part will take up seven firms from the first round of survey and preliminary observations will be made on their competencies, including the switching competence.

Narrative on thirteen firms

These firms are representative, as it were, of the structure of the Indian software sector. Two firms are large (size with reference to number of employees: large with more than 1000, small with less than 100 and medium in between with around 250), six are medium but close to being small and the rest are small. Most firms began operations during the last two to five or six years. The manpower profiles of these firms, indicative of the resources that they command, are rather impressive. A good number of these firms have employees with highest degrees in computer sciences or engineering or in related areas. Only four out of these thirteen firms derive most of their revenue from the domestic market operations. The others derive nearly the entire revenue from export.

It is strange indeed that most small or medium-sized firms that are very close to being small offer products along with providing services. All such firms, however, simultaneously offer services and solutions. Two large firms have products though little of their revenue, or little of their marketing resources or even software writing resources, is spent on products. These firms provided us with data on man-days spent and numbers of products developed and services projects accomplished. Man-days spent indicate apportionment of simple resources. A good number of these small firms spent about 55 per cent of such resources on services and the remaining 45 per cent on product development. To recall the discussion in the preceding chapter, most firms could not spend other resources, particularly marketing resources, on development of a market for their products that could match their investment in product development. It appeared that a firm took up product development more often as a supplementary act (an act that sustains the principal revenue-generating occupation). Product development enables a firm to generate a technological or knowledge platform that, being generic, helps the firm to support crucial high-end application development services. A strategy secured to product alone or product as the principal revenue earner, however, is limited.

A firm, earning principally from services while also earning or expected to earn marginally from subsidiary products, is helped in enhancing its technology profile by resources investment in developing supplementary products. Several small firms adopt this strategy because they lack the wherewithal to support large investment of man-days in the development of products. Five small firms out of this group and one medium-sized firm have invested resources in product development (Table 5.1). Firm '5' is medium-sized and employs only 200 people and hence may be considered as close to being small. A simple ratio of average man-days spent on development of a product to that spent on average service project appears to be a good indicator of structural capability to switch across from projects through intermediate differentiated products. The structural competence to switch from product to services and vice versa, however, may be considered to be somewhat different. One is interested here in observing the structural competence of a firm to switch across projects that demand different types of simple resources or different architectures of resources. These

Table 5.1 Supplementing services by product in six firms

Firm	Average man-days on a product dev.	Average man-days spent on a project	*Rev. from champion prod. In F.E. %	Rev. from champion prod. In Rupees %	Rev. other prod. In F.E. %	Rev. other prod. In Rupees %	Rev services in F.E. %	Rev services in Rupees %	Yrs in op.	Strategy
1	2000	700			45	20	55		6	1
2	600	800		50			16	80	2	3
3	4000	2000	16		47		53	18	4	2
4	2500	2000	10		1		89		8	4
5	40,000	750					14	86	8	4
6	250	250							5	3

* All the percentages of revenue refer to total revenue earning by the firm in year 2000–01.

Strategy: 1 = High end application services development; 2 = New product; 3 = Business consulting; 4 = Others including acquisition.

resources, needless to mention, include technological knowledge and knowledge employees.

The ratio between average man-days spent on development of a product to that on a service, shows that firm '5' stands out. It claimed five champion products and had of late spent most of its resources on development of two products. Over the past years it had supplied 35 service solutions, each consuming a meagre 750 man-days on an average. The entire revenue of this firm, of which 89 per cent is from services, 10 per cent from champion products and only 1 per cent from other products, is from the global market. An insignificant fraction of the available resources have been spent by firm '5' on services, indicating the possibility that its products continued to provide it with a dynamic knowledge or resources platform that could always minimize the specific resources devoted to any particular service project. This is a *'service-product-service'* strategy. This strategy has an advantage in addition to overcoming limitations imposed by paucity of resources that this firm could not muster for marketing of its products. Switching across services (demanded most often by a group of firms, sometimes even a few firms) implies that each service catered to a particular structural demand of its customer and this service in turn generates the next demand for structural change (and hence the next service solution). In short, this is an interesting mode of managing demand. Moreover, internal to firm '5', each service offered is a continuation over a dynamic platform of knowledge, embedded succinctly in a few champion and other products. It follows that this firm can keep dynamically switching its resources architectures that are mounted over and reflected in its product platform.

The ratio values of the other five firms in Table 5.1 have remained scattered in a range. Firms '3' and '6' are very small, employing 20 and 32 people respectively. The rest employ between 50 to 80 people. Strangely enough, notwithstanding the comparatively smaller man-days spent on products vis-à-vis services, most of these small firms earned a fairly large portion of their revenue from products. Firm '3' earned as much as 68 per cent out of its revenue selling the products, of which 50 per cent is from the domestic market. It has one champion product and three other products. Firm '4' earned nearly half its revenue from selling its product in the global market and in doing so it spent about 60 per cent of its marketing resources. Similarly, firm '1' earned nearly half of its revenue by selling its other products in the global market. The revenue of most of these firms was small and hence the small earning through sale of products appears as a significant fraction of its total earning. However, it may be noted that unlike other firms, firm '3' has a product strategy. Other firms have either a strategy for moving into consulting or into increased expertise in certain knowledge or domain.

All firms, except '3', earned more than half of their revenue from services. However, in contrast to firm '5', none had a dominant investment in product. Possibly these firms pursue their services somewhat independently of their product platforms. Firm '5' followed a strategy of investing heavily in the intermediate knowledge platform (of products), while other firms have followed such resources architectures as enable offering succession of services projects. Resources demand more than an ensemble of product knowledge might be able to offer. These firms switch across services projects through meta-products often without the intermediation of the reigning product platform. This strategy may be likened to '*service…[product]…service*'. The intermediation by product is definitely under-emphasized in this latter case. Correspondingly, structural switching in this latter case is necessarily simpler. In the case of firm '5', such a switching necessarily involves the architecture of resources while in the latter cases a switching might get accomplished, even sometimes through rearrangement of simple resources.

Narrative on seven firms

The seven firms studied in the first survey of 1999 revealed another dimension of structural competence in switching (Banerjee, 2003c, 2003d). Of these, professors in computer sciences with little initial capital established the first firm, *Soft1*. Over last two years it has undertaken several projects in high-tech software with very good cash flows. The employees are active in research, publish a lot and frequently travel to destinations in the USA. *Soft1* does not have any plan to launch a product immediately. The next firm, *Soft2*, launched in 1990 by professionals from computer engineering, management and accountancy backgrounds started with supplying software solutions to both domestic and US firms. In general, it does not work on high-technology software solutions and suffers from chronic capital deficiency that limits development of products. A software engineer launched the next firm, *Soft3*, in 1990 to develop a product that was not novel to the global market. Two large global firms had launched in domestic market their products meant for large manufacturing firms. *Soft3* targeted medium-sized enterprises in the domestic market with a low-priced product. Services in software, however, remained its principal revenue earner and provided the knowledge platform based on which its product development could progress. A few software professionals launched *Soft4* in 1988 to support global demands on services. The revenue earning through services has remained lucrative and senior managers do not plan to take up development of products.

Professionals from software and advertising launched the next firm, *Soft5*, in 1992. The entrepreneurs knew about multimedia and the potential of portals. By developing sundry products for the mass consumer market alongside supplying low-technology software projects, it could maintain its revenue-earning potential in a balanced and growing direction. Two associates, from the software profession and from finance, launched the next firm, *Soft6* in 1997. Software professionals had a few special skills and could understand potential market demands, and a product platform could be launched with this small employee base. Constraints on capital forced this firm to the high-technology end of software services. Two young computer scientists and one financial specialist launched firm *Soft7* in 1998, to supply to the domestic market product platform in the area of social applications of computing. Small and differentiated market, flooded with branded products from global large firms, forced *Soft7* to simultaneously deliver software projects to clients in India and abroad. Cash flow has remained a problem for it.

It is worthwhile to consider the values of four competencies (mentioned earlier) of these seven firms through an analysis of *Domain Thrust* (DT). This is the ratio of training received by a weighted number of a firm's employees either on a job or through formal training over the past year in the area of 'domain knowledge', divided by the number of employees who received training on a job or formally over the past year in all the thrust areas. These would include advanced programming, project management, prototype and such like. DT is derived from the architecture of resources and captures the relative thrust accorded to domain knowledge in both the jobs undertaken and in formal training. It is a second-order competency reflecting the direction and dynamism of knowledge upgradation. The next measure of competency, described above, is *Domain Knowledge* (DK). It is derived from a simple first-order combination of resources. Recombination takes into account the quality of manpower, such as educational achievements and experiences. DK is the ratio between the 'product of the number of employees having degrees (bachelor, master, or doctorate) in engineering with their respective weighted experiences in number of years', and the 'product of all the employees with their respective weighted experiences in number of years'. DK, as a simple competency, expresses a firm's willingness to invest in manpower that is highly educated and has long experience.

Product Competence (PC_1) comes next and is a compounded measure, capable of measuring synergistic complementarities (Ichinowski *et al.*, 1997; Porter, 1996) of diverse competencies. PC_1 reflects a competence to combine simple resources and architectures of resources and is the sum of several component indices normalized by the age of the firm. The component indices are:

- revenue earned from champion products and other products divided by total revenue;
- number of champion products divided by total number of products including upgrades in the families;
- number of futuristic products that require creation of a new market divided by total number of products;
- number of markets in which the firm has its own presence divided by the total number of markets the firm accesses;

- ratio between number of products with the firm's brand name and the total number of products;
- ratio between revenue earned through own distribution channel and the total revenue earned.

The final and fourth is *Project Competence* (PC$_2$). This looks into the employment of both simple and secondary resources by a firm for enhancing firm capabilities to supply software service projects or solutions. PC$_2$ is a sum of several component indices that are:

- ratio of revenue earned through projects and through distributing others' products to the total revenue earned,
- number of projects developed and marketed by the firm divided by the total number of projects,
- number of projects earned through competitive bidding in the USA divided by total number of projects earned through competitive bidding,
- number of projects funded through internal accrual divided by total number of projects,
- number of employees who were imparted training on a job or formally in the areas of domain knowledge, technical writing and in project management divided by all the employees provided such training on any areas,
- number of employees sent on clients' jobs divided by total number of employees that worked outstation,
- maximum number of projects taken parallel divided by this number plus the total number of projects handled,
- revenue earned through own distribution channel divided by total revenue earned.

PC$_2$ is the sum of these eight indices divided by the age of the firm.

Table 5.2 shows values of these four competencies for all the seven firms. The DT for the *Soft3* could not be shown because some relevant data was missing. Data on the age of the firm appears unrelated to the values of firm competencies. It may be recalled that data in Table 5.1 also corroborated this observation. Several authors have emphasized that the age of a firm is an important variable, arguing that with age the learning curve goes upward. The rejoinder here is that experience-based learning remains vital for relatively stationary methods of production while for highly dynamic software, whose life cycle is much shorter, such experience in continuous upgradation is of little worth. The last column of Table 5.2 presents another competence: Switching Coefficient (SC). A firm-wise description will be revealing . *Soft1* takes up services alone. It does not have any future plans for product. The domain thrust of *Soft1* is directed to the high-technology end of software services. It also has highly qualified manpower but with little experience resulting in the lower value of DK. Service

Table 5.2 Structural competencies of software firms

Firm name	Domain knowledge (DK)	Domain thrust (DT)	Product competence (PC$_1$)	Project competence (PC$_2$)	Year established	Switching coefficient (SC)
Soft1	73.63	1.37	0	0.14	1996	0.102
Soft2	243.1	0.88	0	0.22	1990	0.244
Soft3	159.56	N.A.	0.33	0.19	1990	N.A.
Soft4	345.26	0.5	0.17	0.25	1988	0.15
Soft5	74.71	0.59	0.16	0.34	1992	0.31
Soft6	53.2	0.31	0.28	1.26	1997	3.14
Soft7	61.44	1	0.92	1.05	1998	0.13

Source: Banerjee (2003d), Technovation, p. 259, table 1.

has commanded the entire simple resources or architecture of resources. Correspondingly, the firm product competency value is zero while the value of PC_2 is not high because this firm has diverted resources to futuristic areas of service.

Soft2 has high DK value because it has manpower with long experience. Few firm resources have been devoted to products and, consequently, its PC_1 is zero while PC_2 is not very high, perhaps because resources have been devoted to current projects that can earn high revenues. The domain thrust thus has an intermediate value. Firm *Soft3* runs on services as well as on a few products. The product-competence value is high and the value of project competence is not negligible. Firm *Soft4* is engaged in low technology and hence the DT is lowest, while the burden of experienced people has rendered DK the highest value. PC_1 and PC_2 are both low, with little difference between them. Firm *Soft5* has, however, not retained people with long experience and its DK has moderate value. The medium-level technology that this firm is in has resulted in lower emphasis on development of domain skills and the DT of this firm has a moderate value. It offers service though it has products and the values of both PC_1 and PC_2 are moderate, with only a small difference between them. The next firm, *Soft6*, is young and supplies niche services. Its PC_2 is highest in this group and PC_1 has a moderate value, indicating a firm's capability to offer a niche product. With no resources spent on training in niche product, it had the lowest value of DT. The concentration of technical knowledge in a few, supported by qualified technical employees with little experience, has rendered DK the lowest value. The last firm, *Soft7*, has high values for PC_1 and PC_2 because its services are in the nature of products and thus the difference between the two competencies are low.

Domain knowledge is a simple competency with single degree of freedom. Large values of this competency indicated that the firms were indeed burdened with highly experienced employees but whose learning the incumbent firm did not know how to employ. The knowledge on recombination of simple competencies generates architectural or knowledge resources. Manpower deployed over current and future service projects or over development of products satisfies the short-term goal of revenue generation and the long-term goal of enhancing capabilities in core areas. Domain thrust captures this aspect and is a second-order competency with two degrees of freedom. Product or project competence can be similarly measured. They are of the second order and enjoy two degrees of freedom. Core competence, by the definition in this account, is independent of content of resources. It is about decision-making capabilities and hence cannot be measured in terms of either simple resources or knowledge or architectural resources.

How would a manager test the efficacy of a decision and the capability to take 'right' decision? Put simply, a manager can infer the efficacy only if a sufficiently long time period has gone by. A past decision is, however, a commitment. A decision commits the firm to a particular resource allocation, a reversal of which is costly. Core rigidities (Leonard-Barton, 1992) result from such commitments. Further, a manager cannot causally associate a decision with the 'respective' result. Some sources of competences are complex enough to be captured and identified (Lippman and Rumelt, 1992). A young firm does not have the advantage of a mass of historical data on decision efficacies and resources for these firms are liquid. The highest investment for a software firm is in its human resources. Such an investment cannot be considered as sunk. This leads a manager to look for a measure of competence defined on structural terms that can capture the ease of switching across structural sorts. In other words, a capability to take good decisions can be indicated by the capability to switch structural sorts. With this reasoning, one can appreciate that a measure of switching competence, which is a structural competence of the third order, is devoid of content of a structure. Being linked *a*-causally by way of reason with the firm's decision, this competence represents equally well the competence to take a decision.

The switching coefficient must reflect the structural ease with which a firm can switch its sorts. The switching coefficient (SC) can be defined as the ratio between the absolute difference between values of product and project competencies to the value of domain thrust. Both the numerator and the denominator are second-order competencies, and SC, because it is derived from the second-order, can logically represent a third-order competency. Second-order competencies are made available in the switching-over function by a firm. With a higher value of the second-order competency such as DT, a switching is easier or less costly and correspondingly the value of SC becomes smaller. A lower value of SC naturally indicates the ease of switching. With close product and project competency values, that is with a lower numerator, switching is easier. The values of this switching coefficient have been computed for these seven firms and are shown in Table 5.2. *Soft6* stands out with a very high value of SC. *Soft6*, it may be recalled, is well-entrenched in the provisioning of a specialized service where it finds little competition. Thus even with high-value domain thrust, the *Soft6* entrepreneur is happy with the current business. Accordingly, structural sorts of this firm are rigidly entrenched. *Soft1*, in contrast, exhibits the smallest value of SC indicating the highest ease. Comparatively higher values are observed with *Soft4* and *Soft5* because the difference between the product and project competencies for them is also low.

Structural competency and co-ordination

The structural decision of a software firm to walk on both legs, switching from product to service and vice versa, is afforded by a capability. This is defined as the core competency because this is purely decisional and is not encumbered with contents of resources. A core competency must remain free of resources and must reflect decision competence. These firms have fairly high domain thrust, which is about the competence to recombine knowledge architectures. High second-order competency enables a firm to switch with cost across product and project competencies. This is an extension of March and Simon (1958) and Nelson (1991). Table 5.2 provides us with an interesting observation that all six firms that have kept the values of project and product competencies close could also retain a high value of domain thrust. This structural quality is attributed to decision. The capability to take decisions on the attributes of a structure without being constrained by the contents of the structural sorts is, as discussed earlier, both a core competency and a competency of the third order.

Switching across projects was discussed in the earlier narrative when it was observed that firms exhibited two modes of switching competence across projects, namely, 'service-product-service' and 'service...[product]... service'. The present narrative has observed switching competence between products and services. Both these types, to recall, are structural competencies. In the former, a product competence is intermediate, and a firm, while moving across services, takes on product development. In the latter discussion, the product is relatively stable but gives way to service. Possibly because of this relatively higher stability, it was easier to construct a switching coefficient in this account, and the position that this coefficient was the core competency could be defended. In the first narrative, however, the product strategy is fluid and a coefficient on core competency might unwittingly have concluded that those firms had core competencies in services.

Such a mode of defining core competency takes one away from some standard definitions – for example, provided by Leonard-Barton (1992) – core competency is what differentiates a firm from its milieu. Three types of differences could be observed: Table 5.2 shows these differences. First, domain-knowledge values based on the allocation of a simple resource vary most widely. Secondly, second-order competencies, such as domain thrust or product or project competencies have relatively lower divergences. Thirdly, switching coefficient, which is free of content, diverges little too. Therefore, firms can retain wide differences across the simple competencies while with higher competencies such divergences will narrow down. The succinct point is that while behaviourally a large divergence appears more meaningful than a small divergence, the import of small differences between switching coefficients, for example, is comparatively much more potent. An observer might conclude wrongly from observations on simple competencies that firms are divergent and that these divergences are strategic. However, the argument here will lead to a different conclusion. It would look into higher orders of competencies in order to measure the divergence that, while numerically small, can strategically differentiate across firm capabilities in a deeply significant manner. From this observation it may be concluded that while differences in values of competencies are valuable, it is strategically significant only when these differences refer to resources of higher order. A difference is most strategic when it refers to capabilities of decisions.

It has been argued that structural competencies (a few have been indicated) are not innate. These competencies are not given a priori nor are they the results of static structural endowments. Received literature has often studied structural aspects from a static perspective, as it were. Structural competencies for these authors are innate. The approach is categorically rejected here. A structure, it is argued, results from strategy, which situates the incumbent's structure in a strategic milieu. The incumbent firm, in order to reap most advantages out of own structural sort and structural sorts of other firms in its strategic milieu, acts strategically locally and switches sorts to activate demand management, for example. The switching coefficient thus refers to a state of affairs, which is by definition dynamic and reciprocal. A firm needs to offer services or products to its strategic milieu or be in competition with the strategic milieu. This milieu demands agility in the incumbent's structure. The incumbent's choice of switching route is a reflection on its strategy. It follows then that structural competency is a result of dynamic co-ordination of structure. Product or services are not determined by innate endowment of resources. Dynamism across service projects or between services and products emanate from the attempts of an incumbent's structure to effect a winning strategy. The structural resolution of the winning strategy in the context of dynamic co-ordination amongst several structures is captured in the indices of structural competencies.

6
Knowledge Strategy and Knowledge Divisions

Manpower, as a resource, is often believed to be homogeneous. If one accepts that experience adds to the quality of manpower, one can also accept that experience always gets an added enhancing quality. Information on quality is, however, primarily private and any contract or negotiation would remain incomplete in the absence of shared and commonly believed and accepted standard of quality (Kennan and Wilson, 1993). Moreover, the holder of private information is an egotist and an opportunist (Williamson, 1981, 1993). This further adds to the vitiated measure of quality. One problem is how exactly quality can act as a signal. Further, a signal is weak and cannot reach distant corners of a market. Firm-internal information on quality, even when it trickles down, reaches only a small local quarter, which often includes only a small number of other firms which are situated in the same strategic milieu as the incumbent holder of that quality manpower. Such a market remains 'uncleared' (Benassy, 1993; Fishback, 1998). There is an additional problem too. Commonly believed theories on wage settlements or valuation of manpower treat a manpower signal quantitatively. Supply-and-demand quantity positions, *à la* Keynes (Leijonhufvud, 1968; Patinkin, 1965), constitute the quantity signals. Such signals are macro by nature. The incumbent firm or the incumbent individual resource-holder acts in the micro domain, and for them, while the quantity signals constitute an important backdrop, the micro quality information remains more important and deciding. In fact, job switching by experienced professionals in the software sector is very large. However, such job switching is almost always non-global or at least partially local. Such a job market is not strictly 'uncleared'. In fact, the software job market is distinctly different from markets that are nearly never cleared, such as in most manufacturing.

Software then presents a novel dilemma. It appears that the software human resources market is a meso-market. It is understood that there are strong indications of denying this 'market' a clearing status, which micro actors enjoy. Again, quantity signals alone are not decisive. Individuals often switch jobs frequently and remain limited in their mobility to a circuit, which could be a circuit of firms or a circuit of a specialist skill or similar others. This 'market' never remains absolutely 'uncleared'. A standard definition of market as one that gets cleared, even if periodically, as in the ups or downturns of business cycles, cannot satisfactorily explain events in this sphere. This leads to the suggestion that this is a peculiar market, hanging in between the micro and macro. This is proposed here to be the meso-market with a pronounced locality. This chapter will speculate on certain characteristics of such a market. The data will be provided by the software manpower situation. One obvious and immediate corollary to this observation is that manpower cannot be considered as resource (Barney, 1986, 1991; Peteraf, 1993). One cannot accept that a resource market that gets cleared exists in this case. It will look into constraints upon the decisions of a firm put up by such meso-markets.

Quality matters a lot. Even so, information on quality is private and is vitiated with egotism and opportunism. An individual cannot be considered as investing in knowledge (Becker, 1962) because information on both current and future demands, available to the individual, is woefully inadequate. This individual has access to information available in the circuit that is local in time and space. Lazear's theory (1979, 1981) of delayed payment would prove inadequate as well. Further, an individual has to write off such apparent 'investments' often because the demands for the knowledge, accumulated in expectation of delayed payment, turn out to be obsolete in the wake of new technological developments. A typical tournament (Carmichael, 1989) can check against a skill getting lost only within a relatively stable technology and in a stable business model, however. It would be difficult to substantiate the claim that wages under this setting are, necessarily, actuarially just (Hutchens, 1989) because one would have doubts about the nature of investments. It appears that knowledge cannot be treated as an accumulated stock that, in any case, does not appear to be the result of a firm, a social organization or an individual investing in generating, maintaining and redirecting or accumulating the stock alone. The consumption of knowledge is an important prerequisite for further generation of knowledge. In most circumstances though, this consumption of knowledge does not limit the scope for further consumption of this same knowledge by others. It follows that knowledge is a special type of joint production. It is argued that joint production of knowledge is an important dimension. Manpower, it will be observed, cannot be treated as human resources as such.

Simon (1991) has pointed out that the role of authority is immense in these acts of generation, maintenance and redirection or reproduction of knowledge. Following Simon, it may be noted that production of knowledge is not a simple joint production where contracting parties enjoy relatively higher degrees of freedom. Authority appears often as coercive. It also follows from the previous observations on locality that the quantity of manpower flowing across production units, and the quality and quantity of manpower that a single unit of production, such as a software firm, can retain gets determined by the local context of the incumbent firm and the local context of the manpower. This context is the strategic milieu. In other words, quantity and quality of manpower in a meso-market result from strategic acts. It is thus argued that unlike the quantity determination in a macro-market or quality determination in a micro context, both local quantity of manpower generation and its flow, and the quality of manpower in a locality gets influenced, if not determined, by strategies undertaken by the firm and acts undertaken by individuals. As a corollary, it is argued, that manpower in a meso-market is an outcome of strategy and co-ordination.

The economics of knowledge

The quality of manpower is private information that experience alone cannot reflect. A contract or negotiation between a firm and its employee remains incomplete if information on quality remains private with an opportunist employee. Quality information can, with limitation, act as a weak signal that fails to reach the entire or the global market. Such information can reach the strategic landscape that is shared by structurally isomorphic firms and such a market remains 'uncleared'. The quantity signals define and clear a market that is macro but the incumbent firm or the incumbent individual resource-holder acts in the micro domain, where quality information proves superior to quantity signals. The partial market of strategic milieu thus trades in quality signals even while remaining dependent on quantity signals – such a market we might call meso, without a market-clearing status. Thus manpower fails to pass as a resource.

The other strangeness lies in knowledge, unlike a typical factor of production, not being an accumulated stock. Several social agents participate in generating, maintaining and redirecting or accumulating knowledge. The production and consumption of knowledge must go hand in hand in a special type of joint production. The local quantity and the quality of manpower generation, its flow are influenced by firm strategies. Thus the production and consumption of manpower or knowledge happening together is referred to as joint production.

Classical and neoclassical economic theories appear inadequate in explaining this strangeness in knowledge. Knowledge production is not technologically determined and its price is not just as per demand. Holding knowledge as an idle capital stock offers little prospect but knowledge can be reproduced, rehearsed or generated anew. Liquidity of knowledge should ensure a higher pay-off from the holding. The concept of obtaining unique prices thus fails and knowledge prices exhibit several degrees of locality. Local markets in knowledge, dictated by firm strategies, influence decisions pertaining to prices, investments and holding knowledge as asset balance.

For a software firm, storage of held back knowledge-asset formation balance *that has been stored and held back* could not, however, be a tradable asset. Tradability implies that all firms have information on the worth of any such balance and that lowers the speculative profit value or the strategic value of such knowledge assets. An ingenuous mode of holding such knowledge is quality manpower that cannot, however, hold the knowledge as specific or tied-up or tacit inaccessible content. A software firm seeks a social net of professionals to serve as a buffer to which it can shunt its temporarily excess manpower and from which it can rehire. This social net must keep on reproducing knowledge. Knowledge held back from immediate consumption represents the first type of distributive aspect that recognized the future. The distributive aspect of a social net spreads over two more horizons. Diffusion or imitation that results in distribution, always follows the future frontier of knowledge provided that knowledge meets with successful innovation. The future frontier of knowledge, consequent to successful innovation, is followed by diffusion or imitation resulting in distribution. The second mode of distribution takes place through a flux of manpower turnover entering the social net that gains in new knowledge and reproduces or generates new knowledge in several organizations.

Limitations on knowledge understanding

Manpower, it would also follow, is not a simple factor of production. Arrow (2000) has noted that the knowledge resident in manpower is a factor of production. Such a statement needs to be qualified though. Knowledge is always about something and the content of knowledge always has a generalized and a particular aspect. Any given industry or period of production exhibits a general aspect but any given organization or individual exhibits particular aspects beyond the generalized aspects. Strategy study is concerned about the edge that an individual might enjoy owing to the particular knowledge that he possesses. Strategy cannot be greatly concerned with the general aspects of knowledge, which, as a factor of production, knowledge captures. Manpower cannot, therefore, be a simple factor of production. Moreover, unlike other factors of production, knowledge, under restricted conditions, such as when it can accumulate, exhibits increasing rates of return. Increasing returns can be expected till the time the current paradigm of knowledge has not been overthrown, assuming that generalized aspects of knowledge are enjoying sufficient diffusion and are, therefore, experiencing a rise in generalized accumulation. This, however, fails as soon as a new paradigm challenges the presiding deity. A firm or an individual thus might enjoy the benefits of generalized accumulation till the paradigm it has been working upon gets challenged. This individual, however, discovers that its investment in the old paradigm has been set to naught by the new paradigm. Often, because of inertia, this individual acts reactively and soon gets replaced. All this reminds us that knowledge is not simply accumulating, or simply diffusing. It cannot be a simple resource whose quality can be measured through the degree of achievement that an individual fine-tuned. In software, there are umpteen numbers of players who did not hone skills but who simply hit upon the new paradigm.

Joint production of knowledge appears to be a rather complex issue and one cannot go beyond discussing some preliminary issues on production of demand and supply. Some aspects of demand management from this joint production perspective were discussed in the previous chapter. Inside a firm, the employees and managers are the co-producers of knowledge. No less important are the roles of other co-producers, such as society and other competing firms. This aspect of co-production refers to the co-operation of social roles. From an economic perspective, knowledge production is intriguingly complex. The difference between cost-based and demand-based pricing approaches, as between the two streams of classical economic thought and the neoclassical (Arrow and Starrett, 1973), was based upon a neglect of joint production. Arrow and Starrett concluded, 'In short, the supplies of labour in general and with particular skills cannot be regarded as completely purchased within the economic system, and therefore the pure capital model seems inadequate. The demand element in the formation of prices seems to us ineradicable' (p. 144). The classical model seems even more inadequate because the produced knowledge is not just technologically determined and it is again knowledge that is the primary factor of production of knowledge. Similarly, the demand-based, neo-classical approach seems inadequate. The price of knowledge produced cannot refashion it except in accordance with the demand of knowledge. In knowledge, as earlier discussed, there are sudden parametric shifts in price, depending on the value of the new knowledge. The value of knowledge has little correspondence with the quantity of knowledge produced. As long as one restricts oneself to knowledge as a factor of production (in the known techniques, for example) only, this quantity matters. However, the significance of the quantity concept of knowledge is made further irrelevant by Arrow's (1962b) observation that knowledge as factors of production is reduced to information, whose value increases instead of getting decreased while allowed to diffuse.

Several other discrepancies can be observed in explaining the economics of knowledge in terms of the existing theories (Machlup, 1963). Knowledge is valued because of its many qualities: an important one being that its value often increases with the increase in its differences from other knowledge. Increasing division of labour justifies this although a pure informational account of knowledge will fail to capture this aspect. Smith's doctrine of equalizing differences (possibly an extension from Leibnitz), whereby individuals are supposed to possess equal abilities but with unequal choice profiles over jobs, fails to account for wage differences corresponding to differences in skills and knowledge. Further, knowledge has the peculiarity of being reproduced, rehearsed and generated anew. Apprenticeship in production or in the institutions of learning ensures reproduction. Continuing with current productive knowledge ensures rehearsal. Experimentation, speculation and imagination or inferences ensure generation of new knowledge. The cost-based classical theory approach surely cannot explain these aspects of dynamism in knowledge: the price of knowledge appears indeterminate and elusive from this approach. Moreover, as in reproduction, the knowledge worker is reproduced from knowledge. This then greatly undermines the quantity determination of knowledge workers that needs to be reproduced. Knowledge workers cannot, therefore, be considered as the primary factor of production.

In the same vein, a pure exchange-based argument following Menger and others or a neo-classical demand-based approach is severely ill-equipped to explain the intriguing complexity of the role of knowledge and its mode of production in the economy. Of the tripartite division in knowledge – the reproduction, the continuation of practice and, finally, the generation of new knowledge – the last cannot be explained in terms of this neoclassical scheme at all. On reproduction and continuation of practice, one observes that an exchange-based argument can explain only severely limited instances. A rather large terrain of both these types of knowledge relates to the production taking place when an apprentice learns on the job. Once a production ceases to continue, the corresponding knowledge cannot continue to get reproduced. Knowledge that is abstracted from its production milieu and does not require continual reference to practice can, however, be exchanged. Certain forms of such knowledge, moreover, can be held back or retained because the holder, caught in uncertainty regarding current prices in exchange, might expect a possibly better future price. As is obvious, only an abstracted knowledge can be thus held back. A patented knowledge must, for example, refer to the specific context of production and competition only. Liquidity alone can ensure a higher pay-off from holding the knowledge and such liquidity must refer to the abstract generalization of knowledge.

In the scheme of Menger, liquidity or marketability is 'due to ubiquity of demand, the number of people dealing in a commodity, the continuity in time of a demand, and the degree of speculation in the commodity in question. It is, he states, due to the existence of well-regulated, competitive markets' (Streissler, 1973: 170) and recalls that such markets are but exceptions. Most markets are different where prices are 'not numbers but stochastic variables' with distribution not only over space and time but also, as stressed by Menger, 'a distribution over persons, different social categories of persons commanding different prices' (*ibid:*, 171). Surely, in the market for knowledge, the price for a knowledge-holding person cannot be understood in terms of certain point price, at which equilibrium is reached. A product in knowledge, for example an individual with certain degree and experience, is not a homogeneous product. This product will have different values to the holder and to its several possible customers. It will have different values to different customers because each customer has a value-profile that depends on the specific strategic milieu of that customer. Most importantly, selling takes place only once or at most periodically and the seller is often not a professional seller having mustered an 'entire spectrum of price offers'. An individual enters into or quits a job only infrequently and even while this seller possesses information on price offers elsewhere, he fails to take a 'rational' decision on very frequent job switching. All this indicates that unique prices cannot be attained and the prices will exhibit several degrees of locality; instead of there being one market, there would be large number of local markets. It is asserted that often regional or strategic milieu based specific markets will be exhibited. Investments in knowledge too, therefore, cannot overcome these limitations on expected prices, non-homogeneity, ignorance and above all rare or at most periodic market transactions.

Following Keynes, one can differentiate between ordinary day-to-day commercial activity and the irregular speculative transactions that offer possibilities of capital gains. Closing a deal and paying on the nail with a certain future expectation or, conversely, holding back a knowledge product from closing the deal on an expectation of speculative gains should thus be separated from the daily activity of knowledge commerce, as exhibited on the job or while writing a standard software. An individual job seeker holds back 'ideas' or a firm holds back another 'idea' in hope of speculative gains. However, what Keynes observed on the role of interest in speculations or of holding-back in stock market, or what Menger observed in general for money cannot be applied as such in the case of knowledge as an asset. It has been observed that knowledge can be held back but with severe limitations. Knowledge may be rendered useless or reduced in value by a new idea or paradigm; or a held-back knowledge, not continually practiced or repro- duced or generated over a new frontier, could very likely be lost to memory. Menger thought that money is held because it enables the holder to take advantage of price variations. The observation in this account is that know- ledge is held but with the limitation that price variations can be destructive, and held-back knowledge, instead of reaping interest income, is liable to perish. The capital account or the speculative part of transactions in knowledge, therefore, demands our attention. Theoretically, daily regular knowledge commerce ought to be differentiated from the speculative account. Another problem is faced here. Unlike money, a regular activity in knowledge-based commercial activity has been known to generate speculative potential. One has often seen that instead of incremental innovation, an idea, when regu- larly worked upon, hits upon a new idea or new knowledge with massive speculative potential. This further proves that regular or mundane activity in knowledge cannot be separated from the speculative account. It is known that a software firm, for example, does not gain from separating its R & D from its regular software writing.

Typically, R & D represented holding back money. Streissler says: '*In order to pursue our irregular business of wealth accumulation, we have to withdraw liquid funds, money, from our regular business*' (1973: 175; italics original). Drawing an analogy, one could ask whether holding back knowledge for future speculative pay-off is a feasible option. Advanced, knowledge-intensive manufacturing has, in general, merged its previously separated R & D with its regular platform of production (Banerjee, 1999). Fordistic R & D referred to structural separation. Contemporary manufacturing, such as in concurrent engineering, must remove such separation, and R & D must become structurally inseparable from other structural elements. At another level though, one might ask if a firm – in Keynesian separation of two accounts – can separate regular production knowledge from the knowledge the firm believes would fetch it speculative bargain. A long quote from Streissler (1973: 176) would be enlightening: '*the greater the degree of variation of price*, which is represented by the average size of the bargain, *the more frequently bargains come along, and the lower the opportunity cost of withdrawing funds, the greater is the expected gain in the irregular business of wealth formation.* "Money" will be held the more in the form of *asset-formation balances* . . . the lower the return in current business, the less well regulated the market is in regard to price' (italics original).

Earlier chapters have shown that a typical software firm holds liquid funds. Holding such liquid funds in the form of 'waiting' and earning merely the prevailing interest income from this asset-formation balance surely indicates that the firms are waiting for bargains to be struck. However, a software firm holds more of its asset-formation balance in the form of liquid manpower. More importantly, it holds them in the form of 'liquid' ideas or prototypes or completed solutions to a futuristic business opportunity. Such assets have very low or zero rate of return compared to returns earned by the assets in regular business, such as from engaging regular manpower in current software writing. A firm, however, would hold such assets in expectation of speculation. The balance between the three types of assets (liquid money, knowledge in waiting and knowledge in regular business) will surely not be determined by the prevailing interest rate in the market and the money supply. The entrepreneur is looking for a profit (as defined by Cantillon and as pointed out by Shackle, discussed in the earlier chapter). In order to earn even a Schumpeterian profit and not a Cantillon profit, a firm would need to go beyond the interest income that it could earn from its liquid money deposits. It follows that money supply will not be a determining factor in the distribution of the firm's asset portfolio. Further, as Streissler points out, such assets distribution will have far-reaching implications on the distributive aspects. Streissler goes further from Keynes when he says the 'the purposes for which, and the forms in which, balances are held are very likely to have distributional effects far exceeding in importance the mere effects on income distribution attributed to the phenomenon of creeping inflation' (Streissler, 1973: 184–5).

Earlier observations on the software market in this account have suggested that it exhibits a degree of price variations far exceeding most other sectors of the economy. A detailed profile of prices, of contract values and contract types is not available but the little data that could be garnered testified to the fact that in software contracts, several types of risk-related and co-shared prices or relational contractual prices prevail. These variations are observed over a single piece of contract, over several pieces of contracts that a single firm enters into with different or the same party/parties over a time or over several contracts that several firms enter during the same period. Moreover, apart from variations in the prices of software services or solutions, each firm experiences a large variation in the input prices of the manpower that it secures from the market. This suggests that variations in prices will give a software firm a higher average size of bargain (or speculative gain). A software firm will, therefore, have higher allocations of its assets to the liquid pool.

Streissler, following Menger, has also asserted that with higher frequency of bargains and with lower opportunity cost of withdrawing assets from the regular business, the expected gains from the irregular business of wealth formation will be higher. In other words, firms will tend to hold more asset-formation balances. On this account, the software market, particularly its demand side, while exhibiting higher dynamism compared to more traditional manufacturing or services, remains limited by the structural rigidities of large corporations that incidentally constitute the principal demand for software services. The last chapter has discussed the influence of structural rigidities in containing demand. Constrained by this limitation, it appears that one strategic task of the asset-formation balance of a software service provider is to manage and create demands for novel services by way of destabilizing the structural rigidities of its clients. The frequency of bargains depends on this critical element of demand management. To recall the earlier discussion on strategic knowledge, the internal processes of firms in the strategic milieu can be influenced by this strategic knowledge, which is different from both knowledge that can be counted as factor of production and knowledge that is structural.

It is doubtful whether strategic knowledge can be considered an asset. An asset must have tradability. A strategic knowledge is not tradable yet it secures for its holder immense strategic advantages. By definition, only knowledge as factor of production is tradable. Structural knowledge, again to recall the earlier discussion, is tradable only in a limited context. It follows that the asset-formation balance reckoned in knowledge, unlike money, is constrained by certain peculiarities. The additional constraints, from the above discussions, are put up by such facts as knowledge that cannot be put on reserve (it must get reproduced) or its content cannot remain stationary. Knowledge generation must always offer new knowledge contents. A firm or an individual cannot put on hold certain knowledge asset as it can with money; at least the liquidity of knowledge cannot be ensured for a long period.

The opportunity cost of withholding knowledge assets from regular production is low for a software firm. The frequency with which a software firm can strike bargains is high though constrained by structural rigidities on the demand side. The knowledge asset withheld cannot earn interest income or be kept as invested in long-term securities. A software firm must then seek avenues for storage, where it can relocate its held-back knowledge asset-formation balance. The tradability of any such balance would immediately lower the strategic value of such knowledge assets. Most of such knowledge is held in the form of quality manpower. One has discussed how decisions of a firm regarding training or continuous learning are determined by this fact of keeping engaged its asset balance or liquid manpower in knowledge reproduction or practice or in generating new knowledge, though this can only accept a limited volume of manpower. A software firm might then look for a social net of professionals that acts as a buffer and where, if required, this firm can shunt its temporarily excess manpower. Such a social net must offer possibilities of knowledge reproduction lest the knowledge asset dries up. In other words, this social net acts like as an investment without return. Menger thought that the asset balance or the withheld asset would earn much lower than what was on offer by the regular production. Similarly, a software firm that earns better than the market interest through its regular production fails to earn interest income from its liquid knowledge asset.

Menger and Streissler pointed out how asset balances implicate distribution. It was argued that this distribution goes much beyond the typically Keynesian income distributions often attributed to inflation. The distributive significance of asset balances in knowledge firms, more particularly in software firms, appears to be far more significant. Money assets when put in long-term securities become distributive over a broad horizon of industrial sectors through selections of portfolios by managers of mutual funds. Such distribution takes places spatially, as it were. Knowledge assets are distributive over at least two horizons. Assets held liquid internal to the firm signify that the firm has expectations on a future frontier of knowledge. This future knowledge will offer bargains and, following a bargain being nailed, there would immediately be diffusion or imitation, resulting in a distribution of new knowledge over a future frontier. This distribution takes place due to firm-internal asset balances and is the first horizon of distribution. The second horizon of distribution is offered by the firm's decision of shunting its quality manpower to the social net. The social net gains in new knowledge and reproduces or generates new knowledge in its organizations, which are other firms or research organizations.

Knowledge, it has been seen, cannot be produced based on cost-based prices and technologically-determined aspects alone. This classical approach has limited applicability to production of knowledge in a firm. One has also examined the neoclassical approach based on demand pricing and exchanges and observed that this approach too could have limited application. It was further learnt that knowledge investment by a firm would be critically dependent on considerations on how to strategically influence the processes of competing firms in its strategic milieu. In other words, decisions regarding knowledge held back from regular production in the form of asset balances would be critically dependent on strategic knowledge that the incumbent firm possesses and on the strategy that it pursues. The incumbent firm would, therefore, look into its own processes as well and, as argued earlier, would like to keep conditions of employment sufficiently attractive to its knowledge employees, such that most of its liquid assets could be retained inside the firm. Knowledge employees and the knowledge with the firm are not just simply assets; they are not simply technologically determined cost-based productions; they are neither simply assets for the purposes of exchange and speculations. Even while they behave as assets, they remain distributed in the structural sorts of a firm and also outside the structural sorts of that firm. These are the limitations within which one might look into the states of affairs in some Indian software firms. While deliberating on their peculiarities, one is constrained by the limits discussed here.

Knowledge specialization divisions of knowledge and co-ordination

The knowledge specialization of a firm and of its employees may be attained through two paths: first, through routinely honing certain skills while continuing with regular production; secondly, through holding back from regular production and investing the asset balance in a strategically chosen area. For an external observer, it is difficult to distinguish between the specializations arrived at through these two divergent modes. Quantitatively both would appear the same. However, their paths being different, the knowledge content and knowledge attitude as well as firm strategies in these two cases would be much different. The path chosen would determine the outcome of investment in knowledge. A detailed history of a firm as a case might enlighten us on this difference. However, these discussions will be limited to non-historical current-event space. This issue was discussed with the firm managers and entrepreneurs and some data was obtained from groups of firms on different occasions, in 1999–2000 and in 2001–02. The following discussion refers to these surveys.

Routine honing of skill takes place often through routine software writing or training on the job. Such routine activities ensure that knowledge acquired previously has been reproduced. Often, however, writing of software mixes up an existing routine with something beyond routine. In this case, even an on-the-job experience entails generation of additional knowledge. It follows then that a routine job of writing entails both reproduction and generation of knowledge. Much of this knowledge, however, is not difficult to reproduce. The reproducible part, which follows logically belongs to the first type of knowledge that is knowledge as a factor of production because reproducible knowledge can be reproduced in another firm and thus such knowledge can be traded as an asset. The other part of the knowledge, which is an outcome of the team work and which, therefore, bears the mark of the structure of the software firm, is not reproducible by any other firm. This latter knowledge is a structural outcome. This component of knowledge is structural. A routine writing or on-the-job experience then leads to a tradable outcome and another outcome, which can be traded between structurally isomorphic firms available only within the limits of the strategic milieu. A strategic milieu shares structural isomorphism and, therefore, a structural knowledge can be used as an asset by another firm with isomorphic structure. Often mixed up with a service software writing project, which generates knowledge of the sort just described, a firm co-generates knowledge on aspects not called for in the service project. This third aspect of generated knowledge stands apart from the routine honing of skill. The generation of this third type of co-generated knowledge depends on the skill in project management. A firm tightly following a project optimization path would not hold its project resources loosely and would, therefore, lose the possibility of co-generation, though Intellectual Property Rights constraints might, through clauses in a contract, debar a firm from co-generation. The tradability of the first aspect of generated knowledge stands against the relative difficulty experienced in trading the second structural knowledge. The third aspect belongs to strategic knowledge and it is not tradable at all.

The gain in structural knowledge is reflected in the structural sorts of that organization. To the extent that structural sorts of several firms who belong to the same strategic milieu share isomorphic structures (and to that extent alone), there can be a market for the structural knowledge. Such a market remains limited to the strategic milieu only. It is most important to recognize, and as argued in the previous chapter, that degree of tradability of knowledge is not at all related to the supposedly existing tacit–explicit domain. In fact, degree of tradability is a function of the market for knowledge, which in turn depends as it were on the extent knowledge participates as a factor of production. Tradability is thus different from the category 'explicit'. Referring to our discussion on this in the previous chapter, we observe that the entire spectrum of knowledge we are concerned about is explicit.

An interesting departure, however, follows from this. A very large literature has evolved over the last few years claiming that knowledge generated over experience or honing is tacit. A tacit knowledge by definition is not tradable. This literature implies that knowledge generated over routine writing is not tradable. The second type of knowledge, which is a structural outcome, according to this received literature, is less tacit and is therefore more tradable. Finally, the third type of knowledge, described as the strategic knowledge and which refers to knowledge about processes in other organizations is, according to the definitions of this received theory, most explicit and hence most tradable.

Our observation in sharp contrast paints a converse picture. Tradability or the asset value of knowledge in the reasoning presented here is an outcome of twin factors: strategy and market for knowledge. The tacit theorist's reasoning forgets market and strategy and remains busy with epistemic considerations alone. From the current reasoning it would follow that the first, knowledge out of routine practice, is most tradable and is easily accepted as an asset that can be traded as an incremental factor of production. Similarly, knowledge sourced in the structural practice is less recognizable as an asset, and knowledge sourced in operations of manoeuvrings on processes of other organizations is the least tradable and has the lowest value as an asset.

The asset value of knowledge depends on the strategy of the undertaker and on the existing market for knowledge. These two factors operate in reverse directions. The more strategic the knowledge, the less its asset value. Further, the larger the market for knowledge as factor of production, the higher the likelihood of getting a value for knowledge as an asset. It will be seen that knowledge is being differentiated more and more along this line of divergence. Hastening up the strategic component of knowledge helps promoting the uniqueness of a firm but does not add to the value of knowledge assets owned by the firm. The strategic component of knowledge ensures that the structural sorts and the processes of the firm have reasonably good control over the generated knowledge. The firm can retain most of such knowledge inseparably from its structure and from its processes. This component is counterpoised by the generation of the other component that is tradable. This latter tradable knowledge is an asset that has a market when the owner of such assets – the firm holds property rights or when individuals can reproduce knowledge unassisted by the structure of the firm – is interested in developing the markets for these assets. This market is Smithian in character. It develops with the hastening up of division of knowledge. Logically, this must be an extremely variegated market and it must thrive on increasing differentiation of knowledge and with increasing specialization.

In order that an incumbent firm can exchange knowledge assets particularly to procure differentiated knowledge assets from the market, it must simultaneously force its structural sorts to accommodate these highly differentiated factors of production. This implies that the firm must encourage divisions of labour inside the organization in as much as what at least the market calls for. This provides the initial condition that the firm must provide internal divisions of labour commensurate with divisions in the factor market. Following a period of production – during which the incumbent has had to generate knowledge and, therefore, differentiate further the internal divisions in knowledge – this firm brings forth to the market a further divided and more specialized set of knowledge as assets. To recall the discussion on the social net that served as a buffer, providing as the pool of human resources, such a net must share with several firms a common minimum division of labour in knowledge assets. A common minimum division of labour across several firms belonging to the same sector or the same region or the same strategic milieu ensures that firms possess a minimum co-ordination. Such co-ordination is secured through similarity in division of knowledge inside and outside the firm.

The received literature argues that division of labour inside and outside a firm is separate and the internal division of labour is a structural outcome. This account offers the understanding that firm-internal division is not a structural outcome and it helps co-ordinate a firm's knowledge generation with the knowledge status of its milieu and of the market that the incumbent operates in. In order to produce, the incumbent firm must access resources from the market that constrain it to undertake division of labour. The structural forms of a firm, to recall the earlier discussion, are not the outcomes of these divisions. The division of labour can thus co-ordinate variegated knowledge resources in a market though the co-ordination can never stay at equilibrium. Following a process perspective and recalling the earlier discussion on the role of strategy in the generation of knowledge, it is recognized that an incumbent firm strategizes to go beyond the current levels of differentiation available in the market. This incumbent pursues an emergent strategy, which in turn offers emergent division of labour that is above and beyond the specializations retained in the market. Temporary differences between division of labour inside a firm and outside in the partial market are thus the cause of dynamism for increasing division of knowledge. The understanding here is that a firm is the active generator of divisions in knowledge; and to gain and sustain competitive advantage, it must hasten the internal divisions in knowledge above and beyond what the market has.

Domain knowledge and specialization modes

'Domain knowledge' is a common term signifying knowledge specialization of a firm in one or more domains that are areas of business applications. A closely similar term is 'verticals'. Hermeneutically speaking, a domain characterizes specialization recognized by, and available currently in a market or a social net. A domain refers to patterns in demands and cannot then reflect types or groups in divisions of knowledge. The market or the social net can only understand language that speaks 'names' of domains that the market is familiar with. 'Names' of domains unknown to the market cannot be recognized then and the current market fails to attach any asset value to such knowledge. However, the incumbent firm in its pursuit of emergent strategy process internally generates domain or specialization names currently unknown to the market. After a period of generation of such specialized knowledge, the market receives new names of domains and such like through mechanisms of diffusion. This account, therefore, is limited by what is currently available in the market vis-à-vis its observation on the internal generation of knowledge names.

Firms recognize several kinds of knowledge. Managers interviewed suggested certain areas and on the basis of these leads, they were asked about the types of knowledge being generated. The nine types identified were: domain knowledge; advanced programming; technical writing; competing products; upgradation of own champion product(s); conceptualization of visionary product; project management; productivity raising tools; and prototyping. Firms impart formal training or deploy or encourage their manpower to hone or generate knowledge through on-the-job or project work. Formal training or recruitment of manpower with the particular knowledge reflects that the firm has identified the required niche. Client-specific software projects also allow some amount of designing for generation of knowledge under the desired type. Moreover, echoing Mintzberg's notion of strategy (1978), one must concede that strategy is not a blueprint of intent of the top management alone. Instead, it is a process shaped by most organizational actors. It follows then that types of specializations developed result from intents of most actors who are writing or doing business in software, as well as from the demands made by clients/market.

The periods of generation of such knowledge were grouped under four time periods: less than one month; between one and three months; between five and six months; and above six months. The period most identified was between one and three months. Data was collected for the number of persons weighted by the period of engagement with honing or generating knowledge under the aforementioned nine types. A plot of the frequency of this weighted variable for 32 firms is shown in Figure 6.1. Domain knowledge

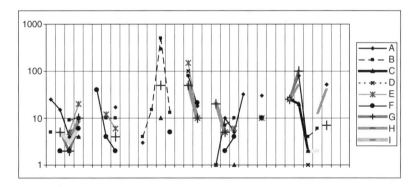

Figure 6.1 Domain knowledge and training in firms

Key: A=domain knowledge; B=advanced programming; C=technical writing; D=competing products; E=upgrading the champion product of the company; F=conceptualizing visionary products; G=project management; H=productivity raising tools; and, I=prototype – are the eight foci of training weighted by number of employees sent for training and for any duration.

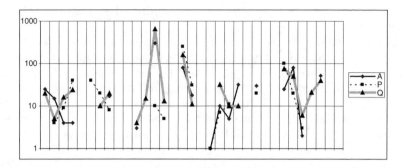

Figure 6.2   Training focus and domain knowledge
Key: A = domain knowledge; B = product competence; and C = advanced programming competence
(weighted by number of people sent for training and for any duration).

received the highest priority. Project management was next in order of importance, followed by the type 'advanced programming'. This same data, when differently grouped, yielded Figure 6.2. Types of knowledge such as technical writing; competing products; upgradation of own champion product(s); conceptualization of visionary product, and such like can be brought under one single type called 'product competence'. Figure 6.2 shows three types: knowledge for product competence and for advanced programming, and domain knowledge. The first two types experienced maximum generation of knowledge. In terms of the earlier discussion on strategies on products or on projects or services, the earlier argument that firms seem to have chosen a path offering minimal cost of switching between the two types is reiterated. All the three types in Figure 6.2 can contribute to the making of a product. Conversely, at least the last two types of knowledge can sustain and raise project or services competency.

Competition ensures that firms invest in such prescribed areas as domain knowledge. However, mere investment in domain knowledge generation does not, in terms of the earlier argument, preclude a firm from generating knowledge that involves further specializations in that domain. Investment in advanced programming too can be made by way of designing a project dexterously while primarily writing routine software belonging to a domain. Working one's way through the competitor's products or designing one's own product while remaining constrained by one's earlier products results in gains in product knowledge of the firm. The figures here indicate varying responses of firms to these categories of knowledge generation. A firm often simultaneously generated several types of knowledge during the same period.

It appears that these types of knowledge can have several degrees of asset orientations, or each knowledge type can have components that either can or cannot be traded. Since a tradable knowledge can be reproduced in another location, a good part of domain knowledge or that of advanced computing can be reproduced in another firm or through another individual. However, each such tradable component will necessarily be immersed in structural and strategic knowledge. Structural knowledge refers to the structural context of generation inside the firm. Strategic knowledge refers to the strategic contexts of processes belonging to other firms. In terms of the discussions in the earlier chapters, it may be concluded that these two types of knowledge are least amenable to such generalizations as can be communicated and hence the abstraction premised upon commonly known theories engender these types.

Context specificity implicates these two types to two sites, namely internal structures of the organization, and the strategic interactions between organizations belonging to a strategic milieu. The tradable asset knowledge begins from particular fact provided by the context but, helped by theories, soon takes flight to abstractions. This does not imply that the structural knowledge and strategic knowledge remain limited to the context. In contrast, these two types also get easily generalized. However, generalized structural or strategic knowledge cannot be communicated and, therefore, cannot be traded as assets. An analogy might help this understanding. Asset knowledge is similar to reasoned knowledge. Knowledge that is structural and strategic is similar to emotionally understood intuited knowledge. The latter can be felt but cannot be explicitly expressed in languages and symbols. Such felt knowledge is as free of context as emotion is. In fact, the structure of a firm or strategic context of a particular intervention recreates in the organization situations that help recalling such expansive knowledge.

Market and specialization

The perspective of the firm as the generator of differentiation in the market has been discussed earlier. It is important to recognize that this perspective is in contrast to what the current paradigm based on Coase's theory of firm (1990) asserts. Coase argued that the transactions costs that are necessarily involved for carrying out a business across differentiated labour get minimized through the formation of a firm. A corollary of this position would be that a firm restrains divisions in labour (or in knowledge). Moreover, Coase does not provide the answer to what causes increase in differentiation. The market appears to retain certain differentiation in this framework. A common observation, following Smith's dictum, is that the market grows with the increase in divisions and it follows then that there must be some generator of divisions. From this reasoning it appears that a firm must necessarily further differentiate between the existing states of affairs in the market while undertaking its own business. This the firm accomplishes through its effort to sustain a degree of specialization or what might be called a strategic edge. A firm retains or sustains its strategic edge by dint of its additional differentiated or specialized knowledge.

The quantity of manpower belonging to a segment of labour division acts as a broad indicator. Domain specialization, for example, including its subdivisions, such as banking or finance or the related computational skills, acts as a variable, which a firm notices while considering its business strategy. A firm guesses quantity that is available in the market and, depending upon the market signal, decides upon its investment in that specific segment. Quantity level judgment is, thus, necessarily limited. Quantity tells us about the macro states of affairs on the broad divisions of knowledge available in the market. A firm, however, cannot look beyond the regional or segmental or beyond the strategic milieu while assessing the demand and supply characteristics of manpower available in a segment. This constraint upon factor availability has been earlier termed as the meso characteristics.

Upon entry or continuation, say in a particular domain, a firm must negotiate with the quality of resources of both what is available in-house and what it can procure from the market. Quality determination is an outcome of negotiation and conversation. Disclosure by an individual or a firm is constrained by both expectations and the ignorance regarding what exactly the useful knowledge could be. Ignorance is important here. A firm does not know, beyond certain broad parameters, the types of knowledge that it might find profitable. Similarly, an individual too is unaware and ignorant about the classifications its knowledge could belong to, and whether such knowledge could indeed generate certain novel products or projects. A broad domain classifier, such as 'banking', therefore, could be currently enjoying certain finer parameters of differentiation, only part of which is common knowledge in the market. Details of such parameters are, therefore, traded across a firm and an individual job seeker during negotiations on what knowledge assets this individual might be able to offer. Sections of a domain market, therefore, could have a currently known finer parameterization and this is part of the common knowledge. It follows then that quantity-determined divisions in a market could currently enjoy several finer divisions that are traded as assets and yet do not appear as market signals to such entrants as a student or an individual from an allied division of labour. Such signals have earlier been described as weak. These entrants receive strong signals available only on broad quantity-determined knowledge divisions. This is the first level of assets belonging to factors of production. However, this same current market also engages in trading signals on finer asset division and such signals fail to get beyond the micro-domain of negotiations. The latter is a second type of asset, which has a limited market and, its signals being weak, it fails to register itself as a broad division or domain. This absence of a powerful signal renders the finer assets tradable only in the local circuit. Following a period of production, these finer divisions become regularized enough and acquire enough strength of signal, whereupon the market can engage in quantity considerations of the second type of asset. It must be noticed that the generation of knowledge in a firm has not as yet entered the stage of finer differentiation. The firm has, however, played its role through acting as a negotiator or a source of demand in furthering the differentiation.

Following a period of production or software-writing, both the firm and the individual arrive at even finer specializations in this domain of 'banking'. The quality signals are weak and limited to negotiated disclosures. The strategy of a firm determines the path that quality-based differentiations would take up. Quantity demands, based on strong market-wide signals, require accumulation of such quality-based finer divisions to take place. A quantity signal follows a period of production and is accompanied by the presence of widespread demands from more than one firm. Strategic decisions of a firm depend primarily on the weak signals, however. Information on quality determines the possible paths that a firm can choose. This information also decides the extent and nature of sustainable strategic advantage. Quantity information decides the resources availability in the market while quality information decides strategy of a firm and the future growth path of knowledge differentiation. Quality information is emergent and belongs to the process perspective of strategy.

A co-ordination process in the market generates information on quantity and types of knowledge divisions on which quantity information is sought. This co-ordination takes place between the demand generated and information leaked out to the public domain by the software firms. Demand by the software user can specify only the broad types of knowledge (such as the domain of banking, for example) and this demand fails to specify the other finer details of the knowledge system. Publicly released information pertains to this broad type that has been specified by the demand pattern. This public information guides the decisions of all other participants, namely other sources of demands, other software firms and the sites of human resources generation at such places as universities. A specific domain-type can thus initiate generation and allocation of human resources on quantity terms across the co-ordinated entities in the market.

A demand articulates several finer types of knowledge required, which however, fails at classificatory attempts. This information on demand remains private to the provider of software services firm who, in consideration of expected gain and the constraints of resources that it faces, provides a shape to the unspecific. Finer specializations are generated in the internal divisions of labour of this firm. Assets thus generated on the fine spectrum have little tradability and hence little market value. Individuals in the firm who possess such finer knowledge too have little tradable value and are, therefore, constrained in switching their jobs. These individuals can articulate such finer divisions to another prospective employer who belongs to the same strategic milieu and who shares similar structural sorts with the firm that the job-switching persons intend to desert. These fine divisions have not yet been accorded a 'name-tag' that the market recognizes as tradable knowledge-asset or a tradable factor of production. Investment by the incumbent firm that has generated these finer divisions of yet-to-be tradable assets is similar to what has been described by Menger as 'asset formation balance'. An asset-formation balance, to recall Menger–Streissler's argument, has little current market value but is a very important distributive implication. Following the earlier reasoning, this balance of increasing division of knowledge can be considered as equivalent to the R & D balance. In fact, R & D balance often generates site-specific assets. In contrast, this asset balance in a software firm is relatively free of site specificity. Consequent to a shift in paradigm of computation or to the firm's failure to successfully innovate upon the finer divisions of knowledge created as asset balance, the finer divisions may even fail to turn up as tradable asset following a period of production. Finally, the distributive and generative (generation of division of knowledge/specialization) significance of a firm's strategic investment in privately held knowledge cannot be glossed over.

A simple example of domain specialization of a few software firms would be interesting at this point. There were 16 firms that responded to queries regarding their involvement in domains, training and other knowledge generative practices, and their strategies. Table 6.1 refers to the data collected during 2002. Of the 16, there were four large firms, six in the middle category but fairly large and the rest small firms but belonging to the middle. The domains indicated by the firms are broad types of knowledge divisions that indicate the types of demands made by the client firms. Information released by the clients and the software firms to the market regarding the divisions of knowledge they are looking for or are working on belong to these broad classes of domains. Finer generative and distributive aspects of information on quality and on finer divisions of knowledge are primarily private or, at the most, leaked through the firms belonging to the strategic milieu by individuals who quit an incumbent firm. The current locales for most firms relate to these broad divisions. The co-ordination between clients and suppliers, and amongst a large number of suppliers, recognizes information on these broad types.

A particular client, however, receives more detailed information. This covers its supplier firm's experience profile in the domain, the qualifications and experience profile of its manpower, the total number of projects belonging to this domain being currently handled by the supplier and the percentage of supplier firm employees working in the relevant domain. This is privileged information and cannot support co-ordination between multiple firms. Table 6.1 shows that variations across domains do not have corresponding variations across qualifications of its manpower. Qualifications appear to be related to the path or the history of a firm. More important than this path

Table 6.1 Domain specialization and knowledge strategy

Firm	DS	Rel Proj To DS	Qual In Comp sc	Qual In Other engg	Qual In Mgt	Exp In DS	Trg In DS	Trg On The job	CC	No. Of Proj In DS	Str For Prod	Str For Con	Str For ser	Emp % in DS Projs
1	Bank security	Y		Y	Y	Y	Y	Y	Same	15	Y	Y		
2	Finance Health telecom	Y		Y	Y	Y	Y		Same	40		Y	Y	
3	Finance R & D	Y	Y	Y		Y			Other	15		Y	Y	80
4	Bank	N	Y	Y	Y	Y	Y	N	Same			Y	Y	
5	Finance	Y	Y	Y	Y	N, Y	N	Y	All Dom		Y			90
6	Engg Bank RTS Tools dev	Y	Y	Y	Y	N, Y	Y, N	Y, N	All Dom	>100	Y	Y	Y	
7	R & D ERP	Y	Y	Y	Y	Y	Y	Y	Same	20	Y		Y	60
8	Engg	Y		Y		Y	Y	Y	Same	50			Y	100
9	Engg	Y	Y	Y		Y	N		Other Serv	5				20
10	Bank RTS	Y	Y		Y	N	Y	Y	Same	10	Y		Y	20
11	Embed Sys RTS	Y, N	Y	Y		Y	N	Y	Same	12	Y		Y	70
12	Telcom Engg	Y, N	Y			N	N	Y	Same	80	Y	Y	Y	
13	Engg	Y	Y			Y	Y	Y	Same	50	Y		Y	
14	Internet Web	Y	Y			Y	N	Y	Same	23	Y	Y	Y	
15	Finance Database	Y	Y		Y	Y		Y	Same	6	Y			
16	Bank taxation	Y	Y		Y	Y	Y	Y	Same	many	Y	Y	Y	

Key: DS=Domain specialization; Rel. = Relation; Qual. = Qualification; CC = Core competence; Str. = Strategy .

dependency is the fact that firms appear to be working towards achieving a competency. Competency to write a software well and manage a project is cultivated through qualified manpower whose entry qualifications testify their competency only. The supplier, therefore, provides the client firm information on the total number of projects in the relevant domain and on previous experience of working in the domain.

The supplier software firm internally generates information on the quality of domain knowledge and retains that as privately held. The quantity signal guides a firm in its decisions on entry. The information on quality guides decisions on what future divisions of knowledge could prove to be profitable. This latter information is emergent and the firm obtains it through working on projects and designing modes of training. An entry decision, based on quantity signal, is then put on a firm footing by the competency function of the firm, one of whose identifying parameter is the number of projects in the domain that this firm is handling in parallel. Competence, however, relates to the quantity identified broad divisions of knowledge. Competence, the firm reckons, cannot provide it with a speculator's or Cantillon profit. In order to get to that, the firm saves up resources as asset in balance and in the form of finer divisions of knowledge that are currently not tradable. This balance based on quality knowledge guides decisions of a firm on its future, reflected under three broad groupings of strategies: product, consultancy and services.

Data in Table 6.1 show that the competency function has not been neglected by any of these firms. Moreover, in order to bid for a new project in the relevant domain and to negotiate, a firm must exhibit enough competencies. Hence no firm can neglect this aspect. The negotiating supplier firm also needs to provide information on the firm's software skills (data on this aspect too was collected but has not been shown above). Such information provides data on the competency of the supplier. The supplier, however, need not provide the actual distribution and the quality aspect of software competency. The client firm, appreciating that it cannot make use of such details, depends on the reputation of the supplier firm. The supplier firm builds up reputation through long periods of software writing and through cultivating internally finer divisions of knowledge. When the software skills of these firms are compiled under quantity classifiers, such as, 'C', 'C++', 'Web Technology', 'Unix', 'Java', or 'Mainframes' and such like, they do not show any significant peculiarity or correlation with the firms' stated domain knowledge. It follows that quantity-type skills are sufficiently general. On any of this quantity-type knowledge division, a firm nurtures finer skills and such finer quality determining internally held information provides this firm with the strategic advantage.

Expectations and training strategy

Kirzner (1997) has described the market process as a state of active rivalry. Rivalrous and opportunity-seeking managers can alter resources imbalances, sometimes by employing persons who, in terms of their professional qualifications, should have been considered unemployable. Further, an entrepreneur can generate and hold as an asset balance resources which currently do not yield profit. This latter type reflects cases where current resources yield only a rent. Given opportunities though, these asset-balance resources yield entrepreneurial profits. In this manner, a firm can invest in and generate resources for several different strategic and uncertain purposes. Sustaining competitive advantages through systematic patterns of resource use, which a traditional resource-theorist has used, can thus be substituted by an apparently disordered and unsystematic pattern of resource use. The latter type of resource use holds scope for the innovator's profit or acts as a buffer to uncertainties in the business environment. These features can be observed in the use of resource by Indian software firms. The equilibrium perspective on competition and on resources fails to offer any concrete and real issue on which a firm's manager can conceive of competing. Managerial discretion and capabilities can undeniably alter weak holding of resources into a commendably competitive and profitable operation (Pfeffer, 2001).

Markets for software projects or services are uncertain. This market's dynamism is often driven by market-making or market-creating. Moreover, firms that offer software products do not have a well-defined market size. The size of product market in software depends on interoperable features. A particular market size is determined by the concurrent operations of a set of other software at the users' platform. Interoperability of software products renders the market uncertain. The resources that a firm believes it should hold depend on criteria that are mostly beyond the structurally determined operational domain of firm-based decisions. Resources often are kept on hold as asset balances. These balances are retained on expectations or promises made by its manpower. Or, they are hired on expectations of a particular inter-firm co-ordination on creating interoperable systems of software. A firm can use resource variously and, in fact, entrepreneurial wisdom resides in sustaining variations of strategic import.

The use of human resources by typical software firms did not yield any systemic pattern. It was, however, observed that very often firms had hired high-quality manpower. The resource theory demands optimality in decisions pertaining to hiring of such high-quality manpower by firms often not having even enough project orders to keep them busy. With high manpower turnover rate (Banerjee, 2003b) no firm could be expected to depend on the tacit aspects of knowledge. Long-term product-development projects, which might call for tacit knowledge and evolutionary routines, can thus be ruled out, more because software exhibits extremely short product life cycle. Hiring behaviour can be better explained through a market-process perspective on strategy formulation. Managers hire manpower more in expectations and in order to react to uncertainties in business environments than simply to use the manpower in optimal jobs. A firm appropriates resources in an emergent strategic manner. There could not thus be any systemic pattern in human resources hiring. Firms, however, behaved strategically. The strategic behaviours of software firms could be attributed to the process perspective. This perspective allows a better appreciation of the emergent nature of knowledge generation, and of training and such others in a software firm. It appears that the training functions in a software firm are much less pre-designed and pre-structured than is the norm in other mature industries.

The supply of human resource is secured from the market, which receives freshers and job switchers, with the latter providing the bulk of the market. A small opinion survey conducted in Bangalore, Kolkata and Delhi found that the average job switch was rather high (Banerjee and Bhardwaj, 2002). An average job switch was defined by the following ratio: Ratio 1 = (Total years in service)/{(Number of jobs switched) × (Years in current service)} The value was found to be 2.28. The average age of these respondents, holding a doctorate or master's or at least a bachelor's degree in engineering, was 31.5. This indicates that job switching is rampant.

In the initial years of Indian software operations, there was poaching of professionals working with firms doing business in other mature industries. Perhaps this practice of poaching institutionalized the practice of hiring from amongst the job-switching professionals. The path-dependency is important. The experienced professionals were mostly from mature industries where tacit knowledge and site-specificity of professional knowledge held true. The result was that the software firms were hiring persons with long experiences in domain knowledge of a kind different from what its emergent strategy was looking for. Higher degrees in computer science, branches of engineering and in other sciences apparently did not have differential advantages vis-à-vis the other domain professionals. Surely, a tension resulted from this. The domain knowledge holders with tacit accounts had to give way to another variant of knowledge. The latter reproduced and expanded on the non-tacit divisions of labour obtained in the external market.

The opinion survey, referred to here, sought opinions regarding constituents of competencies. As may be recalled from discussions in the last two chapters, the possession of higher degrees alone was not considered to be competency providing. Good analytical skill with any degree was accorded highest importance though opinions were not highly discriminating between the choices. Managers however, had higher consensus on the relative weights that 'basic skill holders', 'technology/domain knowledge holders', 'conceptualizer/designer', and 'visionary' manpower ought to have in the total employees. According to the respondents, the average ratio between the total of manpower belonging to 'visionary' plus 'conceptualizer', and the 'domain knowledge' plus 'basic skill' holders, should be around 0.58. There was no clear and sharp preference pattern for the levels of degrees or for disciplines. The contribution of resource to firm competency, measured on information based upon quantity characteristics, did not appear as significant. Professional degrees or disciplines a job seeker studied or years of experience in a publicly known domain of experience provide quantity-information to a firm. Such quantity information pertains to equilibrium features that resources theory argued for. A software firm, instead, is looking for information on resource quality that is not reflected in personnel qualifications and in its experience profiles. Path-dependency has taught an Indian software firm that information on quality gets generated through negotiations and upon working together. Information on quality cannot then be known beforehand and a manager or entrepreneur cannot conceive a strategic plan on its future assets. The manager selects through a strategy process and information on quality gets selected through negotiations within the internal emergent divisions of labour and within the structural sorts of the incumbent firm.

The initial recruitment, however, is dependent upon the choice of quantity-specified knowledge specializations, such as a domain. A comparison was drawn between the firm manpower with disciplinary background in computer science or engineering vis-à-vis those from any other disciplines. Manpower from either of these two groups included all levels of degrees. The comparison indicates that there is no systemic preference for a computer background. Firms appear to have employed manpower in no distinct manner. The ratio between these two groups hovers across a wide range. In the second survey of thirteen firms conducted in 2002, seven firms provided a detailed break-up of manpower. This data too indicated that there is no systemic pattern. In order to know more about the preference of a firm for higher degrees, this data from the first survey was reorganized in three groups: first group with doctorates or MTechs; second group with BTech or equivalents; and the third group with master's degrees in management or commerce. The data shows that the second group is most numerous in general while there are instances where membership of the third group has surpassed that of the second. Naturally, the number of people belonging to the first group remained lower compared to either of the two others. The point of our interest is again that there is no systemic pattern. The initial choice by a firm on quantity parameters is, therefore, also dependent on information that the firm is looking for from aspects of quality. The period that a firm holds its assets for and keeps generating information on quality is reflected by such types as learning on advanced programming, as shown in Figure 6.1. Presumably, this firm picks up a service project during this period. Working on this service project might earn the firm enough revenue for sustenance only while this firm puts in much of its human resources as an asset balance, which could earn it speculator's profit.

Porter's (1980) industry analysis perspective suggests that manpower profiles of firms should correspond to the industry segment they belong to. Industry sector, according to this view, influences strategy and allocation of resources including profile of manpower resource. The differences in man-power profiles of firms from the same segment of industry would then remain unanswered from Porter's perspective. The premises of managerial rational decisions, in contrast to both the frameworks of industry analysis and the resources approach, must take into account features of disequilibria, of expectations on possible future business, and of possible gains in reputation that might come out of higher quality or variations in quality of manpower. According to the resource theorist, a firm hires manpower on current con-siderations of business strategy. Conversely, the observation on the software firm suggests that its managers would dispute the importance of tacit know-ledge. Managers in software would thus be hiring manpower with different qualities and often not according to the current requirement of the firm business.

The initial conditions tell us about the attitudes of the employer towards the quality of manpower. This refers to an evolutionary path which, to recall our argument in the previous chapter, cannot be resident in the behaviour of a single firm. Evolution takes place in the milieu-related firm. Only a Lamarckian account would argue for evolution based on a firm's learning behaviour. It appears that the path or the learning from firm's history influ-ences decisions of a firm regarding maintenance of asset balance and the generation of finer knowledge divisions based on quality. However, such paths for most small firms remained in flux. Opportunities arising out of disequilibria in the market and out of sudden or discovered information or access to a market do always keep changing. A firm cannot sit smugly on a learning strategy. A firm must respond to the contingent situation. This requires that it must have competency to deal with current demands, and highly competent manpower, which, however, might have to remain idle (not working on a revenue-earning project), sometimes for months. Firms generally chose to impart training during these idle times and training imparted on development of a product is greatly reassuring. Most firms being small and located far from the dynamic overseas markets, cannot market their own products. The products, therefore, remained as a default strategy. Manpower profiles reflect such a situation.

7
Manpower Flow and Innovation Strategy

Firms have indefinite boundaries, which are often unlocked by the strategies that firms adopt. Processes internal to a firm and the internal generation of information become dependent on and inseparable from processes that are external to it. Co-ordination theorists believed that such fading away of the boundary occurs because firms, in a milieu, exchange information. Richardson (1997) pointed out that a software firm is an extreme case where co-ordination necessitates not only exchanges of technical and industrial information but also forces it to innovate mutually, in order that software utilities can operate in an environment of interoperability. He argued: 'A software product is of no use in itself, but only when working in conjunction with other complementary products as part of a system. Thus...an operating system, specifically must work with applications and other elements in a hardware platform. In the case of an extended network...the set of related components will be much larger. If these systems, large or small, are to do what we expect of them, then the component parts must be so designed as to inter-operate' (Richardson, 1997: 10–11). Such interoperability of a software service or product appears to be only one aspect, and the interoperable system is itself evolving. In other words, each software product introduces a variation and consequently a change in the system. No prior design exists in any mind on the specific architecture of this system, which is again not stationary at any point of time. A software firm while introducing its product ór service, therefore, does not strive for mute complementarities. Instead, it brings about a change in the existing architecture.

While undertaking concurrent coordination then, a firm introduces another element that destabilizes the co-ordination. Simple co-ordination leads to equilibrium. Interoperability is the condition that forces this movement towards equilibrium. A shift away from interoperability, which is also not as far off from equilibrating conditions so as to disrupt the entire architecture altogether, actively destabilizes equilibrium expectations. The exchange of technical information between software firms helps this concurrent equilibrating co-ordination. Internally, a software firm must utilize a dummy of this technical information to co-ordinate its product planning. Beyond these two variants of information, there must be another creative variant of information that takes away this incumbent firm from equilibrating interoperability. In order that this new software product (or idea as in a service) can become operational in the market, however, firms belonging to the strategic milieu of this incumbent must also commence co-ordination in anticipation – co-ordination in expectation (Rosenberg, 1976). This is a new mode of co-ordination.

Three types of information appear to be in circulation amongst these firms. Richardson (1972) argued for two types of information and consequently two modes of co-ordination, however. Corresponding to each type of information there is an organization. Information is an image of the organization. The technical information of Richardson is the image of the technically equilibrated architecture of firm co-ordination. Business information is the image of the co-ordinated architecture of firms who are in business equilibrium. These two types of information co-ordinate a firm's external and inter-firm relations. Necessarily then, firms must retain sharp and clearly separated boundaries from each other because this separation alone can ensure dispatch or the reception of clear signals. The third type of information invokes a third mode of co-ordination that, however, involves – unlike the hypothetical clear boundaries between firms – the co-ordination between internal processes and expectations of those processes of a set of firms. This mode of co-ordination must engender the breaking up of firm boundaries. Indefinite boundaries of firms and their respective indefinite processes become co-ordinated through this third type of information.

Expectation on expectations of other firms proves to be the driver of this co-ordination, which is never an accomplished act. In other words, we are arguing for a process of co-ordination. This process, unlike the concatenated static and accomplished co-ordination of Richardson, is always a possibility. It thrives on betting. This is engendered through ignorance and, therefore, suffers from chronic uncertainties Co-ordination through integration of stages of production requiring evolutionary co-ordination (Richardson, 1998) under one roof of a vertically organized firm (Perry, 1989) has been a solution to the risks and uncertainties involved in the modes described above. Sometimes firms producing closely similar or otherwise complementary products have managed co-ordination through network or trust (Richardson, 1960). Market co-ordination achieved through movements of distinct yet interdependent intermediate goods (Sraffa, 1963) remained another mode of co-ordination. Undeniably, the regulations determined the outcome of a specific type of co-ordination. Technology too determined this outcome. The mode of co-ordination has, therefore, been the joint outcome of both technology or cost considerations and demand considerations, the two aspects controlled by regulations. Regulations often determined the scale economy, hence the economic batch size as well as the demand characteristics.

The regulation theory points out several factors in an economy that determine a particular outcome on co-ordination. The size of a corporation, nature of technology innovated, chosen and employed, financial regulations including interest rate or even the distribution of wage and the nature of property rights – all this regulate an outcome. The history of co-evolution of large corporations and the corresponding technology (Penrose, 2000) shows a pattern marked by products with longer life cycles. Longer life cycles allowed co-ordinated firms time for investing in capital machinery after any innovation in a large corporation that allowed diffusion through co-ordination. Regulation, according to its proponents, is ubiquitous and the agency of regulation cannot be identified distinctly. Several others who explain diffusion through a market mechanism of the invisible hand provide a contrast. Yet others explain that co-ordination, and hence the structure of an industry, in terms of the invisible hand. Chandler's (1962, 1990, 1992, 2001) visible hand points out to the regulatory power of managers in large corporations. A large part of strategy literature, in particular the entire industrial organization approach (especially Porter, 1985, 1994), is based on the singular understanding that a manager from a large corporation wields sufficient power to influence the outcome of co-ordination in a particular industrial sector to its own advantage. Regulation theorists view this power of the visible hand as an additional support to their conviction.

Regulation by indeterminate agencies or indefinite factors cannot be accepted as sufficiently attractive. One would albeit agree to the contention of these theorists that regulations do take place. A study of co-ordination in software provides another distinct mode of co-ordination, which has been described here as the third mode of co-ordination. This mode takes place, it is argued here, through an exchange of a third type of information. It may be further argued that there evolves a norm since information of this type evokes expectations. Also, parties to an exchange of information act on the basis of expectations on expectations. A norm replaces much of the other modes of co-ordination. This normative co-ordination, as argued here, is a process and is not like an accomplished feat, which the regulation theorist attempts to explain. Normative co-ordination serves the purposes of regulation, and agencies of regulation are widely distributed across firms in a strategic milieu. In other words, normative co-ordination is related to strategies of only those firms that together constitute a strategic milieu, and this mode does not refer to an ubiquitous invisible hand nor to a large corporation as the only regulator. It is also argued here that mode of co-ordination affects the internal process of relevant firms and thereby weakens the boundary of a firm to indefiniteness.

As a corollary to this argument, it may be inferred that vertical integration of firms in a strategic milieu would destroy this mode of normative co-ordination. Both technological or cost aspects and considerations on demand support our belief that software is unlikely to be visited by a large corporation strategy.

This means that there is less likelihood of vertical integration in this sector. The typical classical economic considerations show that the marginal cost of production of software is near zero and investment in fixed capital machinery is comparatively small. The neoclassical demand considerations show that software service produces an apiece product with a very short life cycle. Even more interesting, in software we observe the interplay of joint production. Demand and production costs interplay here. This is corroborated by the fact that most firms do not and in fact cannot undertake proprietary R & D; innovations depend, as it appears, on simultaneity of a publicly available advanced knowledge pool and concurrent expectations of several firms on a new set of interoperable products. This feature of joint production limits the applicability of production function approaches. Historically, cost and technological considerations have shown that co-ordination was achieved most effectively with vertical integration and sometimes even through expansion of the scope. Consequently, competition including potential competition (Gilbert, 1989) depended on such aspects as entry barrier or competitive advantage. With sunk costs approaching zero and prices moving quickly, established firms could earn profits even following entry. Thus the Chicago School variants of efficiency related competence theorists (Demsetz, 1973; Leonard-Barton, 1992; Teece and Pisano, 1994), particularly emphasizing efficiency of resources use (Banerjee, 2003a; Bromiley and Fleming, 2002), appear to be few. The short product life cycle and the vanishing ability of a manager to procure, control and apportion resources internally, only point out the importance of strategies on resources of a group of firms in a strategic landscape/milieu. This strategic capability to control resources of other firms and on what other firms have property rights claims can be achieved by normative co-ordination alone. Dynamic competence refers to a firm's internal capability. It refers to firm-internal apportionment of resources. Normative co-ordination refers to capabilities residing beyond firm boundaries. Thus, if firms have to concurrently expect or to hold expectations on expectations on a set of innovations and, consequently, to apportion resources not only inside the firm but simultaneously amongst the firms in a strategic milieu, it would not be surprising if the strategy-determined, structurally induced apportionment of resources gave way to a new mode of resources acquisition, use and apportionment.

Normative co-ordination is achieved through flow of information, whose carrier is a resource, identified here as the human resource. The extant literature argues that co-ordination is achieved through two parameters of a market: price and quantity. The flow of resources – as observed in the previous chapter – does not follow the quantity approach. In fact, quantity considerations, it was argued, did not apply to the entire market but to a meso level in between, called a strategic milieu. It was also observed that the flow of human resources does not follow only the considerations on price, such as wages or expected wages. Resources flow cannot then follow equilibrium considerations. This violates the basic premise of the resources-based theory of strategy. Further, resources flow in a process, never accomplished and terminated in equilibrium. Resources appear to be an additional parameter in a market that unlike price or quantity has restrictions on its flow and that determines a normative co-ordination in a partial market, called a strategic milieu.

Vertical integration was afforded by considerations of price and price-based information. It is doubtful then that software firms will integrate vertically. Strategy of vertical integration resulted in a structure. Concurrent and normative co-ordination through flow of resources suggests alternative structure. Alongside, this suggests alternative strategies by a firm. The strategy of software firms to co-ordinate resources uses results in alternate structural modes. These two hypotheses are interrelated. Aspects of the Indian software scenario may be narrated to substantiate these two interrelated claims. This will not be an attempt to provide any substantive theory but refers to public policies that can be inferred. This discussion will be limited to the public policy aspects only. The resource that software firms primarily use is manpower, the use of which will be discussed here first by an examination of firm differences from data on resource use. Human resource is generative of imaginative information. Expectations and expectations on expectation are based on such imaginative and speculative use of information that can be provided by human resources flowing across firms in a strategic milieu. Unique resource-use behaviour is uncommon. Normative co-ordination is achieved through information acquired from human elements that provide a unique information generative resource. The manager in a software firm creatively uses this information.

Co-ordination in expectation

The indefinite firm boundaries and interdependent capabilities and processes of firms in a milieu have thrown new challenges to the relevance of strategy for co-ordination. Interdependence of firms coterminus with interoperability of the products of these firms cannot, however, be considered as pre-reconciled. Interoperability and co-ordination in software are emergent and are not results of *ex post* reconciliation. Concurrent co-ordination leads to an equilibrium and interoperability forces movement towards equilibrium. It is argued here that there must be a variant of information other than the two mentioned as business and technical, that can situate a firm from equilibrating interoperability to a process of disequilibria. Co-ordination in expectation, it is argued here, achieves this while not keeping sacrosanct the boundary of a firm as definite. This third variant precipitates co-ordination of expectations. Parties to an exchange of information act on the basis of expectations on expectations through the mediation of norm. Normative co-ordination is a process and refers to capabilities residing beyond firm boundaries. If firms have concurrently to expect or to hold expectations on expectations on a set of innovations, resource or structure-based strategy should give way to a normative expectations co-ordinating norm.

Human resource is the carrier of this third variant of information. Interoperability can be pre-reconciled. It is timeless and non-sequential; or else, it can be an input–output system of interdependent succession of events that can apportion in time intermediate products. Technology can be incorporated in this latter system since it does not depend on pre-reconciliation and on equilibrium conditions. Richardson preferred the first mode. The argument here is for the second mode that allows a strategic move to influence and orient the moves of other firms. This mode is dependent on the expectation on expectations. Normative co-ordination of several intermediate products takes place through an act of deferment of the consumption and we argue for an 'orientation' to this mode. Deferment elongates the period of production and the divisions of labour. The deferment constitutes capital and it increases rate of profit. Strategic acts are then undertaken to increase capital and the rate of profit. Strategic knowledge, which is not a factor of production or tradable, enables normative co-ordination. It follows that strategic knowledge increases capital and often also the rate of profit. Strangely, this knowledge is not a factor of production.

The argument here is for deferment that is not pre-reconciled and allows opportunism, cheating and technological changes. Deferment is capital and happens not because of a 'market failure'. Richardson thinks delay is undesirable and institutions including vertical integration alleviate problems of delay. Systemic innovation is as per pre-reconciled plan although it causes longer delay. Autonomous innovations would experience shorter delays. It is argued, following Shackle, that systemic innovations must appear through an uncertain mechanism of 'orientation' of expectations. The delays in deferment and their lengths are attributable to this orientation. The longer the delay or the 'average period of production', the higher the capital required. An average period is as per the plans made by all the participants to the production net in an epoch. The short period is as per plans made by participants to a systemic technology and a period is even shorter as per plans made by those few who participate in an autonomous technological innovation. The lengths of periods are determined by economic states of affairs, including increase in divisions of labour. A period is less dependent on technological innovation. Technology alone can determine efficiency and the velocity with which an intermediate product might move. Strategic moves bypass technological determinations by inventing and innovating further on economic organization of production, and this takes a firm beyond Schumpeterian technological profit or rent to the Cantillon profit.

Deferment takes place through a norm, which is neither a rule nor a routine. A norm sets in injunctions allowing parties to operate in a dialogue-like normative co-ordination of expectations on expectations. Norm disallows a list of negatives. Ordinary co-ordination depends on durability that must reduce uncertainty through commitment and reciprocation. *Ex post* plans and existing technological paths are durable too. Novelty in technology or innovation and reduced durability of investment allow economic agents to engender differentiation of labour and an increase in lengths and circuits of a production net. Divisions of labour across firms or across several groups are contingent to a situation of expectations. These, therefore, retain fluidity and designing an end product can take several paths and several divisions. Alignment of firms or divisions seeks an institutional solution that is different from organizational solution. Co-ordination too demands an institutional solution. Normative co-ordination is an institutional solution. Vertical integration does not appear to be the only preferred solution to problem of co-ordination with long deferment. Evidence from the Indian software industry points out the undesirability of vertical integration as a solution. The vertical solution is preferred consequent to pre-reconciled plan and durable investment. Durable investment by one party can forcibly bring a closure to several other alternative possibilities.

Irreversible commitment is a closure on increase in division of labour and in the deferment. Cantillon profit vanishes under the above situations. Strategy appears redundant or is reduced to near irrelevance. Irregular writing of software represents reversible investment in manpower as held-back assets that offer prospects of profit through deferment. The quantum of assets and the frequency with which they are held back depend on the opportunity cost of withholding, expected gain in the irregular business and the frequency with which one might strike bargains. The portfolio of a software firm consisting of manpower in regular as well as irregular business, and the liquid money held and the manpower that can be hired at almost zero cost from the social circuit depends on the part of the logistics of expectation that a firm is in.

Normative co-ordination tells one that competency of a firm is not decided internally but evolves over time through negotiations with expectations on expectations. A surprise profit in future appears as a moderated process with several small surprises as strategic steps to broach ignorance. Mutually undertaken small surprise steps would together, at a not-distant future, generate another novel envelope offering profits. Ignorance as a counterfactual to the current knowledge of the *ex post* states of affairs must be based on current knowledge on what others are not expecting. In normative co-ordination, price and quantity data are irrelevant because those refer to the past.

The information exchange in typical co-ordination does not refer to internal processes and structures. Software firms look for carriers of information who can interpret, generate and creatively employ such internal process information. This firm requires intermediate good towards that because deferment necessarily generates elongated intermediation. Manpower flowing between firms can satisfy both these requirements. Manpower flow can offer information beyond the scope of quantity and price data. This we call information-in-expectation that has as its goal disequilibria and refers to ignorance. Expectation is a function of ignorance and common knowledge cannot provide the foundation to expectation. Definite knowledge shapes internal structural sorts, something that ignorance cannot, though it can influence internal processes, which are the sources of expectation.

Job switching defers consumption. Decisions on deferment by a firm do not depend on the quantity signal but on the rate of manpower turnover, which is indicative of the period of production averaged in that partial market. This partial market rate is unrelated to quantity, reflects asymmetric information generative capabilities of personnel and is an indicator of the expectation on the rate of profit in that market. Thus, the internal processes of a firm become directly dependent on the partial market parameters. Differences across firms are a function of delay. The uniqueness of a firm depends on delay function that is a representation of learning and the deferment by a firm is represented in its learning. This partial market deferment acts as a norm that a firm ought to follow. The potential gains of firms do differ owing to differences in learning or in knowledge-generative dimension of the time period of deferment and are thus a function of time. This has been named the delay function here. Firms normatively co-ordinating must consider each other's delay functions.

Given the static average period of production, if firms continue increasing divisions of knowledge in the short period, some divisions are replaced by new incoming divisions. The nature of intermediate good must also keep varying then. Normative co-ordination must exchange not only varying information but also varying intermediated goods that contain capital in the process of deferment. The knowledge resident on an individual alone can ensure this property of capital. This not-yet-complete knowledge of an individual can be completed through inter-firm normative co-ordination. Firm uniqueness in normative co-ordination depends not so much on selection and variation as on the ability to guide generation of information and its use to deflect the expectations of others. Information generative intermediate good helps a firm achieve the strategic vantage point of sustained competitive advantage. Co-ordination and capability are thus interdependent and the site of capabilities is also the site of co-ordination amongst firms. Information-in-expectation is the foundation of innovation that, in all likelihood, is beyond the Schumpeterian technological innovation and supports increase in Cantillon profit. That is named as Shackle space, the private space common to a partial market that brings together internal processes of firms in a milieu through repeated exchanges of intermediate good. A Cantillon innovation, different from the Schumpeterian idea, requires the continuous creation of Shackle space, that is, the space created through repeated flows of intermediate good providing a measure of mutual ignorance. Norms evolve because there is mutual ignorance. Experienced personnel rich in information-in-expectation are attractive to an employer since they assist information passage across firms.

Normative co-ordination and structural aspects: deferment and normative co-ordination

Richardson (1997, 1998) has not elaborated on interoperability. There are two possible courses. In the first, interoperability can be considered non-sequential: when interoperable elements are pre-reconciled and reflect a situation of timeless equilibrium. In the second aspect, it may refer to an input–output system that is an interdependent succession of events through which intermediate products get apportioned to the final consumable products. The input–output system allows for technological changes because consequent to technological changes or changes in tastes and such others, the successions or the relative apportionments might change. This second mode, even if not immediately and directly as in the Leontieff system, conceals the element of time and, therefore, does not depend on pre-reconciliation and on equilibrium conditions. Richardson seems to have preferred the first mode. It is argued instead that the second mode alone can explain time-based, technological and unforeseen changes that remain operative over any interoperable system.

This second mode is close to the Austrian understanding of time dependence of capital and yet significantly different, based as it is on Shackle's (1972) argument. One could begin from Shackle's argument and develop it. The normative co-ordination is this additional element that Shackle did not explain and, as is argued here, is an outcome of 'capital as time' thesis of Shackle. More so because strategy apprehends and orients this dimension of time. The criticality of time in orienting one's product lines or technology constitutes a strategic move and such a move must be able to influence and orient the moves of other firms. This capability to orient the orientations of other firms, dependent on the expectation on expectations, can be achieved by what was described earlier as the strategic knowledge. Two corollaries follow. First, there is now a new definition of capability, that is, the capability to leverage strategic knowledge about others. Secondly, a strategic knowledge is about the processes in other firms and the possibilities of their orientations towards one's own strategic advantages. This dimension of orientation is captured by the second mode of interoperability. Time enters here because orientations appear in possible cascades. A particular *ex post* orientation tells us about the choices committed and acts executed. Success in orienting processes of other firms by leveraging strategic knowledge towards one's own advantage becomes strategic only when this resultant orientation accrues a Cantillon profit or when this *ex post* interoperation appears as 'capital as time'. An orientation through normative co-ordination of several intermediate products is an act of deferment of the consumption. A deferment of consumption achieved through elongation of the period of production or of divisions of labour constitutes capital. It follows then that strategic acts are undertaken to increase capital. The temporal dimension of strategy and of capital permit the collapsing of these two perspectives together. A corollary of this is that strategic knowledge – which, by definition, is not a factor of production nor does it belong to the public space and to the tradable domain in a market – generates capital by acts of strategy. Such strategic acts become possible through normative co-ordination.

Shackle (1972: 304) argued that 'capital is time... capital is the manifestation of the role of time lapse in the productive process... capital is delay. But delay is an inconvenience, a disutility, a discomfort, something which will not be borne except for a reward... capital seems to... offer a prize for, the endurance of delay... [as] a marginal balance.' A pure Austrian approach assumes that deferments are pre-reconciled amongst parties. Pre-reconciliation takes place through co-ordination or interoperability of the first mode, as described above. There is, however, opportunism and cheating, there are technological changes never foreseen and there are changes in utilities. Such changes, moreover, happen along temporal successions. Richardson (1960) does not recognize such changes. In contrast, Richardson's schema fits in with the Austrian schema of plan co-ordination. Departures that Richardson, and following him Leijonhufvud (1993) and Krafft and Ravix (2000), made consisted in recognizing that pre-reconciled plans would still take time: a duration that information needs to flow across firms and a period called 'gestation lags' that would invariably remain across investment commitments of firms. The problem of aligning pre-reconciliation with plans (which in equilibrium surely would be equivalent to strategy) is then a problem of quickening of computation (this alignment is computationally feasible). Krafft and Ravix (2000: 152) find out the computational algorithm with two forms, namely 'maintain competitive investments under a maximum threshold level' and 'maintain complementary investments over a minimum threshold level'. They argue that 'viability of the industrial system is ensured only if the two conditions are proved simultaneously'. This leads them to argue that firms must act for co-ordination of both competitive and complementary investments.

The time lag in this model does not take into consideration delays or deferments owing to possibilities. Technological innovation at any point of time offers the possibility to link up with or be complemented by a set of alternatives. This is the first objection. The second objection is that deferment is capital, and it happens not because of a 'market failure'. In the Richardson type of argument, delay is undesirable. Krafft and Ravix argue for institutions that could alleviate problems of delay. These institutions can take up several forms, such as sequential contract from the property rights approaches of

Hart and Moore (1988, 1990), Grossman and Hart (1990) and others. They involve forms where there is information delay, say, due to uncertainty but there is no investment delay. Or, if there is irreversible investment, a firm needs to make the right decisions regarding the profitability of a competitive investment while there is no information delay (Dixit, 1992). Other forms of co-ordination that might be taken up include informal market relation, licensing, strategic alliances, and formal agreements of various sorts, vertical integration or simply integration. The nature of the institution, it is argued (Langlois and Robertson, 1995; Teece, 1996) would depend on the type and length of delay. Teece (1996) argues that if the delay is caused by an autonomous innovation (which is relatively independent of other stages of production), several types of institutions might emerge depending on the internal capabilities of the relevant firms. In case the innovation is systemic (when simultaneous changes in several stages of production are required), Langlois and Robertson (1995) argue that there is the likelihood of vertical integration. Similarly, when there are delays in both types and the delays are long, vertical integration resolves the co-ordination problems that are simultaneously present. This is because the incumbent will have to generate information on strategies that other firms can implement. Also, the incumbent will have to muster co-ordination of the entire chain of systemic innovation. In case the innovation is autonomous and the delays necessarily shorter a large number of co-operation tools would suffice. When there is only one type of delay, market-based transactions would be able to resolve the coordination problem. When both the delays are of near-zero duration, simple market-based relations would be able to resolve it. Institutional arrangements of the vertical integration type, according to this argument, appear necessary only under specific circumstances.

According to this thinking, the longer delay caused by systemic innovation can be managed as per a pre-reconciled plan. There is little uncertainty involved. Autonomous innovations, according to this argument, would experience shorter delay. Both these appear to be unsustainable. Systemic innovations are understood here as *ex post* and appear through an uncertain mechanism called 'orientation' by Shackle. The delays and their lengths are attributable to this orientation. Delay as deferment refers to the postponement of the consumption with the expectation that there would be a profit at the margin; and the longer the delay or the 'average period of production' the higher the capital. 'It is this orientation of the presently co-existing objects which solely contains what we are measuring when we examine the "period of production". Orientation is thought, design, intention, expectation. Thought is mutable and elusive, thoughts in different minds about "the same" objects need have little in common' (Shackle, 1972: 322). An *ex post* systemic technology offers solution to the plans 'now' made but there is little to ensure that such plans would indeed be executed. The binding or the commitment to plan is ordinarily verified through committed or irreversible investments. The average period of production is computed from such plans 'accepted for the time being as a basis of immediate action, but by no means guaranteed' (*ibid.*). Technology dictates the current configurations that would give the plans stability in some 'short period'. Invariably, advances in technology would tend to shorten this period 'but the pace of innovation would itself be limited by economic considerations, by commercial organization and habits and by contracts' (*ibid.*). An average period may be understood as per the plans made by all participants to be the production net in an epoch. The short period may be as per the plans made by participants to a systemic technology and a period even shorter as per plans made by those few who participate in an autonomous technological innovation. What must be emphasized, however, is that the lengths of periods are determined more by economic states of affairs than by technological innovations. The increase in the average period, for example, Shackle argues, is never realized to the full because the production net is too lengthy and circuitous, and negotiations with the net are too protracted owing to the presence of durable equipment or the inertia caused by irreversible investment.

The epochal increase in the average delay reflects the general rise in capital and in divisions of labour. Systemic increase in delay reflects an increase in divisions of labour. The velocity with which an intermediate product might move reflects technological pace and the productivity but that hastened velocity cannot compensate for the lengthened divisions of labour. Technology is uncertain prior to its appearance and following its appearance, it determines the circuit of production and hence the plans for production. Human ingenuity reflected in the strategic moves, however, bypass such determinations by inventing and innovating further on economic organization of production. A firm takes this step with the hope of reaping a profit, which is beyond technological rent (the Schumpeterian profit) and which belongs to the Cantillon profit. The firm resorts to strategic surprise and evocation of expectation. Modes through which expectations can be definitely raised include lengthening of the production net, bringing about novelties and surprises in combining resources or in design of contracts and, finally, in innovating new technologies and engendering divisions of labour.

Co-ordination under such circumstances must look forward to the future. The co-ordination discussed here referred to earlier plans. Concurrent co-ordination refers to the adjustment process. Plans for deferment of consumption and on surprisingly new forms of intermediate products and combinations thereof are, however, unique to a firm. They refer to the present and the future. The incumbent firm expects that novel routes of the production net will emerge from its strategic choices. Firms belonging to the strategic milieu expect that expectation of the incumbent will chart out a path that is advantageous to them. The situation is analogous to conversation. A speaker does not know the complete sentence that will be uttered while starting to talk and indeed the sentence might get interrupted by an inter-jection from the conversation partner, swerving the dialogue to a path not premeditated by either. Each partner expects to chart out a series of sentences but interventions by others – that expect on the expectation of the speaker – result in the emergence of a unique dialogue path. The major difference with dialogue that strategic acts exhibit is primarily due to the durability of investments that the partners have made. With declining dur-ability, this difference recedes as well. Following this analogy, it is observed that participants enter dialogues in order to achieve fulfilment of certain expectations. If fulfilment is never reached because of the uncertainty of the dialogue paths, a dialogue would never be entered into. This conversation, therefore, has resulted in very interesting structural patterns.

A dialogue is often very long, however, often taking off to a rounding up. As a result it evolves into several nests, nested in other nests. A nested struc-ture evolves and a dialogue is complete after a long journey through such nested structure. This complex yet simple nested formation could not have evolved if there were no norms of dialogue. A norm is not a rule, nor a routine. It is always robust when it speaks only of what parties are not expected to do and when it allows freedom to parties to write whatever their expectation guides them to. A norm then sets in injunctions that allow a very large space to the parties in a dialogue to expect on other's expect-ations. With this analogy, one may briefly compare the strategic expectations of economic agents. A major difference noted is the deterrence caused by durability of investment. Durability reduces uncertainty, shows commit-ment and exacts reciprocal durability of investment from other parties. *Ex post* plans and existing technological paths are durable too. Novelty in technology or innovation and reduced durability of investment allow economic agents to engender differentiation of labour and increase in lengths and numbers of nested circuits of a production net. Drawing upon this analogy, an agent defers the consumption (analogous to completion of a dialogue) with the expectation of profit. This agent would be allowed profit only if there are other agents who participate in the deferment and each of whom holds expectations on profits. The deferment must complete itself at a future time on approaching the average period of production. As in the normative dialogue, these expectations need to follow norms in order to bring about a completion of a particular production net. Norms guide the expectations of agents by disallowing them certain paths and the agents, free to expect on expectations of others, keep generating short-period nests and an average-period dialogue by remaining within the norm. Short periods remain nested within the overall structure of the average period.

Put in another way, it follows from this analogy that divisions of labour do not possess uniqueness or some unique rationale. Such divisions across firms or several groups would then, it is argued, be contingent to a situation of expectations (analogous to a conversational situation). Such divisions retain fluidity. Designing an end consumable product through severalties of co-ordination might take several paths with several alternative and possible divisions amongst the participants, all of whom join in the deferment-based expectations on expectation. The only binding that these groups or firms would consider necessary is what has been called normative binding. A great deal of ambiguity can be allowed in such engagements. Participants who could only guess on the basis of partial and always evanescent evidence offered by the partners, use a mix of axiomatic and subjective probabilities, as it were. Better still, they would think about the potential. This potential gelled in time is the capital. Conversation is then not just an analogy here. Indeed, the participants converse using several modes of signs. The argument here seems to offer a better understanding than Piore, Lester, Kofman and Malek's (1994) arguments have offered. Piore *et al.* offered a hermeneutic argument. It is argued here that conversation better captures the situation than hermeneutics. Others are closer to this understanding even though they used the speech act to explain and not dialogue or dialogical ambience.

The arguments of Krafft and Ravix or Leijonhufvud regarding the failure of the market to offer solutions to co-ordination problem when there are two types of delays – information delay and investment gestation lags – have led to organizational and inter-organizational solutions. They, including Teece and Langlois and Robertson, have found vertical integration of several firms as solutions to longer delays, or varieties of contracts as solutions to shorter delays. It was observed that delays when caused by strategic intentions or by changes in market tastes or through increased divisions of labour and so on, bring about uncertainties or expectations about future. The received argument refers to the alignment between plans made in past and the current states of affairs. The proposed alignment in received theories offers technological solutions (that tend to reduce delays) and organizational solutions. Institutional solutions are, however, different from such organizational solutions. Co-ordination is an institutional problem and, therefore, requires an institutional solution. Normative co-ordination is an institutional solution. In analogy with conversation, which too is an institution, normative co-ordination limits the failures in co-ordination. An institution might not offer a particular organizational solution as the preferred mode. Several organizational or quasi-organizational solutions, including the contractual, might be considered as specific solutions. Vertical solution, it is argued, need not be considered as the only preferred solution to co-ordination with long deferment. The evidence from Indian software points out the undesirability of vertical integration as a solution. Vertical solution can be considered only when information being exchanged across firms refers to pre-reconciled plans. Information that cannot unambiguously describe a situation, or that can remain incomplete evidence and is required to adjust to envelopes of expectations on the future, cannot – even while exchanged – help formation of vertical integration. Moreover, deferment in the received theories is undesirable and technological solutions have been proposed to reduce its length. It is argued that technology fails to reduce the duration of the average period of production. Contrarily, technology increases this period of deferment, which represents capital. Technologies from firms that are not vertically integrated and that make non-durable investment need not reduce the deferment period. In certain circumstances, they might even hasten deferment.

Reversible investment in broaching ignorance

Durability of investment ensures that firms keep to their committed plans. From another perspective, durability is a vehicle for carrying expectations from present to future. Investment currently made in durable technology must, however, make reference to the past because the currently available technology, as an intermediate good, must have been innovated upon or made in the past. Durability refers thus to a sequence of investments. Such a sequence is temporal as well. There can be another temporally non-sequential mode of investing in technology, which Richardson's interoperability is understood to implicate. In this latter case, as in the case with a dominant standard, lateral innovations are supposed to maintain the standard of interoperability alone. It is a timeless system and here, therefore, expansion in the length and breadth of the interoperable domain does not signify a corresponding increase in the capital or in the division of labour. Such interoperability does not throw up challenges to co-ordination because, as through a reigning standard, the plan for co-ordination as a pre-reconciled document exists beforehand and as received. This is a pure case of interoperability. Another interoperability might be conjectured to be temporally sequential or a process. There is no reigning standard or no pre-reconciled plan here. As an emergent envelope or as an ensemble, several firms, by keeping to some normative co-ordination, adjust their futures based on current expectations on expectations. Temporally, non-sequential or timeless interoperability featured a type of durability, which while being a commitment or a commitment-exacting mechanism does not demand anything in the future. In fact, the future remains missing. Vertical integration is unnecessary in this case. A durable asset or a durable machine, however, acts as a vehicle for carrying expectations forward to the future. The irreversibility of investment in such durable goods must then seek to exact reciprocal durable investments by other firms and this so-called systemic innovation or technological system together acts as a deadweight of inertia.

There are umpteen numbers of examples of such systemic inertia. Often in fact, large-scale innovation, especially when undertaken by large corporations or by national governments in the form of a 'national programme', sets standards or exacts commitments from incumbent firms. Had there been no such systemic technology, they might have journeyed through a process of normative co-ordination and offered envelopes of several multiple technological choices and possibilities of divisions of labour. Durable investment, in this case by a reigning player (a corporation or a government), exacts durable investments by others through timeless interoperability and by recalling that these incumbents had no previously made durability. Durable investment by one party can then forcibly bring a closure to several other alternative possibilities. A large number of systemic innovations described by Teece and by Schumpeter fall under this category. Information for co-ordination in this case of dominant technology exists a priori and investment gestation lags are timeless.

The irreversibility of investment can thus exact a commitment. Modes of exacting commitments could be several as discussed above. The invariable consequence of irreversible commitments is a closure to increase in division of labour and in the deferment. Profit under the above situations can either have a falling rate or at most be pepped up to a level through frontiers of technological durability. Cantillon profit vanishes under such situations. Strategy appears redundant or is reduced to near irrelevance. The incumbent firms, under the burden of commitment, can exercise little, if any, strategy in expectation. The alternative is possible only if firms can make reversible investments. The logic here stands on this reversibility of investment by a firm. The firm's investment in manpower, it has been argued or otherwise hinted in earlier chapters, can be made reversible especially if there is little asset specificity in the technology/process of producing the good. Typically, a durable machine or technology with large sunk investment demands a correspondingly large human-asset specificity, which implies that mobility of human resource must remain near zero. Firms took upon this method in their historical path to protect them from uncertainty. If, however, technology can exact little sunk cost or if the reigning standards appear vulnerable or weak, and if investment in durable machinery can be maintained at a sustainable low level, investment in human resources too can be free of asset specificity. In other words, passage or exit/entry of human resources through firm boundaries would be close to zero cost. The investment by a firm in human resources under such a situation can be called reversible.

The software industry is perhaps an excellent example in which firms are able to reverse investments when necessary. Typically, a software firm invests in land, buildings and such investments in hardware–software purchase constitutes a very small fraction of the total revenue of a firm. It is important to note that land or buildings are not required by the technology of software writing and investment in such parts, therefore, cannot indicate capital constitutive investment. These investments appear under capital head only because of accounting tradition. Such investments are not durable either. Durable investment by a software firm is then insignificant. In fact, the durability of hardware–software (used as a tool for writing other software) and the communications system is insignificant, usually for about a year or two. Accounting figures, however, conceal the shaky basis of durability of investment by software firms. Accounting ratio between 'investment' to 'total funds' (as defined in the Annual Reports of the firms) takes up higher values approaching 1 only very occasionally. The value of this ratio for 29 Indian software firms for three years, 1997, 1998 and 1999, revealed that the average value of this ratio was 0.33 for 1998. For 1999 it was 0.04. The distribution of the values is rather skewed (since one or two firms invested heavily in the corresponding year on land, and so on). Ordinarily, the value of this ratio hovered around 0.01. Durable investment in software (as a 'machine to produce other machine' type) is understandably an even lower fraction of total funds.

Durable investment, it has been argued here, can act as a vehicle for carrying expectations into the future. This, in Austrian terminology, can be described as asset-formation balance. R & D investment is believed to belong to this category. Reported R & D investments often, however, follow conventions of accounting and of the capital market. In several cases, R & D investment figures help the valuation of a firm. This presupposes that the capital market, where the incumbent's scrip is traded, has followed a convention of valuing higher investment in R & D. It must be kept in mind that accounting reports have very little to do with Cantillon profit, increase in capital or the rate of profit. It is assumed that with R & D as a separate accounting head, there is a special firm-internal accounting practice or a separate department for it. R & D cannot be reported separately, except under such accounting convention, when technologically inseparable from the act of production. R & D in software writing cannot be separated from the act of writing software. R & D investment in the Austrian sense would have implicated the hastening of division of labour. Increase in division of labour inside a firm never gets captured through accounting figures. This implies that reported R & D investment could be thought of as pertaining to convention, or to making investment as per pre-reconciled plan. In the Austrian sense, R & D cannot be durable. In these conventional senses such figures can represent durability though. Total funds, in accounting terms, indicate investible funds. A study of investments by Indian software firms in R & D suggested that the Indian market does not seem to have the convention of ascribing higher values to a firm that reports R & D. Moreover, software does not demand a separation of R & D from its writing. Rarely would an Indian software firm report an R & D investment. Most such firms deployed investible funds in the money market instruments. Reported accounting figures show that software firms had very little sunk investment.

Accounting convention and the usual practice report investment in manpower as expenditure. The argument here treats this expenditure as an investment to better capture what one may consider 'total personnel cost'. This includes salaries and wages, bonuses, ESOP, welfare, training and such others and the ratio of 'total personnel cost' to the sum of 'cost of sales' and 'cost of communication' is then computed. This ratio can capture several aspects such as the deployment pattern of staff between sales and software writing since a few members of staff work for administration. It captures the capital intensity of software writing that includes use of communications by staff. Data on software purchased as capital item would have shown the ratio in a proper light but most firms do not report on that item. This ratio was computed for 1997, 1998 and 1999 for 14 firms (Banerjee, 2003e). In none of the reporting companies did this ratio take a value lower than 1. In about five companies, it was above or about two and for some it went up to about seven. Since the cost of sales includes all costs, of which salaries constitute a fraction only, it may be concluded that the cost of personnel engaged in writing of software is substantially higher compared to the cost of personnel engaged in sales. In fact, for some firms, the former is several times higher than that of the latter. Both sales staff and software staff share communication costs though, presumably, the former uses it more intensively. This ratio, through the deployment pattern of the human resource in a software firm, provides an imperfect indication. Internal resource deployment characterizes the competency of a firm (Leonard-Barton, 1992). Deployment also refers to the composition of structural sorts. This implies that deployment, apart from referring to competency, also implicates the structure of a firm. Inter-project or inter-functional or inter-knowledge division deployment data is not available though deployment based on firm-internal experience is a common enough practice. Deployment of internally generated components (Amit and Schoemaker, 1993; Galunic and Rodan, 1998) can effect differentiation across firms. Such differentiation, in the terminology here, is based on differences in structural sorts. Differentiation, which is based on resources appropriated from the market that the resources theory proposes, is more driven by the quantity of resource consumed by a firm. The resource market cannot effect differentiation between firms based on structural sorts because structural sorts are an outcome of the strategy of a firm.

Streissler's (1973) asset-formation balance represented assets held back for an expected gain in the irregular business of wealth formation. The interest here is more on this irregular part of 'business in expectation'. Regular writing of software, as discussed here, is burdened little with durable asset. The deployment of human resources from regular writing to the irregular business of writing software is far more important and frequent than deployment inter-projects. This was observed during the field visits to the firms. Irregularly held or held-back assets offer prospects through deferment. Quantity and frequency of such held-back assets depend on the opportunity cost of withholding, expected gain in the irregular business and the frequency with which one might strike bargains. The argument here is that since human resource is the most important and dominant form of asset to a software firm, the asset-formation balance of such a firm would comprise more human resource than the liquid funds. Such a balance would act as the vehicle of carrying forward expectations of the firm. Human resources replace the durable good. A durable good offers inertia and increases the time needed to switch from transactional business to the irregular business. The time needed to do this switch in the case of human resource as the asset balance is near nil.

A software firm, it has been observed, holds enough cash or cash equivalents of money-market investments. The liquidity of such cash represents assets held back but the money is without any intrinsic worth. Human resource is worth as much as its knowledge. Money can buy the plastic human resource from a market, which is fluid and offers little transaction cost. The market or the social circuit of human resources sustains the knowledge levels of human resource by keeping them engaged in certain off-firm or other-firm based knowledge practices. A firm's portfolio will, therefore, have manpower in regular and irregular businesses, in money or its equivalents, and the cost to hire manpower from social circuit. The opportunity cost of withholding, however, also depends on the total manpower withheld by – if not all the firms in a market – all the firms belonging to the strategic milieu. With increasing withdrawal of manpower from regular business by all such firms, the cost of withdrawal too increases since the current return in transaction-based regular business or the interest rate has gone up. The Contagion theory offers the basis of locating a partial market. Any firm withdrawing from this market affects all the firms. This theory or the social interaction theory looks at a partial market where each participant can affect and thus regulate an outcome. To recall, the argument on strategic milieu extended this Marshallian theory of partial market. In such a market with contagion 'changes in interest rates will sometimes have a very small effect on the relative use of money balances and sometimes very large effects depending on which part of the logistic curve one happens to be on.... Profit rates and opportunity costs of consumption foregone may be more important than interest rates' (Streissler, 1973: 177–8).

Expectations on expectations depend on this contagion-affected partial market of the strategic milieu. The portfolio composition of a software firm in terms of the four items, namely, manpower in regular and irregular business, the money held back and the manpower that can be hired from the social circuit, would thus depend on which part of the logistics an incumbent is. The logistics consideration, however, has one limitation. Decisions on composition of a portfolio, according to this argument, depend on the contagion represented, as it were, on the switching points on a logistics. Much depends on two other factors though: the internal processes of an incumbent and its influence on internal processes of other firms in the milieu. These two aspects represent strategic leveragability on which the choice of portfolio depends. It is argued that an incumbent does not have enough information on the knowledge assets belonging to its own processes.

Knowledge is a lumpy asset. A firm, therefore, is uncertain about what it might expect from its own people even if they are withheld from regular writing of software. Cash balance depends not just on interest rate in the market but also, as argued by Streissler, on profit rates and opportunity cost. The ratio between the sum of 'total personnel cost' and 'depreciation' to the 'total revenue' of a firm provides an imperfect picture of this portfolio. The value of this ratio for 51 firms and for the three years, 1997, 1998 and 1999 was computed, its numerator having two types of resources. The first was manpower and the second was based on depreciation (Banerjee, 2003a). The numerator reflects withheld assets. A software firm typically retains a good cash position in the form of several holdings in money market instruments, which can act as a buffer for any sudden demand, say on recruiting manpower, emerging out of a new project. The current revenue of a firm would often get distributed between the regular and the irregular businesses through an initial portfolio selection of this type. One should expect the value of this ratio remaining around 1, which was the confirmed average trend of the value of this ratio.

These two ratios represent the importance of investment in (or cost of) human resources to a software firm. Human-resource investment constitutes the major share in the investment portfolio of a software firm. The liquidity of capital engaged, particularly human capital withheld from the regular business, is represented by the second ratio. The first ratio indicates the use of such a plastic resource by the firm's internal routine, which is geared towards achieving a higher competency. Competency theorists present optimal utilization of resources. Moreover, competency ideas do not recognize the influence of acts of inter-firm co-ordination on competence. A core competency is about differentiating a firm (Nelson, 1991) through firm-internal allocation rule and practices of the firm management (Foss, 1999). Co-ordination amongst firms remains unnoticed and, where competency prevails, it is about adjusting to a pre-reconciled plan. Competing firms, through two modes described by Richardson, business and technical information, can secure information on mutual competencies for securing adjustments to pre-reconciliations.

Normative co-ordination refers to an envelope that unfolds gradually in the future though, and firms expect on the expectations of other firms. Information exchange required for carrying out co-ordination on such an envelope is beyond these two Richardsonian types of information. It follows then that normative co-ordination goes beyond internal determination of the core competency of a firm to a state where core competencies of firms evolve over time on an envelope that unfolds in future with little dead-weights of the past on it. Firm competencies in this latter case evolve mutually over expectations on expectations and not over attempts to adjust to pre-reconciled plans. A simple adjustment can be taken care of by information such as tangible figures publicly reported, as in annual reports. Normative co-ordination would require another type of information. The agent who transmits does not know the value of this information beforehand as happens in the case of a conversation. The value and the nature of such information are generated in a process of evolutionary adjustments. It is argued that such information can be generated in a process based on intangible qualities of the manpower that exits from a firm in a flux to join another firm in the strategic milieu and acts as a carrier of information on the knowledge competency of the firm it has exited from. Manpower then performs the twin role of an intermediate good and the carrier of information. As the flow of intermediate good, manpower lengthens the period of deferment across normatively co-ordinated firms. Deferment of possible consumption enhances capital and the rate of profit. The increase in the rate of profit, it is argued here, is thus attributable to an envelope of innovation to which firms adjust normatively. Simple competency, derived and sustained through an internal mechanism and through adjustments to a pre-reconciled plan, allows a firm to earn only competitive rates of revenue or a Schumpeterian technological rent. Manpower flow through the mechanism of deferment and through generation of information as in a process, allows a firm to earn a Cantillon profit.

Expectations and information-in-expectation

Shackle (1972) argues that with the increase in the dimension of knowledge the scope of ignorance too increases. Knowledge when it refers to the things known with detailed attributes must refer to things or circumstances *ex post*. Things known or believed, especially if through recurrence, generate stereotypes and concepts and the recurrence perpetuates a habit. A habit stereotype or even a concept is less formal than a theory and often employs metaphors, analogies or even heuristics while addressing circumstances *ex ante*. The uncertainty about the future projects to the 'knower's' mind several alternatives, and the hypotheses elude an extension of what is known and sometimes even inferences (including probable inferences). A habitual disposition guides the mind and the pre-reconciled plan is a quasi-agreement on the future. A deviation from this future is adjusted through *tâtonnement*. Richardson has described this co-ordination, which is dependent on 'knowledge' of circumstances as known. Knowledge generates ignorance in equal measure. By knowing what other firms have committed or are capable of doing, a firm attains a position from where it can undertake strategic steps that would take other firms by surprise and which other firms would find difficult to adjust to. Other firms too, through *ex post* knowledge, can take recourse to ignorance of the former firm in bringing about surprises. The objective here is to understand normative co-ordination that can keep together surprises in future brought about by current strategic actions of firms based on their mutual ignorance.

A surprise in future comes not through a blitzkrieg but through a moderated process. Each small surprise as a strategic step is a step in broaching ignorance of the future. It is a step in completing a desire to earn a profit. A long and lone stride could take a firm away from the domain of interoperability. Each step of one firm must receive corresponding surprises from its consorts. Mutually undertaken, small surprise steps would, therefore, generate another novel envelope of a broader and deferred envelope of business at a not-distant future, which offers prospects of profits. In order that a step can broach ignorance, a firm must 'know' the antecedent co-ordination. Again, in order that a surprise step remains a small stride, approachable by succeeding surprises by other firms, a firm must again broach ignorance. Ignorance, as a counterfactual to the current knowledge of the *ex post* states of affairs, must be based on current knowledge on what others are not expecting. It is, therefore, a reading of other firms. Hermeneutic deployment makes such a reading suggestive.

Suggestion is the third function of information. Information on deferment, current strategies and suggestion must continue to be exchanged between firms. A global exchange would be impossible. A conversation cannot be directed globally to an unnamed addressee. Conversation and strategy always address a partial market of the strategic milieu. It is believed here that manpower alone could prove to be a medium or a flux across firms providing such varieties of information. In ordinary exchanges of information various forms of data on quantity and prices are used. These data are, however, on *ex post* circumstances. The medium of exchange must be an intermediate good that has hermeneutic capability. Ordinary exchanges of an intermediate good provide data on price and quantity. In normative co-ordination, as argued earlier, price data is irrelevant because that refers to the past. Quantity data too, while referring to the past, remains restricted to stabilized past platforms of production. Moreover, quantity of manpower entering or exiting a firm cannot remain an indicator because the knowledge level of an individual is not measurable with reference to a standard measure. Firms in traditional sectors employ economic information on competition, consumers, logistics and even trade-related aspects for their business calculations. Technical information regarding the state-of-the-art benchmarking is also used. Co-ordination amongst firms is secured through such information. Normative co-ordination must then be based on exchanges of such intermediate goods as can offer hermeneutic reading and suggestions to parties in exchange. This, to the understanding here, is human resources.

Information exchange as per Richardson and others, does not refer to internal processes of a firm. An incumbent firm, according to this received view, does not search for information on internal processes of firms with which the incumbent adjusts its plan through co-ordination. This information does not generally serve the internal structural purposes of a firm either. In the highly innovative information sector, information plays a radically different role. Economic information on competitors, consumers or about the logistics and the technical information regarding the state of the art, for example, is necessary for firms in this sector. The importance of such information has, however, diminished significantly; firstly because life cycles in software are very short and information through static channels fails to serve purposes of dynamic co-ordination that a software firm must always be looking for. Software firms are looking for carriers of information who can interpret, generate and creatively employ information. A firm requires an intermediate good because deferment necessarily requires elongated intermediation. Such intermediate good must simultaneously prove to be the carrier of suggestive-cues and preferably should be able to interpret and thus generate information not known through quantity and price data. A software firm generates much of the information. Unlike firms in Richardson's schema of co-ordination, it is argued here, software firms that are normatively co-ordinating should each have partly common and partly unique information. Common information between parties in exchange of intermediate good is provided by what the good stands for. Unique information is unshared and generated by one party with the support of the intermediate good. The generation and management of such information, belonging to both the economic and technical types, demand a different perspective. A software firm locates an information-generating resource in the employable and in its employees.

Employees who do not exit a firm become the source of tacit knowledge. Tacit knowledge provides the foundation for asset specificity and is the bedrock on which transaction costs in Williamson (1979, 1985, 1990b) stand. It has been argued here that such asset specificity remains limited to a particular type of technology and to the market structure. The latter was called a stable structure for brevity's sake. An employee, in this case, fails to become a source of both market and technical information and proves to be the source of inertia in such a case. Only when switching jobs and becoming a creative carrier of information, does an employee dismantle the inertia in processes of firms being exited from and entered into. Richardson's talk about business and technical information refers to a market that returns to equilibrium quickly through co-ordinated adjustments brought about by these two types of information. Software goes beyond this to normative co-ordination that, one may recall, is sought through expectation on expectations. The current ensemble of products provides certain co-ordination achieved through stabilization of exchanges by means of business and technical information. The future would be about another ensemble of products and technologies; bringing about novel interoperability and yet-unknown deferments would require exchange of another mode of information. A new type of information, not considered by Richardson, punctuates the interregnum between these two ensembles. Shackle (1972, 1988) provides insights into this new type of information, called here information-in-expectation (Banerjee, 2003a).

Market and technical information refer to the durability or commitment. The durability in the investment profile of a firm belonging to the stable market refers to the durability in several facets including internal processes and, therefore, asset specificity in human resources immobility, and in its product-based production as well as product-centred competence. A product out of a firm's stable is quasi-durable because the marketing of the product, even if it is intermediate, must trace definite, incontrovertible routes. A durable or more properly quasi-durable product, unlike the marketing of a service, cannot get attached to indefinite usage. In other words, such a product would not spawn indefinite divisions of labour and would not encourage indefinite deferment. Durability cannot allow a firm to adjust its competency profile indefinitely and firm competency is decided by the systems and structure of the market as dictated by SCPP or by the resource usage profile of the firm *à la* the resource theorist. Firms in this picture are blocks attempting to adjust internal competencies. Superior technological knowledge or competence in a firm encourages it to enhance both the vertical integration and the scope through mechanisms such as mergers and acquisitions (M and A).

Immediate disequilibria is the goal with information-in-expectation. Equilibrium refers to the plans and knowledge *ex post*. Information-in-expectation refers to ignorance. The source of such information must remain in the expectations of other firms in the strategic milieu. An incumbent firm can expect on expectations of other firms only if information-in-expectation of other firms is available to this incumbent. Firms here cannot generate this information internally. Expectation is a function of ignorance and common knowledge cannot provide the foundation to expectation. The incumbent firm has knowledge about common knowledge shared with other firms but cannot know from business and technical information what another firm perceives as its ignorance and hence its expectations. Thus even if the competency of a firm entitles it to go for M and A, it would stand to lose the information-in-expectation that the unmerged entities could have provided otherwise as independent firms. The source of such an information-in-expectation is entrepreneurial (Hayek, 1949). This information is discovered and, as per Hayek, the market is built upon discoveries by firms. An entrepreneurial firm keeps searching on for this new type of information.

To recall, two internal dimensions of a firm were proposed: structural sorts and the processes. Perceived ignorance rests on the working of internal processes. Definite knowledge, which is not a common knowledge, that a firm possesses shapes up and gets structured in the internal structural sorts of a firm. Ignorance being only cognitive cannot, however, shape the structural sorts. Human resource recognizes the ignorance and, consequently, so do the internal processes. The source of expectation is thus the internal process. The strategic knowledge of a firm, to recall the earlier argument, empowers the firm to influence such processes. Strategic knowledge, it follows, is the cognition of limits of both definite and common knowledge. In other words, strategic knowledge remains diffused through most knowledge employees and the internal processes of a firm. A firm it appears, cannot then sum up strategic knowledge possessed by all, store it as though in a firm-memory or consider strategic knowledge as tacit. It is a knowledge that manifests through working upon it and that shapes up expectations. The processes of a firm provide the conversational or dialogical milieu (Piore, Lester, Kofman and Malek, 1994) where there is no database of definite knowledge. The milieu is a process where each utterance proceeds from the previous utterance and from what is not known and what one expects to achieve. Such a dialogical set-up thus does not depend on hermeneutic entailment as proposed by Piore *et al*. Each knowledge employee acts as an entrepreneur with expectations formed in the manner Cantillon proposed. Strategy-making must then rest on these processes and must attempt to influence, through the wherewithal of strategic knowledge, internal processes and expectations of knowledge employees in both its own organization and other organizations belonging to the strategic milieu. Manpower is thus a resource to a software firm in two respects: first, as a resource as understood by a resource theorist; secondly, as a resource that can provide information-in-expectation. Information resource is dynamic, process-based and information-generative.

The dialogical process and the internal processes of a firm have little respect for the boundary of a firm. Quantified resources, as the resource theorists envision, can be limited by the firm boundary. Information-generating and expectations-making dialogical processes cannot be quantified and the flow of processes, if restricted across the boundary, would fail to continue with the conversations meaningfully (a meaning, it may be recalled is an expectation). The dialogical process must continue to flow through a firm's boundaries into the internal processes of other firms in the strategic milieu. Dialogical or expectations-forming processes must then provide certain common residuum to these firms. The job-switching person acts as the meta-network or as the carrier between firms in competitive expectations or in normative co-ordination and the job switch recognizes this human agency. It helps co-ordination of strategies of firms. Internal processes of the other firm are the sites for securing information. Supply of information-generative human resources causes short-term disequilibria.

Learning and intermediate good

Job switching is a deferment of consumption. The higher and more frequent the manpower turnover, the greater the delay or the deferment of consumption. Had job switching been an industry-wide phenomenon, one would conclude that the industry had deferred consumption and increased profit rate and, therefore, increased capital. This is the situation in software. Industry-wide, higher manpower turnover in software acts as a quantity signal. Manpower turnover along with fresh manpower input into the market together make the quantity signal. How a quantity signal fails when firm-level manpower decisions are considered has been discussed. It was argued that firm-level decisions take into account turnover in the partial market of strategic milieu. A firm taking decisions on the recruitment of fresh manpower takes into account the quantity signal though. Its decisions on manpower are thus separated. The latter quantity-driven decision accepts manpower as a resource in the sense used by resource theorist while decisions that are based on manpower turnover in the partial market consider manpower as an intermediate good, capable of providing suggestions and information-in-expectation.

An interesting observation follows from this description. Deferment caused by industry-wide high.manpower turnover shifts the consumption in the industry as a whole (compared to other non-deferred industry sectors) and thereby increases the rate of profit in that industrial sector. This quantity signal then acts as a signal to other sectors of economy. Manpower turnover across several partial markets in the software sector is, however, uneven and few partial markets are visited by very high turnover while a few others are visited by rather low turnover. The decisions on deferment by a firm in the software sector then depend on which partial market (strategic milieu) the firm belongs to. Internal to the software sector, decisions on deferment by a firm then do not depend on the quantity signal but on the rate of turnover averaged in that partial market. The rate of manpower turnover in a partial market is an indicator of the expectation on rate of profit in it. The rate in this partial market often differs substantially from the average rate prevailing in both the software sector market and in the overall industry. The existence of such differences explains why even internal to a sector, firms exit and enter partial markets.

Partial-market prices (for example, wages) then differ from the sector-market prices, which again differ from the industry prices. It has been argued that quantity-price parameters affect a firm's decision on recruitment of fresh manpower. Partial-market prices are unrelated to the quantity. These latter prices reflect expectations on information-generative capabilities of the manpower and are asymmetric to the quantity in supply. Prices in this partial market, reflecting asymmetric information-generative capability of experienced job-switching personnel, then decide the internal processes of a firm. Job-switching personnel directly enter the calculations on expectations and on strategic knowledge. Thus internal processes of a firm become directly dependent on the partial market parameter. The human resource price to a procuring firm reflects the market condition. Internal resources are thus reflections of the market.

The market here thus recognizes differences in deferment that exist across several partial markets of the strategic milieu. Inter-firm competition and co-operation can only be meaningful when firms do differ. It is also argued that differences in deferment cause inter-partial market. Received theories refer to differences based on technological state of affairs. It is argued here that the differences are based on deferment differentials. In received literature, differences between firms operating in a comparatively static technological environment result from practices internal to those firms (Nelson, 1991), from the dynamic competencies (Teece, 1988) from evolutionary learning (Nelson and Winter, 1982) or else from the mode of resources combinations inside the firm (Peteraf, 1993). The differences in these perspectives belong to the internal domain where, as per Coase (1990), prices, the only distinct signal from the market, do not operate. The position here suggests that either prices or asymmetrically loaded prices affect the internal processes of a firm. Richardson (1998) and Foss and Mahnke (2000) have similarly argued that prices affect internal decisions of a firm.

Differences between firms, it is argued, depend on differences in strategic knowledge. Strategic knowledge reflects the capability to influence the processes internal to an incumbent and its partner firms belonging to the same partial market. This strategic knowledge is a representation of the expectations and of utilization of information-in-expectation. Expectations depend on the deferment or the delay. Differences across firms are a function of delay. The uniqueness of a firm then does not depend on the resources that it has procured. Resources, according to the received theory, are generally defined (Bromiley and Fleming, 2002) as capital, labour, brand, tacit knowledge and such like. Since managerial decisions are assumed to be 'rational' and the markets are supposed to be in equilibrium, the differences in resources endowment alone can explain inter-firm differences. Since bounded rational agents are limited in their decision capabilities, prior conditions of resources, and firm history (Amit and Shoemaker, 1993) would appear to influence differences between firms. Technical and market information cannot be considered as resource. Accordingly, information available equally to other firms cannot be considered as a resource. Barney (1991) attempts to seek explanations for firm differences from information generated within the firm. Information as a resource has to be internal and structural. Firm strategy and aspects of co-ordination then appear irrelevant and the optimality of managerial decisions gets restricted to markets in equilibrium. It has been argued that the uniqueness of a firm depends on the delay function. To extend this argument, a delay function is a function of learning. Partial markets differ by the deferments effected and firms differ by the learning effected through manpower flow on the strategic knowledge. The deferment by a firm is represented in the learning of that firm.

Learning, like R & D, is a deferment of consumption. A firm situated in the context of a partial-market (strategic milieu) is expected to follow the deferment characteristic of that market. This deferment acts as a norm. The delay effected by a firm needs to follow this norm with the exception that even though the length of the period of deferment remains nearly the same for firms in a partial market, the potential gains of firms do differ. Differences in this potential gain mark out the firm's individuality. This potential gain is owing to the learning or knowledge-generative dimension of the time period of deferment. A potential gain is thus a function of time, which is named the 'delay function' here. Learning or generation of knowledge internal to a firm happens through deferment of the intellectual labour from writing of software for immediate consumption. Learning that comes through simple writing of software is different from the one that delay function could offer. The delay function is effected by the strategic deployment of manpower from the regular writing of software. It has been argued here that holding of pure liquid money is only fictional deferment (money can be converted immediately into consumption and is without any 'directedness') but deferment through knowledge employees generates knowledge, which is not necessarily a factor of production and has a certain 'directedness'. This 'directedness' of knowledge thus generated demands that other firms in the partial market too direct their knowledge-generation deferments or the delay functions in the same direction in order that knowledge or its output remains interoperable following a period of deferment. This period of deferment, similar to a period of production, is thus a function of the delay function. Firms in a milieu must then consider each other's delay functions (or equivalently, in-process delay implicated by the knowledge being generated). The normative deferment in a partial market results from the tacitly agreed common minimum delay caused by all firms. It follows then that normative deferment in a strategic milieu results from firm-internal strategic decisions on knowledge generation.

A deferment must also cause increased divisions of labour or knowledge. Capital or increase in (or existence of) rate of profit according to Shackle happens because divisions in knowledge have increased. Consequently, any increase in or bringing into existence of a rate of profit must be visited by an equally increased effort at co-ordination. In fact, every new division in knowledge or in labour must demand new co-ordination. If the long-term or average period of production, apropos of the earlier discussion, remains static while firms continue increasing divisions of knowledge in the short period (as through delay functions and normative deferment), some previous divisions of knowledge must perish, giving room to new divisions. In the short period then, divisions of labour must change while possibly keeping the total quantum of divisions or average period of production (somewhat in correspondence to the input–output table) nearly constant. Each change in division, however, requires changes in the nature of the co-ordination or in the envelope of the emergent co-ordination each time. This envelope is being called the normative co-ordination. A hierarchic corporation created through vertical integration necessarily resists or altogether stops increase in divisions in knowledge or labour. The resolution of co-ordination in favour of vertical integration stops the spawning of divisions in knowledge or consequently in the delay functions of strategic firm. Here the emphasis is on co-ordination as a process, whereas vertical integration, other intermediate forms of quasi-integration or static organization of small producers exhibit an achieved co-ordination. Co-ordination as a process, as in the normative mode, is then different from the co-ordination achieved once as a feat.

A stable division of labour, exhibited for example, in an existing interoperable system exchanges intermediate goods of known kinds. Exchanging firms have prior knowledge of the goods entering or exiting their boundaries. Intermediate goods linking firms and their strategies cannot be defined as resource flows. Similarly, markets with strategic surprises too cannot be analysed if intermediate goods are definitely known beforehand. This discussion on co-ordination as a process has emphasized delay functions of a firm and on the ever-changing divisions in knowledge. The knowledge as deferment takes place as the strategic outcome of activities inside a firm. In order that both divisions in knowledge and the co-ordination remain as processes, the modes of exchange in intermediate goods must not be known beforehand. In other words, the nature of intermediate goods must also keep changing. This implies that normative co-ordination must exchange not only varying information but also varying intermediate goods. Such intermediate goods by definition contain capital in the process of deferment. It is argued here that knowledge alone can ensure this property of capital. An individual in flux across firms in a strategic milieu is the resident of knowledge which is in the process of completion – the resident of not-yet-complete knowledge. Personnel deserting a firm to join another are a strange kind of intermediate goods. Software writing involves cognitive capabilities of a team orchestrated together. Little of this cognitive capacity can be captured in the extant objective hardware or processes and most of this can be located in the human element. The flow of cognitive capacity across firms is tantamount to the migration of an intermediate good between these firms. In Sraffa's model, an intermediate good links possible vertical relations in an industry or an economy. Dynamism in that model is derived from the linkages of the capital-goods producing sector. A capital good is the representation of congealed deferment. A knowledge good in our description is an extension of that argument, however, with a major difference. A capital good in Sraffa is known beforehand and co-ordination is thus pre-reconciled. Knowledge capital or deferments, however, are in-process and indefinite while possessing 'directedness'. Sraffa's model is amenable to organizational integration while the model here is not.

The institutional principle behind Sraffa's or Richardson's systems is organizational formation. This principle allows several, including often the formation of vertical integration. Normative co-ordination does not talk about organizational formation but refers to the evolution of norms. Norms are the principal characteristic of a market and it is argued here that the organizational shape, including vertical organization, is always a contingent outcome. Systemic innovation of Teece or the principles discussed by Langlois and Robertson situate the organizational principle outside economic transactions and they argue for technological or innovational factors. Normative co-ordination attempts to consider both technological and economic methods and, in doing so, arrives at a more general principle, the norm. It might appear intriguing from the perspective of transactions-cost economists that deferment, including deferment owing to learning, raises the time length and hence the accounting cost of a possible transaction that is likely or expected to take place in an indefinite future. The accounting framework of transactions cost goes against the time theory of capital or deferred consumption. A firm appears to be increasing the cost through deferment. Normative co-ordination appears as a necessary solution to a possible overshooting of transactions cost in the event that different firms hold incoherent expectations of others or keep deferring indefinitely. Such an argument saves the transactions cost framework but cannot save Coase's theory on firms that firm-based transactions cost must keep to the minimum and be lower than the costs of market-based transactions. On the contrary, firm-internal transactions are made costlier through deferment.

Trading in intermediate products of a definite kind that are known beforehand by the transacting firms is so conducted as to reduce a possible rise in transactions cost internal to a firm's operation. Sraffa talked about this kind. Trading in intermediate products of an indefinite kind that are not known beforehand by transacting parties, however, cannot be explained on the ground of minimization of transactions cost internal to a firm. Firms in the latter case expect to arrive at a possible interoperable system through offers of partial products. In order that expectations of different firms remain guided by a common systemic feature, it is argued here, co-ordination ought to follow those norms that are not decided by common structural features of the firms in trade.

Strategy and competency of a firm defined on the evolutionary rule or routine can adapt the firm to both the markets in equilibrium and in disequilibria. Firm routines have known definite intermediate products and in case there is a change in these products because of innovation by a firm, adaptive routines, this theory argues, can adjust to that change. Adaptive capability is reflected in the routine or in the learning routine. Common sharing of innate routines ensures that disequilibria are never so far off the mark as adaptability fails. According to the evolutionary rule, the internal and innate structural features of firms then provide the principle of co-ordination. Evolutionary information is akin to generic information. Information must correspond to innate or basic technological features specific to either the industry or the interoperable system. This is similar to what Richardson has described. The uniqueness of a firm arises out of firm-internal adaptive or innovative capabilities, and information usage that this firm has evolved. Such routine on information usage is crucial. Can a software firm possess such generic systems, structures or hardware or software? The development of such interoperable generic software or systems has apparently failed in the case of software. Human-resources practices of a firm failed to evolve into common generic practices based as it were on innate systems (Baron, Burton and Hannan, 1996).

Intermediate good and indefiniteness of firm boundary

Information gets selected in normative co-ordination. In evolutionary affairs, selection is based on innate routine. In normative affairs, selection is based on certain ignorance, more properly on the expectation of what other firms are expecting. It follows that selection criteria are based not on internal structural or otherwise innate forms but in contrast are based upon ignorance (and hence expectation) of the strategy of other firms. A firm must then look for the expectations of other firms that have, in turn, formed their expectations on the expectation of the incumbent. It is a mutual and inter-dependent mode of selecting information. Even in this mutual selection, no firm selects information for a variation-producing cue. Instead, information selected tends to complete a conversational mode of joint development of innovation. In evolutionary and ecological theory, selected information and its effects on the cue of routines in making possible variations differentiate a firm from the rest of the population. The uniqueness in normative co-ordination depends not so much on selection and variation as on being able to guide generation of information and in using information to deflect the expectations of others. The essence of information usage in normative co-ordination is to shape the internal processes of others such that those other firms might now expect differently. Undeniably, the incumbent firm too shapes its own processes through conversational information though this shaping is different, as argued here, from the innate version.

The intermediate good being traded across software firms then informs both the parties in a transaction and the flow of goods thus shapes the expectations as well as the expectations on expectations. Information is constitutive of this expectation. Any organizational shape that could destroy the sources of such information would also destroy expectation and consequently the deferments. A vertically integrated structure or generic structures in general would hit at this expectation formation. Our observation has concluded that Indian software firms have evolved into several types of structures and systems. Such systems do not appear to be generic. Systems are peculiar to a firm, a perspective advocated by the resource theorist. Co-ordination assumes greater significance when firms do not share similar generic structures. A firm must co-ordinate its products, production and resources, especially of information, with its competitors; it must also simultaneously make demands for such information as can differentiate itself from the other firm and it must retain strategic control over the medium of such information. These three purposes can be served by some flux of intermediate goods. Resources theorists cannot offer an explanation for such trades in flux. An intermediate good rich in information serves these objectives fairly well. First, because the firm substantially controls its information or cognitive content; secondly, firms can thus be differentiated; and thirdly, co-ordination of firms in both existing and potential envelopes is made possible. Finally, this good must be indefinite and must provide information along with ignorance. Human resource alone satisfies all these qualities.

The software writing scenario (Kenney, 2000) generally consists of small and numerous start-up firms. Most of them began as spin-offs from large firms in the early phase of this industry in the USA. The Indian scenario is, however, different. Co-ordination amongst firms that share common parentage, or otherwise share a milieu infused with common possibly generic structures, might not insist upon trades in intermediate goods of the kind being insisted on here. The co-ordination issue appears complex in India because start-ups here are not spin-offs from large firms; or else, they do not enjoy the privilege of a common institutional practice regarding resources usage or information to be exchanged. Co-ordination pertaining to products and production planning, technological standards, and innovation envelopes would appear important to these firms. Information required for co-ordination cannot be procured from the typical markets of products, technology or the fresh graduates. An intermediate good that can be generative of information upon demand from the dynamics of the market surprises would serve this purpose. Such an intermediate good could generate information on the expectations of other firms and in the process of generation of this information can also shape the expectations of the incumbent firm. Information-generative intermediate goods help a firm to achieve a strategic and vantage point of sustained competitive advantage. Co-ordination and capability are thus interdependent and, following Richardson, it is argued here that the site of capabilities is also the site of co-ordination amongst firms (Foss, 1999; Krafft and Ravix, 2000). Perhaps this would indicate that the capability of a firm might reside in spaces beyond the firm boundaries. The normative co-ordination is arranged through a flux of intermediate goods. This is a process beyond the boundary of firm yet containing the firm spaces. The capability of a firm, following this logic, cannot then reside only internally. This capability does not seem to reside in specific situations obtaining in the market either. Information-in-expectation is not provided either by the systems and structures of the market and technology or the firm itself. Nor is it provided by a situation obtaining in the market or in the firm's organization. It is resident in the personnel crossing firm boundaries.

The carrier of this information is a person, who is aware of the expectation of the firm being exited from. This person acts as both a carrier and translator and as an active imaginative engine. Information-in-expectation is about situations in a firm but not of these situations. This information relates to the capability, rules and routines and to the expectations of the firm. Such an expectation, though related to firm strategy, is distinct from it and is different from technological expectations described by Rosenberg (1976). Technological expectation in Rosenberg depends on information derived from several public domains such as scientific literature. Public information precludes development of a market on technological expectation. In contrast to the public domain (technological expectation) information-in-expectation refers to non-public domains of internal processes, situations, strategies and expectations of firms in transaction. This expectation depends on an incumbent firm's knowledge on ignorance domain of other firms. Rather often, the incumbent would have public domain access to the knowledge domain of other firms. It follows that mutual knowledge domain between firms is public domain and common knowledge is a quasi-public domain. Firms can infer, reason and take decisions such as on *tâtonnement* adjustment based on this common knowledge. A common knowledge is generally considered as social capital and becomes a factor of production. Both the incumbent and the others, however, remain ignorant about ignorance of the others. Expectation is a function of this ignorance.

Intermediate goods hold the key to deciphering ignorance of both one's own and others'. Each transaction of intermediate goods refers to definite knowledge of the other and, therefore, of ignorance or the domain of indefiniteness of the other. Each such transaction then proves to be an advancement over time in transforming expectations towards the common possible future envelope. Intermediate goods make possible this *tâtonnement*-in-future. Each transaction of intermediate goods through opening up domains of ignorance provides a horizon on which to it is possible to make expectation. Expectation or the information-in-expectation is the foundation of innovation, which in all likelihood is beyond the Schumpeterian technological innovation and which supports increase in Cantillon profit. In order that expectations based on the decipherment of the ignorance of the parties in a transaction converge in future to an interoperable system, the acts of expecting, based on the expectations of others, must continue for a short period in the future. This short period, similar to a conversational period, ends up in a novel innovation of not only a technological system but also a rearrangement, perhaps with new divisions of knowledge, amongst the firms. The continuation of transactions – in intermediate goods and, correspondingly, expectations on the reformulated expectations of others – must take place in a space that cannot be public and that cannot also remain within the boundaries of any participating firm. This space, similar to a conversational space, must (as a private space common to all the firms in a partial market) define a partial market's limit. It follows that in the absence of this space, which supports transactions of intermediate goods and innovations driven by expectation on expectations, there cannot be Cantillon profit. Space internal to a firm and technological expectations based on public domain knowledge can support Schumpeterian innovation. The private space common to a partial market brings together internal processes of firms in a milieu through repeated exchanges of intermediate goods. This may be called the Shackle space.

Schumpeterian innovation can thus attempt to reduce transactions cost through several intra-organizational integrations or else through vertical integration. It does not require information beyond the two types described by Richardson as the business and technical. A public space providing such information at near-zero cost would constitute the social capital on which organizational integrations can aim to reduce transactions cost through technological or organizational innovation. A Cantillon innovation is of a different kind requiring the continuous creation of Shackle space. This space cannot be intra-organizational, neither can it be public. It ceases to exist with the flow of intermediate goods and expectations on expectations stopped. Shackle space is created through repeated actions. A firm receiving the experienced job seeker from the market is in fact in search of the envelope of innovation. This receiving firm cannot, through technical or market information, attempt to co-ordinate its own expectations with the expect-ations of the other firm without having accessed information-in-expectation.

Organizational integration such as through vertical integration would destroy Shackle space and information-in-expectation will cease to be produced. This means that the possibility of Cantillon innovation would be lost. In order to reap Cantillon profit, firms need to innovate in a partial-market Shackle space, while not abstaining from innovations conducted within the organizational boundary. It follows that a software firm seeking Cantillon profit is founded as much externally as it is founded internally. Coase's theory of firm is based on the latter. Richardson (1998) attempted a bridge across the firm-capability, an internally constituted element with problems of co-ordination. He, however, remained limited to the two types of information and to adjustments on the pre-reconciled plan. Shackle space brings to life the transience of partial markets, of alliances effected through passage of human resources and of individual innovations, each of which has an extremely short life cycle.

Strategic knowledge, operational interdependence and Shackle space

The received literature has effected a separation between the operational and the strategic domains. Operational domain takes care of structure. Strategy and structure are separate in the Chandler paradigm. This argument talks of structural sorts and observes that processes, which Weick (1979, 1995) has called organizational processes, link up structural sorts with strategy interdependently. Separation between strategy and structure cannot be retained. The simple observations here on Indian software pointed out inseparability of structure from strategy. Strategy refers to positioning that must refer to other existing or potential firms. Operational aspects reflect current strategic concerns and the structural features of a firm (Chandler, 1990). Software firms must continually keep shifting operational aspects, which are by definition current, to a direction in the future. A firm engaged in current positioning while adjusting to the pre-reconciled plan cannot secure future direction. This firm must position its own operational domain in the context of operational domains of other firms in the strategic milieu and with respect to the future envelope of innovation simultaneously. Software firms are dynamically innovative, product life cycles are very short and marginal costs of production are near-zero. Operational rearrangements too are near-zero cost especially given the continuous flux of human resources across the firm boundary.

It is argued here that firms while expecting on expectations do measure their own ignorance as seen by other firms. An incumbent firm needs to know what another firm perceives as its ignorance. The incumbent must commence operational rearrangements to reshape this ignorance as perceived by others. In other words, each transaction in intermediate goods makes it necessary for the incumbent firm to undertake operational changes. Such operational changes are positioning indeed though never the Chandlerian-type 'strategic positioning'. It appears then that Shackle space forces firms continually to rearrange operational aspects. Structural sorts and the detailed constituents of the structural sorts are, of course, known. Ignorance prevails over strategic knowledge, that is, knowledge about one's processes and those of others. The flow of human resources as the intermediate good affects these internal processes of firms both being exited from and entered into. The reference to rearrangement here does not, however, refer to the effect of the quantity of human resources in transit. Human resources act as the carrier of information on ignorance. Firms position them better with respect to the knowledge now gathered on what is not known. Each positioning implies a new shaping or a novel manner of influencing the internal processes. The incumbent firm shapes its own processes as well as those of other firms. Affecting processes of others are achieved not through gathering up of intelligence as such on others but are achieved in the Shackle space through interventions on mutual ignorance.

Normative co-ordination stands on this mutual ignorance, which sustains expectation on expectation. Norms evolve because there is mutual ignorance. Under other circumstances when firms invest in relation-specific codes and in relation-specific assets, information build-up as a capability or firm strategy address in a fundamental mode the co-ordination aspect described by Richardson. Commitment to durability, as reflected in the development of relation-specific assets, holds back firms from both pre-reconciliation and quick rearrangements of internal processes. Relation-specific durability, studied extensively in recent times, holds back firms from the normative positioning being referred to here. Normative positioning refers to positioning of internal processes with respect to the dynamic contours of expectations on expectation. This expectation is about positioning the firm in a manner that is not strategic in the Chandlerian sense. The objective of positioning must refer to both current markets and the possible future markets. Internal processes of the firm are repositioned in accordance with expectation. This shift in internal domain shapes the strategy of the firm.

The operational aspects of a software firm are highly dynamic. Normative co-ordination consequently influences operational aspects. Operational co-ordination is achieved by the function of expectations on a future envelope of innovation. The structure–conduct–performance paradigm (SCPP) gave way to strategy as a design that transforms capabilities, systems, and structures of a firm. The latter has to be given up if one accepts operational normative co-ordination, which affects the internal processes of firms. Firms concurrently undertake strategies of operational transformation. Richardson (1972) referred to the co-ordination of operational activities effected through a dense network of co-operation and affiliation. Concurrent co-ordination, according to Richardson, offers predictability of what a competing firm is doing. This concurrency must then refer to a pre-reconciled situation. Concurrency is required to create a market for a new product, or to become familiar with what other firms plan to undertake in future or therefore to secure a better predictability of the otherwise uncertain future of innovation. Richardson argues that 'the need for concurrent co-ordination... may reside.... in their *similarity*, in the sense that they require... the same capabilities for their successful undertaking' (Richardson, 1998:5; italics original). This can be called a capability concurrence. A capability, according to Teece, is founded on the internal processes, structures and learning as well as on the path undertaken so far. Concurrent co-ordination achieves similarity in capabilities, according to Richardson and this similarity must then bring about similarities in the operational and structural aspects of the participant firms. Normative co-ordination refers to co-ordination of expectations and as a follow-up similarity in capability – the latter calls for co-ordination of operational aspects. Human resource flow provides the information-in-expectation which co-ordinates expectations on expectations. Shackle space co-ordinates dynamic operational aspects. Nooteboom (1999c) calls similarity a converse of 'cognitive distance'. Here there is reference to ignorance and mutual ignorance based on Shackle. Ignorance refers to cognitive distance, a measure of which is indeed necessary to be able to forge alliance or concurrency. Ignorance affords formation of expectation.

Predictability and the pay-offs of the information secured (Monteverde, 1995), it was argued by received literature, assist vertical integration. The argument here is that these aspects are substituted in normative co-ordination by the increased possibility of convergence of expectations. This is similarity in expectations. Flux of human resources surely helps achieve such similarity in expectations.

Intermediate-good flows across software firms

The manpower turnover rate in software is characterized by peculiarities and a higher rate in several locations, notably in Silicon Valley and in India. In its early years, the Indian software business had seen manpower flowing out slowly, perhaps steadily, from the manufacturing sectors into the software firms. The turnover rate then was low. In fact, the manpower turnover rate in average Indian manufacturing has remained extremely low. Institutional rigidities, in particular, have always prevented exit options in these non-software sectors. Asset peculiarities, asset specificities and the high transfer cost of property rights over specific assets usually prevented manpower turnover in Indian industries. Knowledge industries proved no exception in general but software, strangely, crossed the average. Biotechnology, drugs and pharmaceuticals, for example, belong to the knowledge intensive sector but have not exhibited a similar feature. Possibly product-based competition and stringent control of product-based property rights have prevented bio-technology sectors, in general, to allow a large flux of manpower turnover. Asset specificity is surely the prime factor preventing resources flow. The received literature has often addressed this phenomenon in terms of tacit knowledge and has, in fact, built up the edifice of a transactions-cost based theory of firms primarily on this fact of immobility of manpower. Public domain knowledge and social capital have consequently become important.

Immobility of manpower has spawned growth of little pools of knowledge in each firm. In order to remain innovative, each firm must depend more on knowledge available in the public domain. Public domain knowledge acts as a factor of production. A typical firm, say in biotechnology, has technological expectations (Rosenberg, 1976) but no expectations on expectations. A technological expectation is carried forward through the knowledge available in public domain. Information that a firm in such sectors generates internally on its business and on its own organization tends to gravitate towards lowering of transactions cost through vertical integration (Perry, 1989). It appears, and is argued above, that the nature of innovation depends much on these aspects of specificity of assets, nature of information and the property rights institution and the knowledge available in the public domain. These discussions have pointed out that durability and fixedness of such positioning of a firm can be altered when manpower can flow easily across indefinite boundaries of a firm. Software has achieved this.

In particular, Indian software has had evidence of manpower turnover rates that defy all claims to institutional rigidities of the labour market. Firms in software appear to have taken this turnover with ease and have not taken legal steps or attempted any institutionalization to rigidify the labour institution.

Software has perhaps evidenced the largest number of products, each with apparently the smallest life cycle. Most importantly, following Richardson's observation, at any time there would be a set of products that are interoperable only. Moreover, numerous innovations in software processes remained unnoticed. Process innovations have far surpassed the number of innovations in software products. Biotechnology for drugs and pharmaceuticals or for agriculture belongs to the knowledge sector. Innovations in these sectors – where patenting by large corporations appeared to have severely restricted the spate of innovations – have, however, suffered from overt dependence on the public domain and on property rights protection. Interoperability and lower dependence on the product-centred market have allowed the launching of software products with little capital while biotechnology-based products, especially in drugs, sunk more and more capital. Liquidity of capital and massive generation of divisions of knowledge in software has surely demanded that manpower flows remain unrestricted. These aspects of capital have ensured, as the Austrians have argued, that the rate of profit does not fall in software. Biotechnology, through vertical integration, approached conditions demanded by Schumpeterian technological innovations while software, it has been argued here, through hastened division of knowledge, has approached Cantillon profit based as it is on 'capital as time' hypothesis. In short, the innovation profile in software has exhibited certain unique features.

The argument here is that this novel phenomenon in software rests on structures of knowledge. These structures are derived from knowledge people and divisions of labour amongst them. It is also argued that these divisions of labour and consequently the structure of knowledge have been sustained through the activities of manpower flow in the Shackle space obtaining between firms in a partial market. The explanatory key to this understanding is job-switching personnel. Since its early years, Indian software firms depended on manpower flowing out of other industries. Perhaps this opened up the vision that sources of knowledge could be tapped in the manpower flow. The turnover rates in software firms ranged around 40 per cent in the early nineties and never seem to have dropped. It has been observed here that at least about 25 per cent of turnover rate prevailed around the late nineties (Banerjee, 2003b). Surprisingly, software firms did not appear to have suffered from this. A typical firm experienced an average of above 50 per cent growth throughout this decade. Firms thrived through exporting and in offering BPO services of several types to global clients. This sector grew large with umpteen numbers of small start-ups joining in and the number of entrepreneurial firms increased several fold. Simultaneously, several global corporations opened up their own development or R & D units. In tandem with the growth in the software business, the manpower output from academic institutions increased several fold. The inter-firm flow of manpower and migration of a large number of software personnel to other global locations kept up and sustained the dynamics in the macro market of software manpower. A market for software manpower came into existence.

This macro market deals with quantity data on manpower both available and generated and manpower likely to have crossed floors. Quantity data, it has been argued, appear less relevant to a firm deciding on its questions on strategy. Firms then deal with a meso stage and data from the partial market of strategic milieu are considered relevant for strategy making. It has been observed here that firms look at the Shackle space and consider the social capital or social availability of manpower as secondary. This data can be collected from the partial market where flow of manpower is taking place across strategically related companies. Part of such data can be gathered from the business journals where job advertisements come up on regular basis. Undeniably a large part of floor-crossing manpower switch jobs based on personal knowledge and social networks, which naturally do not appear in public advertisements. Job-switches data were collected from 1,615 advertisements that appeared in a popular business magazine during September 1998 to March 2000 and a database was created from this. Approximately more than 10,000 jobs were covered. The total number of job switches was much higher than the advertisements had indicated.

Advertisements always ask for experienced persons. Freshers are recruited straight from the campus. Only the experienced can provide information-in-expectation. Moreover, most 'experienced' recruitment takes place from the old boys' network and from personal networks. Those recruited from the old boys' network and who are from other firms do indeed provide the information-in-expectation. Advertisements take care of personnel who do not belong to such networks. An advertisement states the kind of experience being sought, desired qualifications, years of experience that could be necessary and broad job categories that are likely to be on offer along with a short profile of what the firm is planning. Only the years of experience required were precisely given. Information in advertisement is in the public domain and hence serves the purpose of co-ordination described by Richardson. A broad classification of these advertised data could be made based on the commonly accepted and identified groups. This has been serialized under several types (Banerjee, 2003e): 25 groups of skill categories with a large degree of overlap between groups, and 20 groups under the experience category. Group divisions could have been created differently but would not have changed the conclusions reached.

A profile of experience against skill required from the job-switching personnel is presented in Figure 7.1. Public declaration and public availability

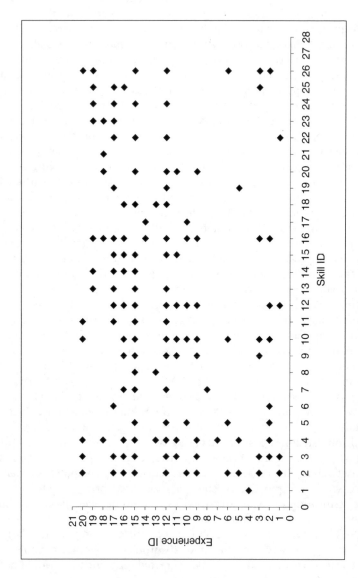

Figure 7.1 Skills by experience demands of firms as reflected in advertisements
Source: Banerjee (2003b) *Global Business Review* 4(1), p. 126, fig. 3.

of information from advertisements have made the groups and the information sufficiently broad based. Similar data have been captured in the following two figures as well (Figures 7.2 and 7.3). Figure 7.2 presents job description against qualification required. Figure 7.3 presents data on job description against experience desired. These three figures together present three facets of signals that advertisements from the firms send to the personnel who intend to switch jobs. Signals from 'experience against skill' conveys that while for certain skills a person can switch jobs having acquired experience in several alternative groups, for certain other groups, experience and skill matching are more sacred. The former types of skills required by jobs in an incumbent firm might be available from several areas of work experience. The employer does not consider the matching between experience and skill acquired as sacrosanct. Further, several advertisers often do not mention the qualification desired and employers seem to exercise wide options. Certain jobs, as the advertisements indicate in Figure 7.2, can accommodate several alternate qualifications. A few jobs are, however, strict about qualifications required. Similar to skill by experience is the profile of job by experience. Certain jobs appear to make demands for persons from wide areas of experience while a few are very selective about the experience profile of the incumbent job seeker.

These three figures represent the quantity signals in a manpower market. Quantity signals present to the software personnel a profile of current and immediate future prospects of experience, years of experiences, skills, and areas as well as qualifications that are on demand currently and that might continue to have demands in the future. The resource market responds to such signals. Fresh manpower often looks at these profiles and selects jobs and skills based on these signals. On-the-job personnel face certain restrictions: the current job might not allow a person to switch over easily to the areas or jobs of preference. A large manpower turnover, however, helps the resource market to clear comparatively easily through the use of these signals. If the manpower market shrinks – if a large-scale vertical integration inter-firm mobility gets severely restricted – scarce signals would fail to clear a market. Similarly, with a paradigmatic shift in technology, a market even with sufficient signal may quantitively fail to clear.

There are limitations to such quantity signals. Information-in-expectation and meso-level signals in the Shackle space have been discussed here. In order to understand the publicly available features of meso-level signals, one can consider plotting experience requirement profiles against each firm and skill requirement profiles against each firm. Data in these cases were collected from a set of advertisements. Both figures plot the requirement features of specific firms. Figures show that certain experience profiles are on demand by almost all firms, while a few other experiences are selectively demanded and firms exhibit specialized divisions of knowledge. The vagueness of skill classifications is sharply clear in skill requirement profiles of

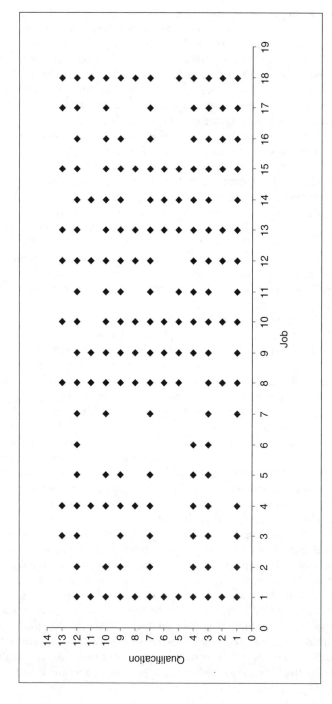

Figure 7.2 Jobs by qualification

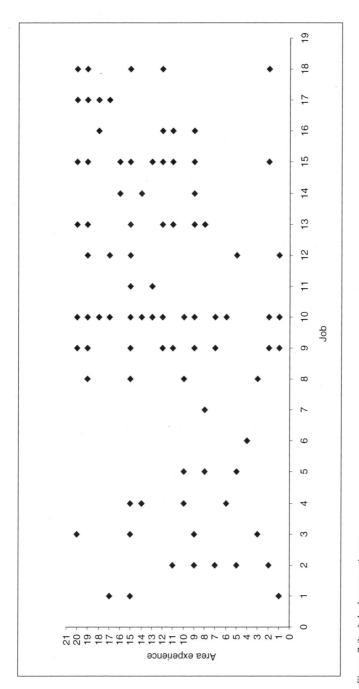

Figure 7.3 Jobs by experience

firms. Here most firms appear to make demands for most types of skills. The skill group divisions here are based on the requirements specified in the advertisements. Public advertisements seem to keep a large amount of details rather vague on the needs of a firm. Quantity information on divisions of knowledge or quality of manpower, therefore, is hardly effective. Quantity information reaches its limit before that.

In order to get at information-in-expectation and gauge ignorance (and hence expectations) profiles of other firms in its strategic milieu, a firm gets closer to the live carrier of information. Declarations in public on skill required display that several areas of work experience count, or conversely, for the same experience type, several types of skills are counted. Needless to say, skills requirement varies widely for similar types of job. Private signals to intending job-seekers from firms in the strategic milieu and public signals, as advertisements, bring forward a number of job seekers. From all of them, the incumbent firm receives information on other firms' profiles of expectations, first through the lengthy process of personal interviews and then following the recruitment of some. Firms follow private definitions on areas of experience, skills that are on offer by the employee and those that the advertised job would require. Firms follow private definitions (as interviews with firm managers reveal) while making judgment on skills, experience and information-in-expectation that a job seeker is able to offer. The figures here suggest, for example, that the nature of job offers and the years of desired experience did not show any specific pattern (Banerjee, 2003g). This was an indication of the failure of quantity signals.

Asset specificity, it was observed, ruined a manpower market. The software manpower market appears to be strong and able to clear effectively at both the macro and meso levels and asset specificity could not develop in software firms. Such assets could have engendered vertical integrations. Manpower is sought for information-in-expectation that is required for future normative co-ordination and for evoking sufficient innovations. In almost all kinds of job offers, persons with experiences of up to eight years appear to be much in demand. Further, persons with up to eight years of experience in any specific areas are equally attractive in the job market. Long experience enriches the manpower on the move with sufficient information on a few firms and about their profiles of expectations. Manpower flow thus first reduces the cognitive distance between the firms expecting to keep on co-ordination. The observation shows that experience makes the personnel even more attractive to the employer in prospect. Under the circumstances, an employee would act forward to carry more information on the firm that is to be exited or on areas of technologies that are related to the current job. An employee has an incentive from the market to act as a carrier of information-in-expectation. This employee also has an incentive to acquire more knowledge on the potential innovation envelope and its technologies. These two aspects assist information passage across firms.

The recruiting firm gathers expectation profiles of firms in the strategic milieu from the employee. The expectations of this recruiting firm change according to the expectations of other firms. The employee, as an intermediate product, reduces the distance between these different kinds of expectations and acts as an active agent in this case. An employee would always like to keep open options on a job switch and, therefore, prefer to be on the frontier of innovations. It has been argued that firms in software look more for Cantillon innovations than for Schumpeterian technological innovations. The former type of innovation is possible through privileged business information; the latter more through public domain knowledge as a factor of production. An employee in the Cantillon mode acts as an active agency in carrying potential information. Such information is about the ignorance profiles of firms exited. The employee does not thus act as an intelligence gatherer but acts to bring about business innovations on the normative co-ordination envelope. Further, organizational integration would have prevented the flow of this active carrier of information. Manpower acts as the interpreter and as the creative resource.

References

Alchian, A.A. and S. Woodward (1987). 'Reflections on the theory of the firm', *Journal of Institutional and Theoretical Economics (JITE)*, vol. 143(1), pp. 110–37.

Alchian, A.A. and S. Woodward (1988). 'The firm is dead: long live the firm', A review of Oliver E. Williamson's 'The Economic Institutions of Capitalism', *Journal of Economic Literature*, vol. 26, March, pp. 65–79.

Alterman, R. (1988). 'Adaptive planning', *Cognitive Science*, vol. 12, pp. 393–421.

Alvesson, M. (2000). 'Social identity and the problem of loyalty in knowledge-intensive companies', *Journal of Management Studies*, vol. 37(8), pp. 1101–23.

Amit, R. and P. Schoemaker (1993). 'Strategic assets and organizational rent', *Strategic Management Journal*, vol. 14, pp. 33–46.

Ansoff, I. (1965). *Corporate Strategy*. Harmondsworth: Penguin.

Antonelli, C. (ed.) (1988). *New Information Technology and Industrial Change: The Italian Case*. Dordrecht: Kluwer Academic Publishers.

Antonelli, C. (1999). 'The evolution of the industrial organization of the production of knowledge', *Cambridge Journal of Economics*, vol. 23, pp. 243–60.

Aoki, M. (2000). 'Information and governance in the Silicon Valley model', in X. Vives (ed.) *Corporate Governance: Theoretical and Empirical Perspectives*. Cambridge: Cambridge University Press: pp. 169–95.

Aoki, M., B. Gustafsson and O. Williamson (eds) (1990). *The Firm As A Nexus of Treaties*. London: Sage Publications.

Aoki, Masahiko (1990). 'Toward an economic model of the Japanese firm', *Journal of Economic Literature*, vol. 28, March, pp. 1–27.

Arora, A., V.S. Arunachalam, J. Asundi and R. Fernandes (2001). 'The Indian software services industry', *Research Policy*, vol. 30, pp. 1267–87.

Arora, A. and A. Gambardella (1990). 'Complementarities and external linkages: the strategies of the large firms in biotechnology', *The Journal of Industrial Economics*, vol. 38, June, pp. 361–79.

Arora, A. and A. Gambardella (1994). 'The changing technology of technological change: general and abstract knowledge and the division of innovative labour', *Research Policy*, vol. 23, pp. 523–32.

Arrow, K.J. (1962a) 'Economic welfare and the allocation of resources for innovation', in R. Nelson (ed.) *The Rate and Direction of Inventive Activity*, Princeton, NJ: Princeton University Press, pp. 164–81.

Arrow, K.J. (1962b) 'The economic implications of learning by doing', *Review of Economic Studies*, vol. 29, pp. 155–73.

Arrow, K.J. (1974) *The limits of organization*. New York: Norton.

Arrow, K.J. (1985) 'Economic welfare and the allocation of resources for innovation', in *Production and capital*, vol.5 of *Collected papers of K.J. Arrow*, Cambridge, MA: The Belknap Press, Harvard University Press, pp. 104–56.

Arrow, K.J. (2000). 'Knowledge as a factor of production', in B. Pleskovic and J.E. Stiglitz (eds) *Annual World Bank Conference on Development 1999*, Washington, DC: The World Bank, pp. 15–20.

Arrow, K.J. and D.A. Starrett (1973). 'Cost and demand-theoretical approaches to the theory of price determination', in J.R. Hicks and W. Weber (eds) *Carl Merger and the Austrian School of Economics*. Oxford: Clarendon Press, 129–48.

Aumann, R. (1976). 'Agreeing to disagree', *The Annals of Statistics*, 4, pp. 1236–9.

Bachelard, G. (1971). *On Poetic Imagination and Reverie*. Tr. by C. Gaudin. Dallas, Texas: Spring Publications, Inc.

Bagwell, L.S. and J.B. Shoven (1989). 'Cash distributions to shareholders', *Journal of Economic Perspectives*, 3(3), Summer, pp. 129–40.

Bain, J. (1956). *Barriers to new competition*. Cambridge: Cambridge University Press.

Balbontin, A., B.B. Yazdani, R. Cooper and W.E. Souder (2000). 'New product development practices in American and British firms', *Technovation*, vol. 20, pp. 257.

Banerjee, P. (1995). 'Nation, distribution and machinery', in A.K. Bagchi (ed.) *New Technology and the Workers' Response: Microelectronics, Labour and Society*. New Delhi: Sage Publications, pp. 47–69.

Banerjee, P. (1997). 'Excess and necessary: redefining skill and the network', in Banerjee, P. and Y. Sato (eds) *Skill and Technological Change*. New Delhi: Har-Anand, pp. 338–60.

Banerjee, P. (1999). 'Bargaining context, entrepreneurial initiative, and society of networked producers', in F.J. Richter (ed.) *Business Networks in Asia: Promises, Doubts, and Perspectives*. Westport, CT: Quorum Books, pp. 253–68.

Banerjee, P. (2000). 'Limits to competition: managing concept, innovation and strategy beyond the firm' 59(8/9), August–September, *Journal of Scientific and Industrial Research*, pp. 65–7.

Banerjee, P. (2003a). 'Resources, capability and coordination in Indian software firms', in Richter and Banerjee (eds), pp. 106–29.

Banerjee, P. (2003b). 'Resources strategy and signals to job market in Indian software', *Global Business Review*, 4(1), *The Knowledge Economy in India*. Houndmills: Palgrave-Macmillan, pp. 115–29.

Banerjee, P. (2003c). 'Some indicators of dynamic technological competencies: understanding of Indian software managers', *Technovation* 23, pp. 593–602.

Banerjee, P. (2003d). 'Resource dependence and core competence: insights from Indian software firms', *Technovation* 23, pp. 251–63.

Banerjee, P. (2003e). 'Employing quality of manpower to leverage emergent strategy: the case of Indian software firms', *Global Business Review*, 4(2) July–December, pp. 239–56.

Banerjee, P. (2003f). 'Imagining organizational transformation through linguistic suggestion', *Journal of Human Values* 9(1), pp. 3–13.

Banerjee, P. (2003g). 'Resources, capability and coordination: strategic management of information in Indian information sector firms, *International Journal of Information Management*, 23, pp. 303–11.

Banerjee, P. and K.K. Bharadwaj (2002). 'Constructivistic management of knowledge, communication and enterprise innovation: lessons from Indian experience', *AI and Society*, 16, pp. 49–72.

Banerjee, A. and E. Dufflo. (n.d) 'Reputation effects and the limits of contracting: a study of the Indian software industry', at http://econ-www.mit.edu/faculty/eduflo/files/papers/sofpap102.1.pdf

Banerjee, P. and F.J. Richter (2001). 'Social management: situating imagination, concept, cooperation and intangible assets in the knowledge business', in P. Banerjee and F.J. Richter (eds) *Intangibles in Competition and Cooperation: Euro-Asian Perspectives*. Houndmills: Palgrave-Macmillan, pp. 289–338.

Banerjee, P. and F.J. Richter (eds) (2003). *Economic Institutions in India: Sustainability under Liberalization and Globalization*, Houndmills: Palgrave-Macmillan.

Banerjee, P. and S. Roy (1999). 'Social partnership and network: CSIR in business', in A.K. Bagchi (ed.) *Economy and organization*. New Delhi: Sage Publications. pp. 350–97.

Barabaschi, S. (1992). 'Managing the growth of technical information', in N. Rosenberg, R. Landau and D. Mowery (eds) *Technology and the Wealth of Nations*. Stanford, CA: Stanford University Press, pp. 407–34.

Barber, B. and R.C. Fox (2000). 'The case of the floppy-eared rabbits: an instance of serendipity gained and serendipity lost', in P.E. Stephan and D.B. Audretsch (eds) *The Economics of Science and Innovation Vol I*. Cheltenham: Edward Elgar, pp. 200–16.

Barnard, C. (1962). *The Functions of the Executive*. Cambridge, MA: Harvard University Press.

Barney, J.B. (1986). 'Strategic factor markets: expectations, luck and business strategy'. *Management Science*, 32(10), pp. 1231–41.

Barney, J.B. (1991). 'Firm resources and sustained competitive advantage', *Journal of Management*, 17, pp. 99–120.

Baron, J.N., M.D. Burton and M.T. Hannan (1996). 'The road taken: origins and evolution of employment systems in emerging companies', *Industrial and Corporate Change*, 5(2), pp. 239–75.

Barr, A. and S. Tessler (1996). 'The globalization of software R & D: the search for talent', Graduate School of Business, Stanford: Stanford University, at http://www-scip.stanford.edu/scip/

Barr, A. and S. Tessler (1997). 'Notes on human resource issues in the software industry and their implications for business and government', Graduate School of Business, Stanford: Stanford University, at http;//www-scip.stanford.edu/scip/

Barron, D.N., E. West and M.T. Hannan (1994). 'A time to grow and a time to die: growth and mortality of credit unions in New York, 1914–1990', *American Journal of Sociology*, vol. 100, pp. 381–422.

Barwise, J. and J. Perry (1983). *Situations and Attitudes*, Cambridge, MA.: The MIT Press. A Bradford Book.

Baumol, W., J. Panzar and R. Willig (1986). 'On the theory of perfectly contestable markets', in J. Stiglitz and F. Mathewson (eds) *New Developments in the Analysis of Market Structure*. Cambridge, MA: Macmillan, pp. 339–65.

Beath, J., Y. Katsoulacos and D. Ulph (1989). 'Strategic R&D policy', *The Economic Journal*, 99, pp. 74–83.

Becker, G. (1962). 'Investment in human capital: a theoretical analysis', *Journal of Political Economy*, October, 70, pp. 9–49.

Bell, D.E., H. Raiffa and A. Tversky (eds). (1988). *Decision Making: Descriptive, Normative and Prescriptive Interactions*. Cambridge: Cambridge University Press.

Benassy, J.P. (1993). 'Nonclearing markets: microeconomic concepts and macroeconomic applications', *Journal of Economic Literature*, 31(2), June, pp. 732–61.

Berle, A.A. and G. Means (1932). *The Modern Corporation and Private Capital*. New York: The Macmillan Co.

Bhatnagar, S.C. and S. Madon (1997). 'The Indian software industry: moving towards maturity', *Journal of Information Technology*, 12, pp. 277–88.

Bhattacharya, S. (1979). 'Imperfect information, dividend policies, and "the bird in the hand fallacy" ', *Bell Journal of Economics*, Spring, pp. 259–70.

Bogaert, I., R. Martens, and A.V. Cauwenberg (1994). 'Strategy as a situational puzzle: the fit of components', in G. Hamel and A. Heene (eds) *Competence-based Competition*. New York: John Wiley & Sons Ltd, pp. 57–74.

Bothner, M.S. (n.d.) 'Structure, scale and scope in global computer industry', at http://gsbwww.uchicago.edu/fac/matthew.bothner/research/structure.pdf

Bourgeois, L.J., III, (1984). 'Strategic management and determinism', *Academy of Management Review*, 9, pp. 586–96.

Boyer,R. and Jean-Pierre Durand (1997). *After Fordism*. Tr. by S.H. Mair. Basingstoke: Macmillan Business.

Boyer, R. and J. Mistral (1982). *Accumulation, Inflation and Crises*. Paris: PUF.

Boynton, A.C. and B. Victor (1991). 'Beyond flexibility: building and managing the dynamically stable organization', *California Management Review*, 34(1), pp. 53–66.

Brandenburger, A. (1992). 'Knowledge and equilibrium in games', *Journal of Economic Perspectives*, Fall, 6(4), pp. 83–101.

Brandenburger, A. and E. Dekel (1989). 'The role of common knowledge assumptions in game theory', in F. Hahn (ed.) *The Economics of Missing Markets, Information and Games*. Oxford: Oxford University Press, pp. 46–61.

Breschi, S., F. Malerba and L. Orsenigo (2000). 'Technological regimes and Schumpeterian patterns of innovation. Economic Journal', April, 110: 463, pp. 388–410.

Bresnahan, T. and A. Gambardella (1998). 'The division of inventive labor and the extent of the market', in E. Helpman (ed.) *General Purpose Technologies and Economic Growth*. Cambridge, MA: MIT Press.

Bromiley, P. and L. Fleming (2002). 'The resource based view of strategy: an evolutionist's critique', in M. Augier and J.G. March (eds) *The Economics of Choice, Change, and Organizations: Essays in Memory of Richard M. Cyert*. Cheltenham: Edward Elgar.

Burgelman, R.A. (1991). 'Intraorganizational ecology of strategy-making and organizational adaptation: theory and field research', Research paper 1122, Stanford University Graduate School of Business.

Burke, K. (1969). *A Grammar of Motives*. Berkeley, CA: University of California Press.

Burt, R.S. and D.S. Carlton (1989). Another look at the network boundaries of American markets, *American Journal of Sociology*, 94, pp. 723–53.

Callon, M. (1994). 'Is science a public good? Fifth Mullins Lecture', *Science, Technology, and Human Values*, 19(4), Autumn, 395–424.

Caporael, L.R., R.M. Dawes, J.M. Orbell and A.J.C. van de Kragh (1989). 'Selfishness examined: cooperation in the absence of egoistic incentives', *Journal of Behavioral and Brain Sciences*, 12, pp. 683–739.

Carmichael, H.L. (1989). 'Self-enforcing contracts, shirking, and life cycle incentives', *Journal of Economic Perspectives*, Fall, 3(4), 65–83.

Casson, M.C. (1990). 'The market for information', in M. Casson (ed.) *Entrepreneurship*. Aldershot: Edward Elgar Pub. Ltd, pp. 202–19.

Castaneda, H.N. (1975). *Thinking and Doing*. Dordrecht: Reidel.

Castaneda, H.N. (1989). *Thinking, Language, and Experience*. Minneapolis: University of Minnesota Press.

Chandler, A.D., Jr (1962). *Strategy and Structure*, Cambridge, MA.: MIT Press.

Chandler, A.D., Jr (1990). *Scale and Scope: The Dynamics of Industrial Capitalism*. Cambridge, MA.: The Belknap Press of Harvard University Press.

Chandler, A.D., Jr (1992). 'Organisational capabilities and the economic history of the industrial enterprise', *Journal of Economic Perspectives*, Summer, 6(3), pp. 79–100.

Chandler, A.D., Jr (2001). *Inventing the Electronic Century*. New York: Free Press.

Cheung, S.N.S. (1983) 'The Contractual Nature of the Firm', *Journal of Law and Economics*, 26, pp. 386–405.

Chomsky, N. (1986). *Knowledge of Language: Its Nature, Origin, and Use*. New York: Praeger.

Chomsky, N. (1993). 'A minimalist program for linguistic theory', in K. Hale and S.J. Keyser (eds) *The View from Building 20: Essays in Honour of S.Broomberger*. Cambridge, MA: MIT Press.

Christensen, C.M. (1997). *The Innovator's Dilemma: When New Technologies Cause Great Firms to Fail*. Boston: Harvard Business School Press.

Clark, J.M. (1961). *Competition as a Dynamic Process*. Washington, DC: Brookings Institution.

Clark, K. and T. Fujimoto (1991). *Product Development Performance*. Boston, MA: Harvard Business School Press.

Clower, R. and A. Leijonhufvud (1975). 'The coordination of economic activities: a Keynesian perspective', *American Economic Review*, 65(2), pp. 182–8.

Coase, R. (1990). 'The nature of the firm', in O.E. Williamson (ed.). *Industrial Organisation*. Aldershot: Edward Elgar, pp. 3–22 .

Cohen, M.D., R. Burkhart, G. Dosi, M. Egidi, L. Marengo, M. Warglien and S. Winter. (1996). 'Routines and other recurring action patterns of organizations: contemporary research issues', *Industrial and Corporate Change*, 5(3), pp. 653.

Cohen, W. and D. Levinthal (1989). 'Innovation and learning: the two faces of R & D', *The Economic Journal*, 99, pp. 569–96.

Cohen,W.M. and D.A. Levinthal (1990). 'Absorptive capacity: a new perspective on learning and innovation', *Administrative Science Quarterly*, 35, March, pp. 128–52.

Cohendet, P., F. Kern, B. Mehmanpazir and F. Munier (1999). 'Knowledge coordination, competence creation and integrated networks in globalised firms', *Cambridge Journal of Economics*, 23, pp. 225–41.

Cohendet, P. and W.E. Steinmueller (2000). 'The codification of knowledge: a conceptual and empirical exploration', *Industrial and Corporate Change*, 9(2), pp. 195–210.

Conlisk, J. (1996). 'Why bounded rationalty?', *Journal of Economic Literature*, June, vol. 34(2), pp. 669–700.

Cowan, R., P.A. David and D. Foray (2000). 'The explicit economics of knowledge codification and tacitness', *Industrial and Corporate Change*, 9(2), pp. 211–53.

Cusumano, M. (1992). 'Shifting economies: from craft production to flexible systems and software factories', *Research Policy*, 21, pp. 453–80.

Cyert, R.M. and J.G. March (1963). *A Behavioral Theory of the Firm*. Englewood Cliffs, NJ: Prentice-Hall.

Dasgupta, P. and P. David (1986). 'Information disclosure and the economics of science and technology', in G. Feiwel (ed.) *Essays in Honour of K.J. Arrow*. London: Macmillan.

Dasgupta, P. and P.A. David (1994). 'Toward a new economics of science', *Research Policy*, 23(5), September, pp. 487–521.

David, P.A. (1997). 'From market magic to calypso science policy: a review of T. Kaely's Economic Laws of Scientific Research', *Research Policy*, 26, pp. 229–55.

David, P.A. (2001). 'From keeping "nature's secrets" to the institutionalization of "open science". A Contribution to the University of Siena Lectures on 'Science as an Institution and the Institutions of Science' (mimeo), available at paul.david@ economics.ox.ac.uk

David, P.A. and D. Foray (1996). 'Information distribution and the growth of economically valuable knowledge: a rationale for technological infrastructure policies', in M. Teubal *et al.* (eds). *Technological Infrastructure Policy: An International Perspective*. Dordrecht: Kluwer Academic Publishers, pp. 87–116.

David, P.A., D. Foray and W.E. Steinmueller (1999) 'The research network and the new economics of science: from metaphors to organizational behavior', in A. Gambardella and F. Malerba (eds), *The Organization of Inventive Activity in Europe*. Cambridge: Cambridge University Press, pp. 303–42.

David, P.A. and B.H. Hall (1999). 'Heart of darkness: public–private interactions inside the R & D black box', contact authors: paul.david@economics.ox.ac.ul, bronwyn.hall@nuff.ox.ac.uk

Davidson, D. (1984). *Inquiries into Truth and Interpretation*. Oxford: Oxford University Press.

Davidson, P. (1991). 'Is probability theory relevant for uncertainty? A post-Keynesian perspective', *Journal of Economic Perspectives*, Winter, 5(1), pp. 129–43.

Dawes, R.M. and R.H. Thaler (1988). 'Anomalies: cooperation', *Journal of Economic Perspectives*, vol. 2(3), pp. 187–97.

Demsetz, H. (1973). 'Industry structure, market rivalry and public policy', *Journal of Law and Economics*, 16, pp. 1–9.

Demsetz, H. (1982). 'Barriers to entry', *American Economic Review*, March, 72, pp. 47–57.

Dierickx, I. and K. Cool (1989). 'Asset stock accumulation and sustainability of competitive advantage', *Management Science*, 35, pp. 1504–11.

Dixit, A. (1992). 'Investment and hysteresis', *Journal of Economic Perspectives*, 6(1), pp. 107–32.

Dixit, A. and B. Nalebuff (1991). *Thinking Strategically*. New York: Norton.

Dosi, G. (1982). Technological paradigms and technological trajectories: a suggested interpretation of the determinants and directions of technical change, *Research Policy*, 11(3), pp. 147–62.

Dosi, G. (1988). 'Sources, procedures and the microeconomic effects of innovation', *Journal of Economic Literature*, 26, September.

Dosi, G. and L. Marengo (1994). 'Some elements of an evolutionary theory of organizational competencies', in R. England (ed.) *Evolutionary Concepts in Contemporary Economics*, Ann Arbor, MI: University of Michigan Press, pp. 157–78.

Dosi, G. and D. Teece (1998). 'Organizational competencies and the boundaries of the firm', in R. Arena and C. Longhi (eds) *Markets and Organization*. New York: Springer-Verlag, pp. 281–301.

Drejer, A. (2001). 'How can we define and understand competencies and their development', *Technovation*, 21, pp. 135–46.

Drucker, P. (1988). 'The coming of the new organization', *Harvard Business Review*, 66(1), pp. 45–53.

Dutrenit, G. (2000). *Learning and Knowledge Management in the Firm*, Cheltenham: Edward Elgar.

Dutta, S. (2003). 'Using offshore software development to drive value: the experience of Motorola in India', in Richter and Banerjee (eds) *The knowledge Economy in India*. Basingstoke:Palgrave-Macmillan, pp. 87–105.

Earl, M. and D. Fenny (2000). 'How to be a CEO for the information age', *Sloan Management Review*, Winter, 41, pp. 11–23.

Elster, J. (1989). 'Social norms and economic theory', *Journal of Economic Perspectives*, Fall, 3(4), pp. 99–117.

Elster, J. (1998). 'Emotions and economic theory', *Journal of Economic Literature*, 36(1), pp. 47–74.

Englander, E.J. (1988). 'Technology and Oliver Williamson's transaction cost economics', *Journal of Economic Behavior and Organization*, 10, pp. 339–53.

Fischhoff, B. (1975). 'Hindsight is not equal to foresight: the effect of outcome knowledge on judgment under uncertainty', *Journal of Experimental Psychology: Human Perception and Performance*, August, vol. 104(1), pp. 288–99.

Fishback, P.V. (1998). 'Operations of "unfettered" labor markets: exit and voice in American labor markets at the turn of century', *Journal of Economic Literature*, 36(2), pp. 722–65.

Fisher, F. (1989) 'Games Economists Play: A Noncooperative View', *RAND Journal of Economics*, vol. 19, pp. 113–24.

Fodor, J.A. (1981). *Representations: Philosophical Essays on the Foundations of Cognitive Science*. Cambridge, MA: Bradford Books/MIT Press.

Fodor, J.A. (1983). *The Modularity of Mind*. Cambridge, MA: Bradford Books/MIT Press.

Foss, N.J. (1996). 'Research in strategy, economics, and Michael Porter', *Journal of Management Studies*, 33(1), pp. 1–24.

Foss, N.J. (1999). 'Capabilities, confusion and the costs of coordination: on some problems in recent research on inter-firm relations', DRUID Working Paper no. 99–7, Aaolborg: DRUID.

Foss, N.J. and B.J. Loasby (eds). (1998). *Economic Organization, Capabilities, and Coordination: Essays in Honour of G.B. Richardson*. London: Routledge.

Foss, N.J. and V. Mahnke (eds). (2000). *Competence, Governance and Entrepreneurship*. Oxford: Oxford University Press.

Foss, N.J. and P. Robertson (eds). (1999). *Resources, Technology and Strategy*. London: Routledge.

Galambos, L. (1988). 'What have CEOs been doing?', *The Journal of Economic History*, 48(2), June, pp. 243–58.

Galunic, D.C. and S. Rodan. (1998). 'Resource recombinations in the firm: knowledge structures and the potential for Schumpeterian innovation', *Strategic Management Journal*, 19, pp. 1193–201.

Gambetta, D. (ed.). (1988). *Trust: Making and Breaking of Cooperative Relations*. Oxford: Basil Blackwell.

Gardenfors, P. (1988). *Knowledge in Flux*. Cambridge, MA: MIT Press.

Gardenfors, P. and N.S. Sahlin (eds) (1986). *Decision, Probability, and Utility: Selected Readings*. Cambridge: Cambridge University Press.

Garvin, D. (1994). 'The processes of organization and management', Harvard Business School Working Paper.

Geanakoplos, J. (1992). 'Common knowledge', *Journal of Economic Perspectives*, 6(4), pp. 53–82.

Gibbard, A. (1995). 'What "rational" could mean in the human sciences', in Andler, D., P. Banerjee, M. Chaudhury, and O. Guillaume (eds) *Facets of Rationality*. New Delhi: Sage Pub., pp. 58–78.

Gibbons, M.T. (ed.) (1987). *Interpreting Politics*. Oxford: Basil Blackwell.

Gilbert, R.J. (1986). 'Preemptive competition', in J.E. Stiglitz and F. Mathewson (eds) *New Developments in the Analysis of Market Structure*. Cambridge, MA: MIT Press, pp. 90–125.

Gilbert, R.J. (1989). 'The role of potential competition in industrial organization', *Journal of Economic Perspectives*, Summer, 3(3), pp. 107–27.

Goldman, A. (1986). *Epistemology and Cognition*. Cambridge, MA: Harvard University Press.

Grant, R.M. (1996). 'Prospering in dynamically-competitive environments: organizational capability as knowledge integration', *Organization Science*, 7(4), p. 375.

Groner, R., M. Groner and W.F. Bischoff (eds) (1983). *Methods of Heuristics*. Hilsdale, NJ: Lawrence Erlbaum Assoc. Pub.

Grossman, S. and O. Hart (1990). 'The costs and benefits of ownership: a theory of vertical and lateral integration', in O.E. Williamson (ed.). *Industrial Organization*. Aldershot: Edward Elgar, pp. 252–80.

Haley, J.O. (1997). 'Relational contracting: does community count?', in H. Baum (ed.) *Japan: Economic Success and Legal System*. Berlin: Walter de Gruyter, pp. 167–83.

Hamel, G. (1991). 'Competition for competence and inter-partner learning within international strategic alliances', *Strategic Management Journal*, 12, pp. 83–103.

Hamel, G. and A. Heene (eds) (1994). *Competence-Based Competition*. New York: John Wiley & Sons Ltd.

Hands, D.W. (1993). 'Popper and Lakatos in economic methodology', in U. Maki, B. Gustaffson, and C. Knudsen (eds) *Rationality, Institutions and Economic Methodology*. London: Routledge, pp. 61–75.

Hannan, M.T. and J.H. Freeman (1984). 'Structural inertia and organizational change', *American Sociological Review*, 49, pp. 149–64.

Hannan, M.T. and J.H. Freeman (1989). *Organizational Ecology*. Cambridge, MA: Harvard University Press.

Hanusch, H. (ed.) (1988). *Evolutionary Economics: Applications of Schumpeter's Ideas*. Cambridge: Cambridge University Press.

Harman, G. (1973). *Thought*. Princeton, NJ: Princeton University Press.

Harman, G. (1986). *Change in View: Principles of Reasoning*. Cambridge, MA: Bradford Books/MIT Press.

Hart, H.L.A. (1961). *The Concept of Law*. Oxford: Clarendon.

Hart, H.L.A. (1982). *Essays on Bentham: Studies in Jurisprudence and Political Theory*. Oxford: Clarendon.

Hart, H.L.A. (1983). *Essays in Jurisprudence and Philosophy*. Clarendon: Oxford.

Hart, O. (1988). 'Incomplete contracts and the theory of the firm', *Journal of Law, Economics and Organization*, 4(1), pp. 119–40.

Hart, O. and B. Holmstrom (1987). 'The theory of contracts', in T. Bewley (ed.) *Advances in Economic Theory*. Cambridge: Cambridge University Press.

Hart, O. and J. Moore (1990). 'Property rights and the nature of the firm', *Journal of Political Economy*, 98(6), pp. 119–58.

Haveman, H.A. (1993). 'Organizational size and change: diversification in the savings and loan industry after deregulation', *Administrative Science Quarterly*, 38, pp. 20–50.

Hayek, F.A. (1949). *Individualism and Economic Order*. London: RKP Ltd.

Hayek, F.A. (1967). *Studies in Philosophy, Politics and Economics*. London: Routledge & Kegan Paul.

Hayek, F.A. (1973–8). *Law, Legislation and Liberty*. 3 volumes. Chicago: University of Chicago Press.

Heeks, R.B. (1996). *India's Software Industry*. New Delhi: Sage Publications.

Heeks, R.B. (1998). 'The uneven profile of Indian software exports', Working Paper no.3, IDPM, Manchester: University of Manchester, at http://www.man.ac.uk/idpm_dp.htm#devinf_wp

Heeks, R.B. (2000) 'Software strategies in developing countries', Development Informatics Working Paper no.6, IDPM, Manchester: University of Manchester, at http://www.man.ac.uk/idpm/di_wp6.htm

Heeks, R.B. (2000). 'India's Software industry', IDPM, Manchester: University of Manchester, at http://www.man.ac.uk/idpm/isi.htm

Hempel, C.G. (1965). *Aspects of Scientific Explanation*. New York: The Free Press.

Henderson, R.M. and K.B. Clark (1990). 'Architectural innovation: the reconfiguration of existing product technologies and the failure of established firms', *Administrative Science Quarterly*, 35, pp. 9–30.

Henderson, R.M. and I. Cockburn (1994). 'Measuring competence? Exploring firm effects in pharmaceuticals research, *Strategic Management Journal*, Winter Special Issue, 15, pp. 63–84.

Henderson, R., L. Orsenigo and G. Pisano (1999). 'The pharmaceutical industry and the revolution in molecular biology: exploring the interactions among scientific', institutional and organizational change, in D.C. Mowery and R.R. Nelson (eds) *Sources of Industrial Leadership: Studies of Seven Industries.*, New York: Cambridge University Press, pp. 267–311.

Hirschfeld, L.A. and S.A. Gelman (eds). (1994). *Mapping the Mind: Domain Specificity in Cognition and Culture*. Cambridge: Cambridge University Press.

Hodgson, G. (1998). 'Competence and contract in the theory of the firm', *Journal of Economic Behavior and Organization*, 35, April, pp. 179–201.

Hodgson, G.M. (1993). *Economics and Evolution: Bringing Life Back to Economics*. Cambridge: Polity Press.

Hodgson, G.M. (1998). 'The approach of institutional economics', *Journal of Economic Literature*, 36(1), March, pp. 166–92.

Hodgson, M. (1993). 'Organisational learning: a review of some literatures', *Organisation Studies*, 14(3), pp. 375–94.

Holmstrom, B. (1990). 'Moral hazard in teams', in O.E. Williamson (ed.) *Industrial Organisation*. Aldershot: Edward Elgar, pp. 162–78.

Holmstrom, B. and J. Roberts. (1998). 'The boundaries of the firm revisited', *Journal of Economic Perspectives*, 12, pp. 73–94.

Holmstrom, B. and Tirole, J. (1989). 'The theory of the firm', in R. Schmalensee and R.D. Willig (eds) *Handbook of Industrial Organization*, vol.I. Amsterdam: North Holland, pp. 61–133.

Hounshell, D.A. (1984). *From the American System to Mass Production, 1800–1932: The Development of Manufacturing Technology in the United States*. Baltimore, MD: Johns Hopkins University Press.

Hovenkamp, H. (1988). 'The classical corporation in American legal thought', *The Georgetown Law Journal*, June, 76(5), pp. 1594–689.

Hsiao, R.L. and R.J. Ormerod (1998). 'A new perspective on the dynamics of IT-enabled strategic change', *Information Systems Journal*, 8(1), pp. 21–52.

Huberman, G. (1984). 'External financing and liquidity', *Journal of Finance*, July, 39(3), pp. 895–908.

Hutchens, R.M. (1989). 'Seniority, wages and productivity: a turbulent decade', *Journal of Economic Perspectives*, Fall, 3(4), pp. 49–64.

Iansiti, M. and K.B. Clark (1994). 'Integration and dynamic capability: evidence from product development in automobiles and mainframe computers', *Industrial and Corporate Change*, 1(3), pp. 557–606.

Ichinowski, C., K. Shaw, G. Prennushi (1997). 'The effects of human resource management practices on productivity: a study of steel finishing lines', *American Economic Review*, 87(3), p. 291

Ingrao, B. and G. Israel (1990). *The Invisible Hand: Economic Equilibrium in the History of Science*. Tr. by I. McGilvray. Cambridge, MA: The MIT Press.

Isenberg, D.J. (1988) 'How Senior Managers Think', in Bell, Raiffa and Tversky (eds) *Decision Making: Descriptive, Normative and prescriptive Interactions*. Cambridge: Cambridge University Press, pp. 525–39.

Itami, H. and T. Roehl (1987). *Mobilizing Invisible Assets*. Cambridge, MA: Harvard University Press.

Jacob, P. (1996). 'What Can Minds Do' (mimeo). Paris: CREA.

Jain, S. (2003). 'Globalization, legal institutions and values', in Banerjee and Richter (eds) *The Knowledge Economy in India*. Basingstoke, Palgrave Macmillan, pp. 351–70.

Jensen, M. and W. Meckling (1976). 'Theory of the firm: managerial behavior, agency costs, and capital structure', *Journal of Financial Economics*, 3, pp. 305–60.

Jessop, B. (1990). 'Regulation theory in retrospect and prospect', *Economy and Society*, 19(2), May, pp. 153–216.

Jovanovic, B. and R. Rob (1987). 'Demand driven innovation and spatial competition over time', *Review of Economic Studies*, 54, pp. 63–72.

Kahneman, D., P. Slovic and A. Tversky (eds) (1988). *Judgment Under Uncertainty: Heuristics and Biases*. Cambridge: Cambridge University Press.

Kahneman, D. and A. Tversky (1979). 'Prospect theory: an analysis of decision under risk', *Econometrica*, 47, pp. 263–91.

Kaldor, N. (1972). 'The irrelevance of equilibrium economics', *Economic Journal*, 82, pp. 1237–55.

Kennan, J. and R.B. Wilson (1993). 'Bargaining with private information', *The Journal of Economic Literature*, 31(1), March, pp. 45–104.

Kenney, M. (2000). 'A note on the comparison between Cambridge, England and Silicon Valley'. BRIE Research Note 6, *Berkeley Roundtable on the International Economy*, University of California.

Kern, T. and L. Willcocks (2000). 'Exploring information technology outsourcing relationships: theory and practice', Templeton Research Paper 2000/00-08, Templeton College, Oxford: Oxford University.

Kirzner, I. (1973). *Competition and Entrepreneurship*. Chicago, Ill: University of Chicago Press.

Kirzner, I. (1997). 'Entrepreneurial discovery and the competitive market process: an Austrian approach', *Journal of Economic Literature*, 35, pp. 60–85

Kitchener, R.F. (1986). *Piaget's Theory of Knowledge: Genetic Epistemology and Scientific Reason*. New Haven, CT: Yale University Press.

Kittler, F.A. (1990). *Discourse Networks 1800/1900*. Tr. by M. Mettcer, with C. Cullens. Stanford, CA: Stanford University Press.

Kleinknecht, A. and J.O.N. Reijnen (1992). 'Why do firms cooperate on R & D?', *Research Policy*, 21, pp. 1–13.

Klepper, S. (1996). 'Entry, exit, growth and innovation over the product life cycle', *American Economic Review*, June, 86(3), pp. 562–83.

Kogut, B. and U. Zander (1996). 'What firms do? Coordination, identity and learning'. *Organization Science*, 7(5), pp. 502–18.

Kornblith, H. (ed.) (1985). *Naturalizing Epistemology*. Cambridge, MA: Bradford Books/MIT Press.

Krafft, J. and J.L. Ravix (2000) 'Competition and Industrial Coordination', in J. Krafft (ed.), *The Process of Competition*. Cheltenham: Edward Elgar, pp. 143–164.

Kripke, S.A. (1982). *Wittgenstein on Rules and Private Language*. Oxford: Basil Blackwell.

Kuhn, T. S. (1962). *The Structure of Scientific Revolutions*. Chicago, Ill: Chicago University Press.

Lacity, M.C. and L.P. Willcocks (2000). *Information Technology Outsourcing – Practices, Lessons and Prospects*. Templeton Research Paper # 2000/00–05, Templeton College, University of Oxford, Oxford.

Lacity, M.C. and L.P. Willcocks (2001). *Global Information Technology Outsourcing*. Chichester: John Wiley & Sons, Ltd.

Lakatos, I. and A. Musgrave (eds) (1970). *Criticism and the Growth of Knowledge*. Cambridge: Cambridge University Press.

Langlois, R.N. (ed.) (1986). *Economics as a Process: Essays in the New Institutional Economics*. Cambridge: Cambridge University Press.

Langlois, R.N. (1992). 'Transaction-cost economics in real time', *Industrial and Corporate Change*, 1(1), pp. 99–127.

Langlois, R.N. and P.L. Robertson (1995). *Firms, Markets and Economic Change*. London: Routledge.

Lateef, A. (1997). 'Linking up with the global economy: a case', New Industrial Organization Programme DP/96/1997, Geneva: International Labour Organization.

Lazear, E.P. (1979). 'Why is there mandatory retirement?', *Journal of Political Economy*, December, 87, pp. 1261–84.

Lazear, E.P. (1981). 'Agency, earnings profiles, productivity, and hours restrictions', *American Economic Review*, 71, pp. 606–20.

Lazear, E.P. and S. Rosen (1981). 'Rank order tournaments as optimal salary schemes', *Journal of Political Economy*, pp. 841–64.

Lazonick, W. (1991). *Business Organization and the Myth of the Market Economy*. New York: Cambridge University Press.

Lazonick, W. (1992). *Organization and Technology in Capitalist Development*. Aldershot: Edward Elgar.

Lazonick, W. (1993). *Business Organization and the Myth of the Market Economy*. Cambridge: Cambridge University Press.

Leijonhufvud, A. (1968). *On Keynesian Economics and the Economics of Keynes*. New York: Oxford University Press.

Leijonhufvud, A. (1986) 'Capitalism and the factory system', in R.N. Langlois (ed.) *Economics as a Process: Essays in the New Institutional Economics*. Cambridge: Cambridge University Press.

Leijonhufvud, A. (1993) 'Towards a Not-too Rational Macroeconomics', *Southern Economic Journal*, vol. 60(1), pp. 1–13.

Leiponen, A. (2000). 'Competencies, innovation and profitability of firms', *Economics of Innovation and New Technology*, 9, pp. 1–24.

Leonard-Barton, D. (1992). 'Core capabilities and core rigidities: a paradox in managing new product development', *Strategic Management Journal*, Summer Special Issue, 13, pp. 111–126

Lewontin, R.C. (1985). 'The organism as the subject and object of evolution', in R. Levins and R.C. Lewontin (eds) *The Dialectical Biologist*. Cambridge, MA: Harvard University Press.

Libecap, G.D. (1989). 'Distributional issues in contracting for property rights', *Journal of Theoretical and Institutional Economics*, 145, pp. 6–24.

Lippman, S. and R. Rumelt (1982). 'Uncertain imitability: an analysis of interfirm differences under competition', *Bell Journal of Economics*, 13, pp. 418–38.

Lippman, S.A. and R.P. Rumelt (1992). 'Demand uncertainty and investment in industry-specific capital', *Industrial and Corporate Change*, 1, pp. 235–62.

Loasby, B.J. (1976). *Choice Complexity and Ignorance*. Cambridge: Cambridge University Press.

Loasby, B.J. (1986). 'Organisation, competition, and the growth of knowledge', in R.N. Langlois (ed.) *Economics as a Process*. Cambridge: Cambridge University Press, pp. 41–57.

Loasby, B.J. (1989) *The Mind and Method of the Economist*. Aldershot: Edward Elgar.

Loasby, B.J. (1990). 'The firm', in J. Creed, (ed.) *Foundations of Economic Thought*. Oxford: Basil Blackwell, pp. 212–23.

Loasby, B.J. (1994). 'Organizational capabilities and interfirm relations', *Metroeconomica*, 45(3), pp. 248–65.

Loasby, B.J. (2000). 'Decision premises, decision cycles and decomposition', *Industrial and Corporate Change*, 9(4), pp. 709–32.

Machlup, F. (1963). *Essays on Economic Semantics*. Englewood Cliffs, NJ: Prentice Hall.

Machlup, F. (1980). 'Knowledge: its creation, distribution and economic significance', *Vol.1: Knowledge and knowledge production*. Princeton, NJ: Princeton University Press.

Macneil, I. (1985). 'Relational contract: what we do and do not know', *Wisconsin Law Review*, 483.

Madhok, A. (1996). 'The organization of economic activity: transaction costs, firm capabilities, and the nature of governance', *Organization Science*, 7, pp. 577–90.

Maki, U. (1990). 'Practical syllogism, entrepreneurship, and the invisible hand', in D. Lavoie (ed.) *Economics and hermeneutics*. London: Routledge, pp. 149–76.

Malerba, F. (1992). 'Learning by firms and incremental change', *Economic Journal*, 102, July, pp. 845–59.

Malerba, F. and S. Torrisi (1992). 'Internal capabilities and external networks in innovative activities: evidence from the software industry', *Economics of Innovation and New Technology*, 2, pp. 49–71.

Mansell, R. and U. Wehn (1998). *Knowledge Societies: Information Technology for Sustainable Development*. New York: The UN/Oxford University Press.

Mansfield, E. (1995). 'Academic research underlying industrial innovations: sources, characteristics, and financing', *Review of Economics and Statistics*, 77(1), February, pp. 55–65.

March, J.G. (1975). 'Science, politics and Mrs. Grunberg', in J.G. March (1999) *The Pursuit of Organizational Intelligence*, Malden, MA: Blackwell.

March, J.G. (1981). 'Footnotes to organizational change', *Administrative Science Quarterly*, 26, pp. 563–77.

March, J.G. (1991). 'Exploration and exploitation in organizational learning', *Organization Science*, 2(1).

March, J.G. (1999) *The Pursuit of Organizational Intelligence*. Malden, MA: Blackwell.

March, J.G. and H.A. Simon (1958). *Organizations*. New York: Wiley.

Marshall, A. (1919). *Industry and trade*. London: Macmillan.

Marshall, A. (1920). *Principles of Economics*, 8th edn. London: Macmillan.

Marshall, A. (1925). 'Some aspects of competition'. Reprinted in Pigou (ed) *Memorials of Alfred Marshall*. London: Macmillan.

Marsili, O. (2001). *The Anatomy and Evolution of Industries: Technological Change and Industrial Dynamics*. Cheltenham: Edward Elgar.

Menard, C. (1994). 'Organizations as coordinating devices', *Metroeconomica*, 45, pp. 224–47.

Merleau-Ponty, M. (1962). *Phenomenology of Perception*. Tr. by C. Smith. London: Routledge & Kegan Paul.

Merton, R.K. (1957). 'Priorities in scientific discovery: a chapter in the sociology of science', *American Sociological Review*, 22(6), December, pp. 635–59.

Merton, R.K. (2000). 'Priorities in scientific discovery: a chapter in the sociology of science', in P.E. Stephan, and D.B. Audretsch (eds) *The Economics of Science and Innovation, vol I*. Cheltenham: Edward Elgar, pp. 217–41.

Miles, R.E. and C.C. Snow (1984). 'Fit, failure and the Hall of Fame', *California Management Review*, 26(3), pp. 10–28.

Miles, R.E. and C.C. Snow (1992). 'Causes of failure in network organizations', *California Management Review*, 34(4), pp. 53–72.

Miles, R.E. and C.C. Snow (1995). 'The new network firm: a spherical structure built on a human investment philosophy'. *Organizational Dynamics*, 23, pp. 4–8.

Milgrom, P. and J. Roberts (1990). 'The economics of modern manufacturing: technology strategy and organization', *American Economic Review*, 80(3), June, pp. 511–28.

Miller, M.H. and K. Rock (1985). 'Dividend policy under asymmetric information', *Journal of Finance*, 40(4), pp. 1031–51.

Minkler, A.P. (1993). 'The problem with dispersed knowledge: firms in theory and practice', *Kyklos*, 46, pp. 569–87.

Mintzberg, H. (1978). 'Patterns in strategy formation', *Management Science*, 24, pp. 934–48.

Mintzberg, H. (1979). *The Structuring of Organizations*. Englewood Cliffs, NJ: Prentice-Hall.

Moad, J. (1995). 'Object methods tame reengineering madness', *Datamation*, 15, May, pp. 43–8.

Modigliani, F. and M.H. Miller (1958). 'The cost of capital, corporation finance and the theory of investment', *American Economic Review*, pp. 261–97.

Montgomery, C.A. and M.E. Porter (eds) (1991). *Strategy: Seeking and Securing Competitive Advantage*. Boston: Harvard Business Review Book.

Montgomery, C.A. and B. Wernefelt (1988). 'Diversification, Ricardian rents, and Tobin's q', *RAND Journal of Economics*, 19(4), pp. 623–32.

Montverde, K. (1995). 'Technical dialog as an incentive for vertical integration', *Management Science*, 41, pp. 1624–38.

Mori, P.A. (1991). 'Job signaling and the returns to private information', *Oxford Economic Papers*, 43, pp. 351–67.

Mowery, D. (ed.) (1996). *The International Computer Software Industry: A Comparative Study of Industry Evolution and Structure*, Oxford: Oxford University Press.

Mowery, D.C. and R.R. Nelson (eds) (1999). *Sources of Industrial Leadership: Studies of Seven Industries*. New York: Cambridge University Press.

Muffatto, M. and M. Roveda (2000). 'Developing product platforms: analysis of the development process', *Technovation*, 20, pp. 617.

Nahpiet, J. and S. Ghoshal (1998). 'Social capital, intellectual capital, and the organizational advantage', *Academy of Management Review*, 23(2), pp. 242–66.

Nakahara, T. (1993). 'The industrial organization and information structure of the software industry: A US–Japan comparison'. CEPR Discussion Paper, No. 346, Center for Economic Policy Research. Stanford, CA: Stanford University. May.

Nalebuff, B. and J. Stiglitz (1983). 'Information, competition and markets', *American Economic Review*, 73, pp. 278–83.

Narduzzo, A., E. Rocco and M. Warglien (2000). 'Talking about routines in the field: the emergence of organizational capabilities in a new cellular phone network company', in G. Dosi, R.R. Nelson and S.G. Winter (eds) *The Nature and Dynamics of Organizational Capabilities*. New York: Oxford University Press, pp. 27–50.

Nelson, R.R. (1991). 'Why firms differ and how does it matter?', *Strategic Management Journal*, 12, pp. 61–74.

Nelson, R.R. (1992). 'What is "commercial" and what is "public" about technology and what should be?', in N. Rosenberg, R. Landau and D. Mowery (eds) *Technology and the Wealth of Nations*. Stanford, CA: Stanford University Press pp. 57–72.

Nelson, R.R. (ed.) (1993). *National Innovation Systems: A Comparative Analysis*. Oxford: Oxford University Press.

Nelson, R.R. and P.M. Romer (1996). 'Science, economic growth, and public policy', in P.E. Stephan and D.B. Audretsch (eds) *The Economics of Science and Innovation, vol II*. Cheltenham: Edward Elgar pp. 425–37.

Nelson, R.R. and S.G. Winter (1982). *An Evolutionary Theory of Economic Change*. Cambridge, MA: Harvard University Press.

Nelson, R.R. and S.G. Winter (2002). 'Evolutionary theorizing in economics', *Journal of Economic Perspectives*, Spring, 16(2) pp. 23–46.

Newell, A. and H. Simon (1972). *Human Problem Solving*. Englewood Cliffs, NJ: Prentice Hall Inc.

Nonaka, I. (1994). 'A dynamic theory of organizational knowledge creation', *Organization Science*, vol. 5, pp. 14–37.

Nonaka, I. and H. Takeuchi (1995). *The Knowledge-Creating Company*. Oxford: Oxford University Press.

Nonaka, I. R. Toyama and A. Nagata (2000). 'A firm as a knowledge-creating entity: a new perspective on the theory of the firm', *Industrial and Corporate Change*, 9(1), pp. 1–20.

Nooteboom, B. (1999a). *Inter-firm Alliances: Analysis and Design*, London: Routledge.

Nooteboom, B. (1999b). 'Innovation, learning and industrial organization', *Cambridge Journal of Economics*, 23 pp. 127–50.

Nooteboom, B. (1999c). 'Discovery and organization: priorities in the theory of innovation', Paper for the DRUID Conference, 9–12 June, 1999.

Nooteboom, B. (2001). 'From evolution to language and learning', in J. Foster and J.S. Metcalfe (eds) *Frontiers of Evolutionary Economics: Competition, Self-organization and Innovation Policy*. Cheltenham: Edward Elgar pp. 41–69.

North, D.C. (1989). 'A transaction cost approach to the historical development of polities and economies', *Journal of Institutional and Theoretical Economics*, 145, pp. 661–8.

Nuki, T. (1997). 'Craftisatisation of industry: to comply with the genuine-product-oriented age', in P. Banerjee and Y. Sato (eds), *Skill and Technological Change*. New Delhi: Har-Anand, pp. 237–52.

Oberquelle, H. (1987). 'Human–machine interaction and role/function/action nets', in W. Brauer, W. Reisig and G. Rosenberg (eds) *Petri Nets: Applications and Relationships to Other Models of Concurrency*, Berlin: Springer-Verlag.

Oberquelle, H. (1988). 'Role/function/action-nets as a visual language for co-operative modeling', in H. Finkelstein (ed.) Proceedings of IFIP Workshop on Human Factors of Information System Analysis and Design (WHISAD), London: Imperial College.

O'Driscoll, G. and M. Rizzo (1985). *The Economics of Time and Ignorance*. New York: Basil Blackwell.

O'Driscoll, G.P. Jr (1986). 'Competition as a process: a law and economics perspective', in Langlois (ed.) *Economics as a Process: Essays in the New Institutional Economics*. Cambridge: Cambridge University Press, pp. 153–70.

Orihata, M. and C. Watanabe (2000a). 'The interaction between product concept and institutional inducement: a new driver of product innovation', *Technovation*, 20, pp. 11–23.

Orihata, M. and C. Watanabe (2000b). 'Evolutionary dynamics of product innovation: the case of consumer electronics', *Technovation*, 20, pp. 437–449.

Orsenigo, L. (1995). *The Emergence of Biotechnology*. London: Pinter.

Papineau, D. (1987). *Reality and Representation*. Oxford: Basil Blackwell.

Patinkin, D. (1965). *Money, Interest and Prices*, 2nd edn. New York: Harper & Row.

Pearce, M.R.N. and D. Pearce (1989). 'Economics and technological change: some conceptual and methodological issues', *Erkenntnis*, 30, pp. 101–27.

Penrose, E.T. (1968). *The Theory of the Growth of the Firm*. Oxford: Basil Blackwell.

Penrose, E.T. (2000). 'Vertical integration with joint control of raw material production: crude oil in the Middle East', in P. Stevens (ed) *The Economics of Energy, Vol. II*. Cheltenham: Edward Elgar, pp. 230–46.

Perry, M.K. (1989). 'Vertical integration: determinants and effects', in R. Schmalensee and R.D. Willig (eds) *Handbook of Industrial Organization, Vol. 1*. Amsterdam: North Holland: pp. 183–255.

Peteraf, M.A. (1993). 'The cornerstone of competitive advantage: a resource-based view', *Strategic Management Journal*, 14(2), pp. 179–91.

Pettit, P. (1992). *The Common Mind*. New York: Oxford University Press.

Pfeffer, J. (1981). *Power in Organizations*. London: Pitman.

Pfeffer, J. (2001). 'Fighting the war for talent is hazardous to your organization's health', Research Paper No. 1687, Graduate School of Business, Stanford University, Stanford.

Piatelli-Palmarini, M. (1980). *Language and Learning: The Debate Between Jean Piaget and Noam Chomsky*. Cambridge, MA: Harvard University Press.

Piatelli-Palmarini, M. (1994). 'Ever since language and learning: afterthoughts on the Piaget–Chomsky debate', *Cognition* pp. 315–46.

Pigou, A.C. (ed.) (1925). *Memorials of Alfred Marshall*. London: Macmillan.

Piore, M.J., R.K. Lester, F.M. Kofman and K.M. Malek (1994). 'The organization of product development', *Industrial and Corporate Change*, 1(2), pp. 405–34.

Pohl, H. (ed.). (1988). *The Concentration Process in the Entrepreneurial Economy Since the Late 19th Century*. Stuttgart: FSVW Gmbh.

Polanyi, K. (1957). *The Great Transformation*. Beacon Hill, Boston, MA: Beacon Press.

Polanyi, M. (1962). *Personal Knowledge: Towards A Post-critical Philosophy*. New York: Harper, Torchbooks.

Polanyi, M. (1966). *The Tacit Dimensions*. New York: Doubleday.

Popper, K.R. (1959). *The Logic of Scientific Discovery*. New York: Basic Books.

Popper, K.R. (1963). *Conjectures and Refutations: The Growth of Scientific Knowledge*. London: Routledge & Kegan Paul.

Porac, J. and J.A. Rosa (1996). 'Rivalry, industry models, and the cognitive embeddedness of the comparable firm', *Advances in Strategic Management*, 13, pp. 363–88.

Porter. M. (1980). *Competitive Strategy*. New York: The Free Press.

Porter. M. (1985). *Competitive Advantage: Creating and Sustaining Superior Performance*. New York: The Free Press.

Porter, M. (1990). *The Competitive Advantage of Nations*. London: Macmillan.

Porter, M. (1994). 'Toward a dynamic theory of strategy', in R. Rumelt, D. Schendel and D.Teece (eds) *Fundamental Issues in Strategy: A Research Agenda*. Boston, MA: Harvard Business School Press, pp. 423–61.

Porter, M. (1996). 'What is strategy?', *Harvard Business Review*, November–December, pp. 61–78.

Prahalad, C.K. and G. Hamel (1990). 'The core competence of the corporation', *Harvard Business Review*, May–June, pp. 79–91.

Putnam, H. (1981). *Reason, Truth and History*. Cambridge: Cambridge University Press.

Putnam, H. (1995). *Pragmatism: An Open Question*. Oxford: Basil Blackwell.

Quine, W.V. (1986). 'Reply to Morton White', in L.E. Hahn and P.A. Schlipp (eds) *The Philosophy of W.V. Quine*. La Salle: Open Court, pp. 663–5.

Rabin, M. (1998). 'Psychology and economics', *Journal of Economic Literature*, 36(1), pp. 11–46.

Radner, R. (2000). 'Costly and bounded rationality in individual and team decision making', *Industrial and Corporate Change*, 9(4), pp. 623–58.

Reed, R. and R.J. DeFillippi (1990). 'Causal ambiguity, barriers to imitation, and sustainable competitive advantage', *Academy of Management Review*, pp. 88–102.

Reinganum, J.F. (1983). 'Uncertain innovation and the persistence of monopoly', *American Economic Review*, 47, pp. 341–48.

Richardson, G.B. (1960). *Information and Investment*. Oxford: Oxford University Press.

Richardson, G.B. (1972). 'The organization of industry', *Economic Journal*, 82, pp. 883–96.

Richardson, G.B. (1996). 'Competition, innovation and the increasing returns', DRUID Working Paper no. 96-10, Aaolborg: DRUID.

Richardson, G.B. (1997). 'Economic analysis, public policy and the software industry', DRUID Working Paper no. 97-4, Aalborg: DRUID.

Richardson, G.B. (1998). 'Production, planning and prices', DRUID Working Paper no. 98-27, Aaolborg: DRUID.

Richter, F.J. and P. Banerjee (eds). (2003). *The Knowledge Economy in India*. Basingstoke: Palgrave-Macmillan.

Rizzo, M.J. (1980). 'Law amid flux: the economics of negligence and strict liability in tort', *Journal of Legal Studies*, 9(2), pp. 291–318.

Robertson, P.L. and R.N. Langlois (1994). 'Institutions, inertia and changing industrial leadership', *Industrial and Corporate Change*, 1(2), pp. 359–78.

Romer, P.M. (1987). 'Growth based on increasing returns due to specialization', *American Economic Review*, 77(2), pp. 56–62.

Rosenberg, N. (1976). 'On technological expectations', *The Economic Journal*, September, 86, pp. 523–35.

Rosenberg, N. (1982). *Inside The Black Box: Technology and Economics*. Cambridge: Cambridge University Press.

Rosenberg, N. (1990). 'Why do firms do basic research (with their own money)?', *Research Policy*, 19(2), April, pp. 165–74.

Rosenberg, N. (1994) *Exploring the Black Box: Technology, Economics, and History*. Cambridge: Cambridge University Press.

Rumelt, R. (1984). 'Towards a strategic theory of the firm', in R. Lamb (ed) *Competitive Strategic Management*. Englewood Cliffs, NJ: Prentice-Hall.

Rumelt, R., D. Schendel and D. Teece (eds). (1994). *Fundamental Issues in Strategy: A Research Agenda*. Boston, MA: Harvard Business School Press.

Russell, B. (1984) *Theory of Knowledge: The 1913 Manuscript*. Edited by E.R. Eames and K. Blackwell. London: Allen & Unwin.

Ruttan, V. (1959). 'Usher and Schumpeter on invention, innovation and technological change', *Quarterly Journal of Economics*, November, pp. 596–606.

Ryle, G. (1949). *The Concept of Mind*. London: Hutchinson.

Sah, R.K. (1991). 'Fallibility in human organizations and political systems', *Journal of Economic Perspectives*, 5(2), Spring, pp. 67–88.

Sappington, D.E.M. (1991). 'Incentives in principal–agent relationships', *Journal of Economic Perspectives*, 5(2), Spring, pp. 45–66.

Sauer, C. (1997). 'Deciding the future for IS failures: not the choice you might think', in W. Currie and R.D. Galliers (eds) *Rethinking MIS*. Oxford: Oxford University Press.

Sauer, C. and L.P. Willcocks (2002). 'The evolution of the organizational architect', *MIT Sloan Management Review*, Spring, 43(3), pp. 41–9.

Schelling, T. (1960). *The Strategy of Conflict*. Cambridge: Harvard University Press.

Scherer, F.M. (1999). *New Perspectives on Economic Growth and Technological Innovation*. Washington DC: British-North American Committee and Brookings Institution Press.

Schmalensee, R., R.D. Willig (eds) (1989). *Handbook of Industrial Organization*. Amsterdam: North Holland.

Schotter, A. (1981). *The Economic Theory of Social Institutions*. New York: Cambridge University Press.

Schumpeter, J. (1928). 'The instability of capitalism', *Economic Journal*, pp. 361–86.

Schumpeter, J. (1950). *Capitalism, Socialism and Democracy*. New York: Harper and Row.

Schumpeter, J. (1961/1934). *The Theory of Economic Development*. New York: Oxford University Press.

Schutz, A. (1971). 'Concept and theory formation in the social sciences', in K. Thompson and J. Tunstall (eds) *Sociological Perspectives*. Harmondsworth: Penguin.

Scott-Morton, M. (ed.) (1991). *The Corporation of the 1990s: Information Technology and Organizational Transformation*. Oxford: Oxford University Press.

Sengupta, S. (2003). 'Facing hypercompetition in world software markets: global strategies for India', in Richter and Banerjee (eds) *The Knowledge Economy in India*. Basingstoke: Palgrave Macmillan, pp. 58–78.

Shackle, G.L.S. (1949/52). *Expectation in Economics*. Cambridge University Press.

Shackle, G.L.S. (1972). *Epistemics and Economics: A Critique of Economic Doctrine*. Cambridge: Cambridge University Press.

Shackle, G.L.S. (1988). *Business, Time and Thought*, edited by S.F. Frowen. London: Macmillan.

Shane, S. (2001). 'Technological regimes and the new firm formation', *Management Science*, 47(9), pp. 1173–1190.

Shapiro, C. (1989a). 'Theories of oligopoly behavior', in R. Schmalensee and R. Willig (eds) *Handbook of Industrial Organization*. New York: North Holland.

Shapiro, C. (1989b). 'The theory of business strategy', *RAND Journal of Economics*, 20(1), Spring, pp. 125–37.

Simon, H.A. (1961). *Administrative Behavior*, 2nd edn. New York: Macmillan.

Simon, H.A. (1972). 'Theories of bounded rationality', in C.B. Macguire and R. Radner (eds) *Decision and Organization*. Amsterdam: North Holland, pp. 161–76.

Simon, H.A. (1979a). *Models of Thought*. New Haven, CT: Yale University Press.

Simon, H.A. (1979b). 'Rational decision making in business organizations', *American Economic Review*, 69, pp. 493–513.

Simon, H.A. (1983a). *Models of Bounded Rationality. Vol. 1. Economic Analysis and Public Policy*. Cambridge, MA: MIT Press.

Simon, H.A. (1983b). *Reason in Human Affairs*. Stanford, CA: Stanford University Press.

Simon, H.A. (1991). 'Organisations and markets', *Journal of Economic Perspectives*, 5(2), Spring, pp. 25–4.

Singh, N. (2003). 'Information technology as an engine of broad-based growth in India', in Richter and Banerjee (eds) *The Knowledge Economy in India*. Basingstoke: Palgrave Macmillan, pp. 24–57.

Sraffa, P. (1963). *Production of Commodities by Means of Commodities*. Bombay: Vora & Co.

Stalnaker, R.C. (1987). *Inquiry*. Cambridge, MA: Bradford Books/MIT Press.

Staudenmayer, N., M. Tripsas and C. Tucci (2001). 'Development webs: a new paradigm in high technology product development', HBS Working Paper 01-007, Harvard Business School, Harvard.

Stephen, P.E. (1996). 'The economics of science', *Journal of Economic Literature*, 34(3), September, pp. 1199–235.

Sternberg, R.J., L.A. O'Hara, and T.I. Lubert (1997). 'Creativity as investment', *California Management Review*, 40(1), Fall, pp. 8–21.

Stitch, S. (1990). *The Fragmentation of Reason*. Cambridge, MA: Bradford Books/The MIT Press.

Streissler, E. (1973). 'Merger's theories of money and uncertainty – a model interpretation', in J.R. Hicks and W. Weber (eds) *Carl Merger and the Austrian School of Economics*. Oxford: Clarendon Press, pp. 164–89.

Stuart, T.E. (1999). 'Interorganizational endorsements and the performance of entrepreneurial ventures', *Administrative Science Quarterly*, 44, pp. 315–49.

Stuart, T.E. (2000). 'Interorganizational alliances and the performance of firms: a study of growth and innovation rates in a high-technology industry', *Strategic Management Journal*, August.

Suppe, F. (ed.) (1974). *The Structure of Scientific Theories*. Urbana: University of Illinois Press.

Sutton, J. (1997). 'Gibrat's legacy', *Journal of Economic Literature*, 35, pp. 40–59.

Szulanski, G. (2000). 'Appropriability and the challenge of scope: Banc One routinizes replication', in G. Dosi, R.R. Nelson and S.G. Winter (eds) *The Nature and Dynamics of Organizational Capabilities*. New York: Oxford University Press, pp. 69–98.

Teece, D. (1980). 'Economics of scope and the scope of the enterprise', *Journal of Economic Behavior and Organization*, 1(3), pp. 223–47.

Teece, D. (1986). 'Profiting from technological innovation: implications for integration, collaboration, licensing and public policy', *Research Policy*, 15, pp. 285–305.

Teece, D. (1988). 'Technological change and the nature of the firm', in G. Dosi, C. Freeman, R. Nelson, G. Silverberg and L. Soete (eds) *Technical Change and Economic Theory*. London: Pinter, pp. 256–81.

Teece, D. (1996). 'Firm organization, industrial structure and technological innovation', *Journal of Economic Behavior and Organization*, 31, pp. 193–224.

Teece, D. and G. Pisano (1994). 'The dynamic capabilities of firms: an introduction', *Industrial and Corporate Change*, 3(3), pp. 537–56.

Teece, D., G. Pisano and A. Shuen (1997). 'Dynamic capabilities and strategic management', *Strategic Management Journal*, vol. 18(7), pp. 509–33.

Teece, D., R. Rumelt, G. Dosi and S. Winter (1994). 'Understanding corporate coherence: theory and evidence', *Journal of Economic Behavior and Organization*, 23, pp. 285–305.

Tessler, S. and A. Barr (1997). 'Software R & D strategies of developing countries', Graduate School of Business, Stanford: Stanford University, at http://www-scip.stanford.edu/scip/

Thagard, P. (1989). 'Explanatory Coherence', *Behavioural and Brain Sciences*, 12, pp. 435–502.

Tilton, J.E. (1971) *International Diffusion of Technology: The Case of Semiconductors*. Washington, DC: Brookings Institution.

Tirole, J. (1990). 'Hierarchies and bureaucracies: on the role of collusion in organisations', in O.E. Williamson (ed.) *Industrial Organisation*. Aldershot: Edward Elgar pp. 179–212.

Torrisi, S. (1998). *Industrial Organization and Innovation: An International Study of the Software Industry*. Cheltenham: Edward Elgar.

Tripsas, M. (1997). 'Surviving radical technological change through dynamic capability: evidence from the typesetter industry', *Industrial and Corporate Change*, 6(2), pp. 341–77.

Tripsas, M. and G. Gavetti (2000). 'Capabilities, cognition and inertia: evidence from digital imaging', *Strategic Management Journal*, 21, pp. 1147–61.

Tversky, A. and D. Kahneman (1971). 'Belief in the law of small numbers', *Psychology Bulletin*, August, vol. 76(2), pp. 105–10.

Tversky, A. and D. Kahneman (1982). 'Judgments of and by representativeness', in D. Kahneman, P. Slovic and A. Tversky (eds) *Judgement Under Uncertainty: Heuristics and Biases*. Cambridge: Cambridge University Press, pp. 84–98.

Tversky, A. and D. Kahneman (1988) 'Rational Choice and the Framing of Decisions', in Bell, Raiffa & Tversky (eds) *Decision Making: Descriptive, Normative and Prescriptive Interactions*. Cambridge: Cambridge University Press, pp. 167–92.

Usher, A.P. (1954). *A History of Mechanical Inventions*. Harvard University Press.

Usher, A.P. (1955). 'Technical change and capital formation', in *Capital Formation and Economic Growth*, National Bureau of Economic Research, pp. 523–50.

Utterback, J.M. and W.J. Abernathy (1975). 'A dynamic model of process and product innovation', *Omega*, December, 3(6), pp. 639–56.

Valax, M.F. and F. Sarocchi (1989). 'Structure of action plans and the notion of temporal stop', *European Bulletin of Cognitive Psychology*, 9(2), pp. 223–38.

Van de Ven, A., A.L. Delbecq and R. Koenig (1976). 'Determinants of coordination modes in organizations', *American Sociological Review*, 41, pp. 322–37.

Van Fraassen, B.C. (1980). *The Scientific Image*. Oxford: Clarendon Press.

Veblen, T. (1919). 'Why is economics not an evolutionary science?', in *The Place of Science in Modern Civilization*. New York: W.B. Huebsch.

Vickers, J. (1995). 'Concepts of competition', *Oxford Economic Papers*, 47, pp. 1–23.
Von Hippel, E. (1988). *The Source of Innovation*. New York: Oxford University Press.
von Savigny, E. (1988). *The Social Foundations of Meaning*. Berlin: Springer-Verlag.
Warnock, M. (1976). *Imagination*. London: Faber & Faber.
Weber, Max. (1978). *Economy and Society: An Outline of Interpretive Sociology. Vol. II*, (ed. by G. Roth, and C. Wittich). Berkeley, CA: University of California Press.
Weick, K. (1979). *The Social Psychology of Organizing*. Reading, MA: Addison Wesley.
Weick, K. (1995). *Sensemaking in Organizations*. London: Sage.
Weisbrod, B.A. (1989). 'Rewarding performance that is hard to measure: the private non-profit sector', *Science*, May 5, p. 244.
Wernerfelt, B. (1984). 'A resource-based view of the firm', *Strategic Management Journal*, 5(2), pp. 171–80.
White, H.C. (1981). 'Where do markets come from'? *American Journal of Sociology*, 87, pp. 517–47.
White, H.C. (2001). *Markets and Networks*, Lazarsfeld Center for Social Sciences, Columbia University.
Williamson, O.E. (1975). *Markets and Hierarchies*. New York: The Free Press.
Williamson, O.E. (1979). 'Transaction cost economics: the governance of contractual relations', *Journal of Law and Economics*, 22(2), pp. 233–61.
Williamson, O.E. (1981). 'The modern corporation: origin, evolution, attributes', *Journal of Economic Literature*, 19, pp. 1537.
Williamson, O.E. (1985). *The Economic Institutions of Capitalism*. New York: Free Press.
Williamson, O.E. (1988). 'Technology and transaction cost economics: a reply', *Journal of Economic Behavior and Organization*, 19, pp. 355–63.
Williamson, O.E. (1990a). 'Transaction cost economics: the governance of contractual relations', in O.E. Williamson (ed.) *Industrial Organisation*. Aldershot: Edward Elgar pp. 223–251.
Williamson, O.E. (1990b). 'A comparison of alternative approaches to economic organization', *Journal of Institutional and Theoretical Economics (JITE)*, 146, pp. 61–71.
Williamson, O.E. (1993). 'Calculativeness, trust, and economic organization', *Journal of Law and Economics*, 36, April, pp. 453–86.
Williamson, O.E. (1996). *The Mechanisms of Governance*. New York: Oxford University Press.
Williamson, O.E. (1999). 'Strategy research: governance and competence perspectives', *Strategic Management Journal*, 20, pp. 1087–108.
Winter, S. (1964). 'Economic "natural selection" and the theory of the firm', *Yale Economic Essays*, 4.
Winter, S.G. (1987). 'Knowledge and competence as strategic assets', in D.J. Teece (ed.) *The Competitive Challenge: Strategies for Industrial Innovation and Renewal*. Cambridge, MA: Ballinger, pp. 159–84.
Winter, S.G. (1993). 'On Coase, competence and the corporation', in O.E. Williamson and S.G. Winter (eds) *The Nature of the Firms*. New York: Oxford University Press, pp. 179–95.
Yano, S. (ed.). (1993). *Global Management and Innovation Strategies: Towards a New Frontier in Theory and Practice*. Tokyo: Chikura Shobo Co. Ltd.
Yetton, P.W., K.D. Johnson and J.F. Craig (1994). 'Computer-aided architects: a case study of IT and strategic change', *Sloan Management Review*, 35(4), pp. 57–67.
Zajac, E.J., M.S. Kraatz and R.K.F. Bresser (2000). 'Modeling the dynamics of strategic fit: a normative approach to strategic change', *Strategic Management Journal*, 21, pp. 429–53.

Zander, U. and B. Kogut. (1995). 'Knowledge and the speed of transfer and imitation of organizational capabilities: an empirical test', *Organization Science*, 6(1), pp. 76–92.

Zucker, L.G., M.R. Darby and M.B. Brewer (1998). 'Intellectual human capital and the birth of U.S. biotechnology enterprises', *American Economic Review*, 88(1), March, pp. 290–306.

Index